THERAPEUTIC
COMMUNICATION

For Marcia

THERAPEUTIC COMMUNICATION

Developing Professional Skills

HERSCHEL KNAPP

Mental Health Clinician and Health Science Researcher

SAGE Publications
Los Angeles · London · New Delhi · Singapore

For information:

Sage Publications, Inc.
2455 Teller Road
Thousand Oaks, California 91320
E-mail: order@sagepub.com

Sage Publications Ltd.
1 Oliver's Yard
55 City Road
London EC1Y 1SP
United Kingdom

Sage Publications India Pvt. Ltd.
B-42, Panchsheel Enclave
Post Box 4109
New Delhi 110 017 India

Printed in the United States of America.

Library of Congress Cataloging-in-Publication Data

Knapp, Herschel.
Therapeutic communication : developing professional skills / Herschel Knapp.
    p. cm.
Includes bibliographical references and index.
ISBN-13: 978-1-4129-3774-0 (pbk.)
    1. Communication in psychiatry. I. Title.
RC437.2.K63 2007
616.89—dc22

                                        2006028042

This book is printed on acid-free paper.

07   08   09   10   11   10   9   8   7   6   5   4   3   2   1

Acquisitions Editors:	Arthur Pomponio, Kassie Graves
Editorial Assistant:	Veronica Novak
Project Editor:	Tracy Alpern
Copy Editor:	Robert Holm
Typesetter:	C&M Digitals (P) Ltd.
Proofreader:	Kevin Gleason
Indexer:	Rick Hurd
Cover Designer:	Candice Harman

Contents

Preface

Therapy is essentially composed of communication. Enhancing the communication pathway serves to facilitate the mutual cognitive and emotional exchanges between you and the client, thereby advancing the therapeutic process. The purpose of this book is to introduce the fundamental principles and communication skills used in psychotherapeutic and other helping settings. The skills detailed in this book are aimed at building rapport and enhancing factual and emotional understanding while respectfully promoting client self-determination, independence, and empowerment. As these are virtually universal principles among health and human service providers, the text does not embrace or promote any particular theoretical orientation, intervention method, or treatment modality. It is up to you to selectively combine and utilize the skills in order to best serve the unique needs of each client.

Although the text and examples are written in terms of therapist-client interaction, the skills detailed in this book are applicable for a variety of practitioners including but not limited to chaplains; community outreach workers; counselors; crisis and disaster relief workers; educators; group (co)facilitators; help line staff; human resources; leadership (managers and directors); marriage, family, and child therapists; nurses; peer counselors; pharmacists; physical therapists; physicians; psychiatrists; psychologists; psychotherapists; rehabilitation workers; social workers; substance abuse recovery workers; and volunteers seeking to improve their person-to-person contact in both therapeutic and nontherapeutic capacities.

The text consists of five cumulative chapters and several appendixes:

Chapter 1, "Defining the Therapeutic Relationship," delineates the multidimensional differences between the casual helping relationships that you are familiar with involving friends, family, and acquaintances compared with your professional contact with clients in four domains: (1) the therapeutic process, (2) social/emotional factors, (3) professionalism, and (4) self-disclosure.

Chapter 2, "Getting Started," provides guidance on initiating the therapeutic process in a thorough and compassionate manner. This chapter lays the groundwork for developing an effective therapeutic alliance between you and the client and identifying the client's initial problem.

Chapter 3, "Following," covers the most essential skill for the competent clinician, *listening*, which entails attending to verbal and nonverbal cues, and skills for progressively verifying and correcting your perception of the client's story.

Chapter 4, "Emotional Communication," offers a framework for identifying and effectively working with the multifaceted emotions that emerge throughout the therapeutic process for both you and the client.

Chapter 5, "Leading," details skills for keeping sessions on track, advancing your understanding of the client's circumstances, interpreting your impressions, resolving discrepancies, and educating.

Appendixes A, B, and C contain full transcriptions of three successive 50-minute therapy sessions exemplifying the principles and skills presented in this text, combined and applied in a natural clinical setting.

There are a number of unique attributes to this book: The text presumes no prior knowledge of behavioral science principles; hence, it is ideal for beginning practitioners. Each skill is discussed using clear, jargon-free language, accompanied with a dialogue between a client and therapist demonstrating various uses of every skill. The dialogue examples are presented with two streams of text: (1) Italicized text represents the script of the spoken words. (2) Text that is printed in straight font provides a running commentary detailing the therapist's thought process, progressive impressions, intentions, and rationale. Postdialogue debriefings provide supplemental discussion of each skill including variations, implementation tips, and constructive alternatives. For brevity, these examples are set in individual (one-to-one) therapy sessions; however, the skills covered in this book are equally applicable in other modalities such as couples, family, group, and peer support.

For sake of educational clarity, the demonstration dialogues used throughout the text highlight only one communication skill at a time, whereas one would likely utilize a broader array of skills in real-life settings, as in Appendixes A, B, and C.

Although there is considerable social science theory and research associated with the therapeutic process itself, the actual practice of effective clinical communication skills ultimately happens spontaneously in a real-time interactive environment. As such, one may consider understanding each skill from a textual standpoint as step one. Step two involves building proficiency by actually applying these skills. Metaphorically speaking, it is one thing to merely read about how to juggle, whereas it is quite another thing to actually become an agile juggler—this can only be achieved through practice. To help facilitate this essential leap from the printed page to real life, each chapter concludes with five role-plays, offering the opportunity to actively practice and refine your utilization of the principles and skills presented.

Though communication skills themselves may be considered relatively public domain, the implementation of these skills is not necessarily generic. Along with discussion of personal differences in the communication styles among clients, relevant multicultural references indicate additional considerations that should be taken into account when applying particular skills with individuals from backgrounds that differ from your own.

At the conclusion of the final chapter, there are guidelines for doing the Video Interview Self-Critique Exercise. This project will give you the opportunity to make key observations as to how you actually look and sound when interacting with a (simulated) client. An outline is included to guide you in documenting your observations, detailing your strengths, and improving your performance.

Proficiency in clinical communication guided by theory, your intellect, intuition, feelings, receptiveness, compassion, and the desire to help builds the pathway to understanding the unique world that is each client. Tread gently but purposefully as you respectfully enter the client's realm. Welcome the privilege to be an active instrument in helping to improve the quality of people's lives.

Guidelines for Implementing Role-Play Exercises

There are role-play exercises at the end of each chapter that provide opportunities to practice the principles and skills presented. The performance parameters specified for the client and the therapist should be considered suggestive only. Take the liberty to spontaneously enhance or modify the existing role-plays, within reason, or invent additional role-play scenarios of your own. This can help to bring a sense of realism to these practice situations.

The person playing the client should tune the implementation of the role-plays according to the skills of the person acting as the therapist. For instance, if as the client you are finding that a role-play is too easy for the therapist, consider incrementally including additional complicating factors. Conversely, if the role-play seems too confounding, you may want to reduce the client's circumstances or needs by simplifying the story somewhat.

The person playing the therapist may use the skills suggested but need not necessarily constrain him- or herself to that limited list. As your clinical

xiv   Therapeutic Communication

communication skills accumulate, consider saying, within reason, whatever you need to proceed effectively through the role-plays.

The characters in the role-plays have been assigned unisex names and gender-free circumstances; hence, either a female or a male can plausibly play the part of the client. After completing a role-play and debriefing, you may choose to exchange roles and rerun the exercise for additional practice. The role-plays may be executed using a more limited set of skills; multiple iterations of the role-play may be performed, each time emphasizing different skills.

If you wish to specify supplemental client characteristics that are not stated in the text, then briefly negotiate this with your partner prior to embarking on the role-play. For instance, as you gain more experience and comfort in performing the role-plays, you may want to consider portraying the client as coming from a cultural or ethnic background that is different from your own, thereby giving the therapist the opportunity to implement the therapeutic skills in a fashion that is conducive to the client's unique social attributes.

If while engaged in a role-play you find yourself stuck or having an unexpected emotional reaction as the therapist, client, or observer, raise your hand and say *"Wait"* or *"Stop,"* indicating that you need to suspend the role-play. This provides an opportunity to confer with your partner, peers, or instructor to process your questions or feelings. Also, if you notice your role-play partner or someone else present is having an adverse reaction to the role-play, consider halting the role-play to tend to their reaction. It is up to the participants to mutually decide if and when a role-play should be resumed from where you left off, restarted from the beginning, or abandoned.

Debriefing

A role-play should run about 5–10 minutes; a stopwatch may be helpful. To terminate a role-play, say something like, *"Okay, let's come out of the role-play."* This explicit statement cues both participants that the role-play is over and to halt their portrayal of the factitious characters.

Sometimes partaking in or merely observing a role-play can conjure up strong feelings within you. After each role-play, participants should be encouraged to talk about their feelings. Consider discussing how you felt portraying or working with this character, as well as how you feel about your performance. After the initial feelings have been processed, take turns discussing your experience in the role-play:

- What skills did you feel comfortable with?
- What skills do you feel you need to work on?

- What parts of the role-play did you find most challenging?
- What did you wish you would have done or said differently?
- What was your goal?
- Did something unexpected happen?

Providing Feedback

As this is a learning process, feedback is an essential tool for identifying strengths as well as opportunities to improve. Nobody enjoys criticism; however, it is important to provide honest feedback. Courteously withholding or diluting negative feedback essentially robs the person of the opportunity to further develop his or her skills.

It is recommended that after each participant has discussed his or her feelings, the person playing the client provide feedback to the individual who portrayed the therapist. Feedback, both positive and negative, is most useful when it is phrased *as specifically as possible*. It is okay to initially provide general feedback (*"You seemed very accepting of the client."*), but to the extent possible, provide specific instances supporting that generalization; make an effort to identify actual quotes or paraphrase specific components of the interview that corroborate your claims (*"It felt good when you said 'XYZ.' That really showed me that you were on my side. It helped build some good rapport."*). It may be useful to take some notes during these learning exercises in order to provide more focused feedback.

Begin with positive feedback. Describe the skills that the person demonstrated most proficiently. Next, select one or two of the most important things that you feel require further development. Make an effort to phrase your feedback in a positive fashion: Instead of saying, *"You weren't very empathetic,"* consider saying, *"I was hoping you'd express more empathy."*

Next, the person who played the therapist may provide some feedback to the person who played the client.

If there are observers, they can offer their impressions of the therapist's performance. Observers may reiterate positive feedback, but each observer should limit negative feedback to one recommendation. Do not repeat negative feedback that has already been given.

Allow the person who is being reviewed an opportunity to summarize the feedback—and his or her feelings related to it. The ultimate goal of this process is for the person playing the therapist to assemble a meaningful educational "to do" list. (*"Okay, so it sounds like I'm good with A and B. I felt pretty comfortable with those skills, but it looks like I need to spend some time working on X and Y. Right now, those don't come so naturally to me."*)

Advanced Feedback Techniques

As you become more proficient in the role-play process, the person play-ing the client may include some feedback in the voice of the client *without* halting the role-play. In the following example, the bold text indicates feed-back that the client gives during the role-play:

Cl: *When I came home, there was nobody there, just a note.*

Th: *Uh-huh.*

Cl: *It was my birthday.*

Th: [Silent]

Cl: *We were supposed to have dinner together.*

Th: *Yeah.*

Cl: **It sounds like you don't even care.**

Th: *Oh, I'm sorry, I do care. So, all you got on your birthday was a note?*

Cl: *A note! Right. Can you believe that?*

Th: *Wow.*

Cl: **Don't you want to know what the note said?**

Th: *Oh, yes, please . . . what did it say?*

This embedded feedback allows the person playing the therapist the chance to improve his or her performance here and now as opposed to waiting for a similar opportunity in a future role-play.

Such feedback need not always be negative; it may be useful to remark on an improvement in the use of a skill—or a particularly effective use of a skill:

Cl: *I don't know, with my dad being in the hospital, and my mom crying all the time, and finals coming up, it's practically a miracle that I can even get up in the morning and get anything done.* [Crying]

Th: *It's okay to cry. You've got a lot going on right now, and the tears are totally appropriate. None of this is easy, but it seems to me that con-sidering all that you're dealing with, you actually appear to be coping very well: You're tending to your family through a difficult time, and it looks like you're going to finish up the term with some pretty decent grades. This is all commendable.*

Cl: Thanks ... you know, it's like you're the only one who **really** *understands.*

Notice that the client stays in character and does not resort to clinical language when providing feedback. Per this example, the client would never say, *"Your use of empathy, normalizing, and validation were highly effective here."* These terms should be reserved for the feedback given after the role-play.

Because it can be difficult to provide extensive detailed feedback while portraying a client, consider including the feedback given within the role-play as part of the post-role-play debriefing discussion also, noting the therapist's performance before and after the within-role-play feedback was given.

Depending on the role-play, it can be challenging to remain in character while spontaneously providing meaningful feedback. If this does not come naturally, it is okay not to use this technique; just proceed in character and save your feedback for the regular post-role-play debriefing. Alternatively, you may wish to pause the role-play, provide some brief feedback (out of character), and then resume.

Last, try not to be too hard on yourself or your peers. Therapeutic communication is challenging in that it takes place in real time: You will need to learn to think on your feet. Depending on your prior experience, it can take some time to build proficiency. Despite your enthusiasm, be patient with yourself. Nobody becomes an expert overnight. Even the most capable therapists misspeak or misunderstand from time to time. As with any learning process, as you practice these skills, they will become second nature to you. In time, you will find yourself intuitively employing these skills, enabling you to devote more of your attention to the client's issues. Enjoy the process.

Acknowledgments

Sage Publications gratefully acknowledges the following reviewers:
    Luther Brown, Castleton State College
    Michael Waldo, New Mexico State University
    Chester R. Robinson, Texas A&M University
    Cindy Pharaz, University of South Alabama
    Michael J. Constantino, University of Massachusetts, Amherst
    Valorie Thomas, Rollins College

*What psychologically troubled people most need
is not to be analyzed, judged or advised, but simply to be
heard—that is, to be truly understood and respected by
another human being.*

—Dr. Carl Rogers

1

Defining the
Therapeutic Relationship

This chapter contrasts the role of the casual helper—who informally provides help or guidance to friends and family—with the role of the professional helper.

Therapeutic Figures

Our conception of a proper therapeutic relationship may come from a variety of sources: We may have been involved in therapy as a client and seek to emulate various aspects of the therapist that we utilized. Readings of various therapeutic orientations can also influence our ideas as to the kind of therapist we aspire to be. Undeniably, another influential source of our conception of therapy is the media. There is no shortage of fictional therapists and television/radio "shrinks" providing some sense of entertainment. In some cases, such intervention efforts may be facilitative; however, for the sake of theatrical performance or literary license, much of what is depicted as therapy in movies or other popular media cannot be thought of as appropriate models for more traditional therapeutic practice.

Each of us has, on occasion, provided guidance, advice, and help to family, friends, and acquaintances in an informal manner. Typically, good intentions, common sense, personal experience, and the wish to be helpful provide a good compass for these facilitative efforts. The purpose of this chapter is to delineate the therapeutic role by contrasting social relationships with the client-therapist relationship in four domains: (1) the therapeutic process, (2) social and emotional aspects, (3) professionalism, and (4) self-disclosure.

The Therapeutic Process

Selection

Typically, we think of ourselves as free to select our friends at will based on personal preferences. A variety of things can attract us to an individual: similar interests, physicality (overall appearance, fashion, grooming, stature, etc.), talents, common backgrounds, ethnicity, attitudes, demeanor, and common friends. In a professional setting, there is usually no such privilege. Your role as a therapist involves the commitment to provide quality care to clients without bias with respect to age, ethnicity, culture, race, disability, gender, religion, sexual orientation, or socioeconomic status (*Ethical Standards of Human Service Professionals,* Statement 17; Council for Standards, 1996).

It is common that managers will assign clients based on the expectation that you possess the skills necessary to competently provide services to the client. Skilled supervisors may choose to take into account such attributes as gender, age, ethnicity, specialized training, or expertise when considering making such assignments, such as by assigning an adolescent boy who is exhibiting conduct problems to a male therapist, whereas a female rape survivor would likely be paired with a female therapist. Generally, as a professional therapist, you do not get to select who your clients will be; in fact, it is likely that the individuals who present themselves as potential clients are not going to be the specific types of individuals that you would voluntarily select for friendship.

Unlike social relationships, the selection process involves some deliberate information exchanges: A potential client is usually required to schedule an appointment, complete forms, and be screened for eligibility for services and identification of the primary problems (Neukrug, 2002).

Additionally, an agency or organization may be set up to provide only a selected set of services to those who meet a particular set of needs criteria such as homeless, substance addicted, low income, young mothers, HIV positive, or over 65. Unlike in social settings, there may be any number of eligibility criteria that may contribute to client selection.

Initial Contact

Social relationships can begin in a variety of ways, such as introductions through friends; incidental conversations at parties, with coworkers, with fellow students; or Internet contact. Additionally, there are no fixed ground rules that need to be articulated or followed in order to start a friendship or relationship; social and personal norms guide this process. In the professional realm, clients may be self-referred or they may seek out a facility based on a referral from another such as a family member, significant other, friend, physician, or a member of the clergy. The initial contact may also include a professional disclosure statement detailing the therapist's characteristics, which may contain information regarding qualifications, education, license status, treatment modalities, or specialties. The potential client is also given information regarding the agency's policies involving such things as appointment cancellations, fee structure, and services provided and not provided. The client signs an appropriate "consent for treatment" form, which typically spells out the information and legal parameters regarding confidentiality (Corey, Corey, & Callanan, 2006).

Termination

Social relationships may end in a variety of ways for a variety of reasons, ranging from irreconcilable differences to geographical relocation. Such deliberate endings may be gradual or abrupt. Alternatively, people may drift apart or become more occupied with other people, projects, or interests. Unlike social relationships, which may last a lifetime, the professional therapeutic relationship is ultimately meant to be finite. The termination phase of the therapeutic process is handled in a purposive and deliberate manner; termination often involves a systematic review of the progress that the client has achieved in therapy and issues that will require continued work, along with strategies and resources for the client to continue this work after therapy ends. As the final session approaches, feelings regarding termination are discussed and processed by both the client and therapist. Occasionally, termination may happen abruptly. A client may quit therapy with little or no notice. Termination is discussed in more detail in "Overview of Appendixes A, B, and C."

Time

When it comes to friends and family, we usually do not think about the duration of the relationship. Such relationships are typically considered as enduring over time. Although we may set a time to meet with such acquaintances, less often is there a predetermined end time. Spontaneous or unannounced visits may also be characteristic of our social contacts. In a therapeutic setting, time is considered to be a more crucial factor. Your professional contact with a client may be limited by a fixed number of sessions, or termination may be indicated upon the accomplishment of the designated goal or goals. Unlike casual contacts, therapeutic appointments are scheduled with a specified beginning and ending time. Usually clients establish a standing weekly appointment, traditionally 50 minutes in duration and typically not extended with the exception of genuine crisis situations.

Despite wishes to methodically fit clients into consistent appointment time slots, it is important to be flexible when working with some Latino clients, who by tradition may place a higher priority on the task completion—such as tending to a friend—than adherence to a rigid appointment time (Martinez, 1986; Sue & Sue, 2003). Similarly, traditional American Indians may perceive time as a naturally occurring event, as opposed to a phenomenon that controls their lives (Barcus, 2003; Ho, 1992; Sue & Sue, 2003).

Goal

Social contacts need not be goal-directed. Sometimes, we just choose to visit and casually "shoot the breeze" with friends. It is socially appropriate and common to desire friendly companionship with or without a particular task or project in mind. Conversely, effective psychotherapy largely depends on the identification of specific goals and consistent efforts directed toward advancing the accomplishment of such goals (*Ethical Standards of Human Service Professionals,* Statement 1; Council for Standards, 1996).

In social circumstances, there are no enforceable guidelines with respect to setting goals. Either individual may submit a goal. In professional settings, you will collaborate with the client to articulate appropriate goals that are acceptable to him or her (*Ethical Standards of Human Service Professionals,* Statement 1; Council for Standards, 1996). In your role as the therapist, you may provide recommendations with respect to setting goals, but despite your good intentions, it is essential to resist the temptation to unilaterally set goals for the client. The client's self-determination must remain at the forefront at each step of the therapeutic process (*Ethical Standards of Human Service Professionals,* Statement 8; Council for Standards, 1996). Provisional goals can be established by engaging the client to thoughtfully discuss the problem. Consider asking the client what, if anything, he or she has tried in the past to address the problem, the outcome of these efforts, and what the client's life might be like once the problem is reduced or resolved (Sperry, Carlson, & Kjos, 2003).

There are no practical limitations on setting socially defined goals. As such, one may encourage or coordinate with a friend to carry out a vengeful or illegal goal, such as formulating a retaliatory plan against a disliked person or organization, whereas in your professional role as a therapist, you are constrained by legal and ethical considerations and cannot suggest, condone, or facilitate the setting, planning, or execution of any such illegal, unethical, or (self-)destructive goals. In such cases, your familiarity with and commitment to the professional code of ethics pertaining to your particular field of practice should provide a useful framework for making responsible clinical judgments (Brammer, 1993). Case in point: Suppose a client presents that the ex-spouse persistently fails to provide child support as specified in their divorce agreement. In your role as a therapist, you are ethically and legally obliged to discourage illegal actions. As an alternative to participating in or encouraging any possibly illegal actions that the client may be considering or fantasizing about, you may provide an environment for venting and processing such feelings along with appropriate referrals for legal or arbitration services that could be used to address this problem within legal and ethical boundaries.

For some cultures and individuals, it is customary to engage in some initial "small talk" as a warm-up prior to embarking on clinically goal-related discussion; in the interest of facilitating rapport, you may find it useful to engage the client in such dialogue and then appropriately guide the discussion to address the therapeutic issues at hand. In order to enhance your effectiveness as an evolving therapist, it can be useful to orient yourself to the multicultural characteristics of your community and the social norms of such groups (Pendersen, Draguns, Lonner, & Trimble, 1996; Sue, 1992). Specifically, Latino clients may prefer to engage in some brief nontherapeutic chatting (*la plática*) as a customary warm-up prior to embarking on therapeutic issues (Martinez, 1986). Conversely, this practice would be inappropriate for Asian clients who, per cultural practice, may perceive such social conversation as an unnecessary delay to discussing tangible immediate goals (Root, Ho, & Sue, 1986; Sue & Sue, 2003).

Occasionally, the client may enter the session with a crisis issue that may be unique from the predominate goal for therapy. In such cases, a temporary departure from the primary goal may be appropriate in order to help the client manage such acute circumstances.

Goals must also be consistent with the client's belief system. For example, suppose a client expresses that he or she has a problem with alcohol addiction and that it is mutually agreed that the client will attend AA meetings daily for the next 90 days; however, the client's spiritual beliefs require ceremonial attendance at some point during that period, which interrupts the 90-day commitment. Although you are welcome to address concerns regarding the impact that this may have on the client's sobriety, you are not in a position to insist on the client's strict compliance with the 90-day plan. Again, the client is recognized as the chief decision maker in his or her life. One way to conceptualize your role might be to think of yourself as the client's "mental health consultant." In this case, you would work with the client to arrive at alternative ways of coping with the recovery issue. This might involve the client calling to check in with his or her sponsor on missed meeting days, thus respecting the client's spiritual beliefs.

Topic of Conversation

Social conversations have no particular limitations in terms of subject matter; participants may raise any topic at will. In a therapeutic setting, topics of conversation are not necessarily limited, but they are typically more focused. Topics of conversation are guided in order to address those issues specifically related to the therapeutic goals. Unlike casual conversations, wherein the participants typically discuss things that they mutually want to discuss, therapeutic discussions may involve emotionally challenging issues that the client may be hesitant to discuss but which are essential to addressing and resolving the problems at hand (Kadushin, 1990). Whereas casual conversations are free to drift seamlessly or abruptly from one topic to the next, therapy is typically more focused. When a client drifts off topic, part of your role is to recognize this departure and assess the value of such conversation. Valuable ancillary information may be revealed in the content of such discussion. Conversely, you may feel that it is beneficial to discuss the nature of this shift by asking the client some questions about it: Did the client feel anxious and feel the need to switch to a more comfortable line of discussion? Did some critical piece of information suddenly come to mind? As the therapist, it is your responsibility to keep the discussion on track. This may involve deliberately directing the discussion back to the (most) relevant therapeutic issues. Specific techniques for *redirecting* and *refocusing* are discussed further in Chapter 4.

Social conversations are usually balanced between the members in terms of who the subject of the conversation will be. For instance, sometimes Jane will tell Mike about what is going on in her life, and sometimes Mike will tell Jane about his life issues. This reciprocity is not characteristic of the therapeutic process. The client consistently remains the focal point of the discussions; typically you would not indulge in confiding in the client. Exceptions to this rule may include profession-related inquiries, such as the client seeking information regarding the therapist's education, qualifications, clinical experience, special training, or certifications. Guidelines for the use of therapeutic self-disclosure are discussed later in this chapter.

Advice

Social conversation is often laced with casual advice, suggestions, recommendations, and sometimes even firm demands. Such guidance can be based on anything including empirical research, personal opinions, anecdotes, impulsive ideas, or belief systems. Though well intended, there are no formal guidelines with respect to the quality or appropriateness of recommendations given in the role of the casual helper. As a therapist, advice giving is typically not the first order of business. Prior to submitting recommendations, you would typically take the time to assemble a comprehensive profile of the client to better ensure that the advice will be suitable to the unique attributes and circumstances of the client. Factors that should be taken into account include the client's perception of the problem and internal factors, which might include the client's personality, prior coping, motivation, belief systems, personal ethics, spiritual base, physical health, and external factors such as social system, family, friends, community resources, and culture. Advice that is given prematurely is less likely to fit within the boundaries of the client's life. Haphazardly given advice is likely to be a mismatch to the client's characteristics and is seldom followed. The better the fit, the better the likelihood that the client will actually follow through.

In social settings, one has the privilege to, with good intention, unilaterally insist that a particular action be taken. In concordance with the ethical standards of health and human services professionals, it is essential to genuinely respect the client's right to self-determination and facilitate empowerment at each phase of the therapeutic process. Consider the client as an expert on his or her own life and work collaboratively with the client to flesh out a facilitative course of action suitable to the unique needs and attributes of the client. This can involve prompting the client to discuss the (problematic) circumstances, identify functional and dysfunctional components, and select which part(s) of the problem that the client is motivated to resolve. This is not to say that as the therapist you withhold potentially useful advice waiting for the client to stumble upon it. Quite the contrary. Through your education and experience, you may possess and propose specialized clinical knowledge or experience that may be suitable to addressing the problem at hand. Additionally, you may have knowledge of, or access to, reputable resources. Providing meaningful referrals is an essential supplement to the therapeutic process.

There are no constraints on what sort of advice can be given in social settings. Socially, one might offhandedly recommend that a friend try hypnosis to help control an eating disorder, discuss an herbal remedy for severe headaches, or refer a friend to a promising Web site for health information, products, or services that may be helpful. Such benevolent recommendations may indeed turn out to be beneficial. In your role as a mental health professional, you are obliged to provide reputable referrals that have been adequately researched.

In casual settings, there are no binding rules as to who the beneficiary of such advice may be: John may attempt to persuade Kate to take actions that are not necessarily exclusively beneficial to Kate; John may be motivated for others to be the primary, or perhaps secondary, beneficiary of Kate's modified behavior. This is contraindicated in therapy. Per ethical and legal rules, as the therapist, you cannot be the beneficiary—primary or otherwise—of professional interventions (Ivey, 1983). The client must consistently remain the focal point of therapeutic planning and interventions. Specific techniques for *informing* and *advising* are presented in Chapter 5.

Perspective

Social relationships and conversations can be driven as much by fact as by feeling. In such relationships, what is said from one member to another can be comprised of a combination of such things as intuition, knowledge of one's self and the other person, personal opinions, life circumstances, and experience. In the therapeutic relationship, the perspective is not that different from the casual relationship. In your evolving role as a therapist, you will be aware that you are not completely objective. You do have personal opinions about what you think a client should or should not do; however, in light of the ethical principles promoting each client's right to self-determination, a clinician's personal opinion has lower priority in a professional setting. Bearing in mind that although you have good intentions on behalf of your clients, it is the client who holds the privilege and responsibility for determining the shape of his or her life and ultimately carrying out those plans or not.

As in social contexts, you accumulate a level of understanding about the client, both in terms of the data provided and also from a sense of feeling and intuition that is a natural part of the communication process. Although the efforts of a trusted friend may indeed be helpful in providing support and solving problems, in your capacity as the therapist, you have the advantage of a social science education. This more objective perspective enables you to utilize the appropriate theoretical framework(s) to gather and process information and feelings in a systematic manner, identify source problems, formulate diagnostics, and collaboratively assemble and implement appropriate therapeutic treatment.

Social/Emotional Factors

Emotional Involvement

It is appropriate and expected that we have close emotional relationships with the people in our lives. We do not exist in an isolated intellectual realm. We are social, feeling beings. In our contact with others, we have the privilege of experiencing a wide spectrum of emotions, ranging from the joy of a loving relationship to profound hurt and sense of loss. Much of our identity is characterized by our emotional characteristics. Often when describing a person, we may refer to his or her social or emotional hallmark. (*"He's the kindest person I know." "In the morning she's a little rough around the edges." "He's good with kids." "She can make anyone laugh without even trying."*) The therapeutic relationship is by no means devoid of feelings; in fact, effective therapy largely depends on expressing, perceiving, and processing feelings as they pertain to the client's life circumstances. Therapy largely consists of acknowledging such feelings and sensitively working with emotionally laden issues while maintaining a professional emotional distance. Issues related to effectively identifying and working with the emotional aspects of the therapeutic process are addressed in Chapter 4.

Objectivity

It is difficult to achieve a sense of objectivity in close personal relationships. Personal involvement with friends and loved ones appropriately confounds our sense of objectivity. We are not indifferent or uninvolved in the lives of others. Quite the contrary. We do have opinions about the quality of our friends' lives and the choices they make. Some of these choices may affect or involve us personally. In the professional setting, it is essential to identify and take into account the client's feelings. It is equally important to keep an appropriate emotional distance in order to maintain a less obscured view of the client and his or her problems. That is to say, in your capacity as a therapist, you have the unique opportunity to provide an additional perspective to the problem: *What might this problem look like with the emotions subtracted?*

Consider a case in which the well-meaning client describes how each Sunday is dedicated to personally supervising an alcoholic friend so that the friend will be sober for work on Monday. As the therapist, your objectivity affords you the opportunity to convey critical observations: (a) This activity is well-meaning. (b) This friend is failing to take responsibility for his or her own actions and inactions. (c) The client's rescuing efforts serve to cushion the friend from the reality of this situation, which in turn is unintentionally delaying the pathway to a meaningful recovery. (d) The client may be holding resentments against this friend for consuming half of each weekend. Hence, your objective perspective may enable the client the opportunity to view and present problems *with* and *without* the emotions in place, which may provide alternative routes to the problem-solving pathway.

Rescind Your Ego

Although it may seem overly simplistic, it is worth stating that as thinking, feeling, social beings, we take our personal lives personally. You care about the people in your life and you want them to care about you as well. To varying degrees, it matters to you what family and friends think and feel about you, just as your thoughts and feelings matter to them. This sense of cognitive, emotional, and social reciprocity can be thought of as the basis for such relationships. Your close relationships are far from objective. You are not impartial to the people in your life. Appropriately, you have strong feelings about the people that you are close with; you care what happens to them; and presumably, you care about their opinions and interactions with you.

The therapeutic setting is somewhat different. Although the therapeutic process is a collaborative relationship, rich with feelings and a sense of connection, the therapist maintains a certain level of objectivity with respect to the client.

Objectivity enables you to embark on providing effective therapy, placing the appropriate ethical principles first. Though you are entitled to form and express your impressions and opinions in a professional manner, client self-determination must remain at the forefront of the therapeutic process. At times, your clients may thank you for your helpful efforts or blame you for failing to fix their problems; it is critical to remember that though your mission is to be helpful in improving the quality of client's lives, the client is the primary decision-maker and actor in his or her life. As a therapist, you may think of yourself as a kind of emotional consultant (the client solicits your professional opinion and guidance with respect to some form of problem solving). Although it is your job to collaborate with the client using social science principles to process issues, it is the client who is responsible for his or her life. Although it may be tempting to assume an inordinate amount of credit for a client's successes or failures, ultimately, the client's decisions, actions, inactions, and outcomes are ultimately in the client's hands, not yours.

Personal Contact

Personal relationships are comprised largely of personal contacts, which can take a variety of forms including spontaneous telephone calls, social lunches, leisure activities, or visits. A social relationship may consist of a single role, such as tennis partner, or multiple roles wherein one person may be your best friend, confidant, work-out partner, and travel companion. The therapeutic relationship differs in that out-of-the-office contacts are contraindicated; ethical and legal statutes regulate the extent of such contact. As a therapist, you are obliged to separate your social life from your professional life. Dual or multiple relationships wherein the therapist socializes with clients or has friends as clients are contraindicated, thereby facilitating the preservation of the professional contact. Dual relationships have the potential of harming the therapist's sense of professionalism and objectivity. Additionally, in a dual relationship, the client may continue to perceive the therapist as an authority figure, creating the risk of a potentially exploitive relationship (*Ethical Standards of Human Service Professionals,* Statement 6; Council for Standards, 1996). In short: Your friends cannot become your clients, and your clients cannot become your friends.

In some ways, the personal friend has advantages over the therapist: The personal friend has the opportunity to make first-hand observations of a person in a variety of natural settings (the breakfast table, the bowling alley, interacting with family at home, etc.), whereas in your role as therapist, you will typically see the client outside his or her "natural habitat," leaving you largely dependent on the client's report of circumstances and events occurring outside the office between sessions.

Lacking observations of the client in his or her natural settings, such as home or with friends, it is possible that social desirability can be a confounding factor wherein the client may distort or choose not to discuss selected events, thoughts, or feelings for fear of being negatively judged (Rubin & Babbie, 1993). Another possibility is that the client may not see a particular event occurring outside the session as relevant to the therapy; hence, the client may not feel that it is worthy of mention. Without presuming a suspicious stance, it is not unreasonable to consider the likelihood that the client may only be telling half a story or skewing a story. Such conveyance is not necessarily attributable to social desirability. Rather, the client only has a single point of view. At best, a story can only be told in the way that it is initially perceived and later remembered.

Often strong emotions are woven into the memory of events, which may compromise the accuracy of otherwise objective information. With the client's written permission, it can be advantageous to the therapeutic process to have access to collateral information. This may include relevant records, consults with other health care professionals—specifically physicians, psychiatrists, and prior therapists—or it may involve including other significant people in the therapy (McClam & Woodside, 1994). For example, a solo female client may describe her boyfriend as consistently late coming home, verbally cruel, and physically withdrawn. Our initial impression may lead us to conclude that this is an abusive or neglectful relationship. Upon including the boyfriend in the therapy, we may find out that he is a part-time college student working a night job and that he becomes verbally abrupt with his girlfriend when she forcefully awakens him for further attention. In short, supplemental information, appropriately gathered, can provide you with a more comprehensive understanding of the client's life circumstances, thereby better focusing the assessment, treatment planning, and interventions.

Involvement

In personal relationships, when it comes to helping, there are no limitations with respect to involvement. As an illustration, suppose an individual has lost a job. As a friend, in addition to consoling, you may choose to step in and skillfully craft the résumé and cover letter, write a letter of recommendation, help shop for appropriate interview attire, perform the job searches, submit résumés, schedule interviews, and may even go so far as to transport the person to the interviews. Each of these is a valuable service. It is socially appropriate for friends to help each other per their talents and needs. Additionally, in this case, it is clear that the workload is unevenly distributed: About 90% of the work is being done by you and about 10% by your friend. In a social or friendship setting, there is nothing inherently wrong with this balance. In a professional helping relationship, this workload distribution would be inappropriate. The fundamental ethical principles of therapy involve empowerment, self-determination, self-efficacy, and the right to refuse services (*Ethical Standards of Human Service Professionals,* Statement 8; Council for Standards, 1996). Essentially, instead of doing this work for the client, as the therapist, your role would be more in the capacity of coaching the client to do as much for him- or herself as possible by collaboratively identifying meaningful goals and providing feedback and encouragement, thereby fostering personal growth and facilitating independence. In this case, it may be appropriate to utilize the sessions to help the client to cope with the emotional stresses related to unemployment such as self-esteem issues, depression, anxiety, frustration, or financial concerns. The therapy may also take the direction of identifying and resolving emotional roadblocks that may encumber the rigors of the job search.

In terms of the mechanics of achieving employment—which may include activities like refining the résumé, crafting a clear cover letter, and job hunting—as the therapist, you would take a more directive and less active stance. For instance, as opposed to your actually writing or editing the résumé, it would be more appropriate to recommend that the client confer with a résumé service or vocational guidance counselor. In terms of the job search itself, you may possess useful knowledge of some job search resources. Providing information regarding reputable Web sites, job boards, or reliable employment services would be appropriate, whereas performing the actual search for the client would likely be considered to be beyond the scope of your professional responsibility.

Professionalism

Legal

There are no special laws that govern the social conduct between friends. As such, there are no grounds for legal action with respect to such unfortunate happenstances as disappointment, rudeness, or hurt feelings, whereas there are clearly defined ethical and legal rules that govern the client-therapist relationship: Unlike casual friendships which typically have no supporting documentation, therapists are obliged to maintain thorough client records—including information detailing the consents for treatment, initial problem, diagnostic information, therapeutic goals, progress notes, and collateral information—in order to review clinical progress and as a professional service to other providers who may be involved with, or take over the care of, the client (Committee on Professional Practices and Standards, 1993).

As a health care practitioner, you must also adhere to laws and procedures governing mandated reporting, requiring you to breach the client's confidentiality under special circumstances. In instances when you believe that a client poses a plausible physical threat to him- or herself or others, as a therapist, you are legally mandated to notify the appropriate parties of the potential threat (Tarasoff warning; Kagle & Kopels, 1994). Additionally, as a therapist, you are required to understand potential compulsory breaches to confidentiality in terms of the laws regarding mandated reporting should you reasonably suspect that a client has perpetrated child abuse (Hepworth & Larsen, 1993). You must also be knowledgeable regarding your legally mandated responsibilities and protocol with respect to promptly reporting suspected abuse or neglect of a child, dependent adult, or elderly person. Those who submit such reports in good faith are protected from legal recourse from those named in the report (Lindsey, 1994). In your professional capacity, you must also know where you stand in terms of responding properly to subpoenas, depositions, and court orders, which varies from state to state. These legally enforced limitations regarding confidentiality may be provided to the client in the form of intake documentation. Other times, they may be a point of discussion early in the initial session.

Although avoiding social contact with clients is typically considered to be an ethical issue, engaging in sexual contact with a client, even among consenting adults, is both unethical and illegal (*Ethical Standards of Human Service Professionals*, Statement 7; Council for Standards, 1996). Laws vary considerably from state to state with respect to the therapist having sex with ex-clients; as with confidentiality, you are responsible for knowing and adhering to the laws of the states in which you practice.

Confidentiality

In casual relationships, individuals are free to exchange information and opinions with each other. For instance, John is free to tell Jane of his afternoon spent with Scott, which may include details regarding activities, conversations, or impressions. John may also choose to disclose one of Scott's secrets; although this may be perceived as a breach of trust among friends, such disclosures are not illegal, per se. In your role as a health care provider, confidentiality is legally and ethically paramount. As a therapist, you are committed to protecting an individual's confidentiality. The content of therapy is considered privileged information, which can only be disclosed to others with the client's written consent, except for special circumstances delineated by law (Kagle & Kopels, 1994; *Ethical Standards of Human Service Professionals*, Statements 3 & 5; Council for Standards, 1996).

You may partake in professional peer consultations with another therapist. Such consults should be conducted privately, as opposed to in open or public spaces where one could be overheard, and only the essential details should be provided. Take care to preserve the client's anonymity by omitting potentially identifying information. Make a consistent effort to protect the identity of clients by conducting therapy in a private sound-protected setting, properly storing client files and related data and, when indicated, properly destroying and disposing of identifying material. It is your responsibility to actively protect client identity, including confidential record management protocol as it pertains to current, ex-, and deceased clients. Additionally, as a professional, you are responsible for exercising appropriate protocol related to sharing client information with other practitioners, specifically signed consents when disclosures could suggest the identity of the client. This practice is also applicable to those requesting information via phone or other media. Haphazard breaches in confidentiality will cost you and your colleagues the trust and support of clients and compromise public opinion of such services (Crenshaw, Bartell, & Lichtenberg, 1994).

Depending on the state laws governing therapists' privilege, your notes may be subject to subpoena or court order, and depending on the case, you may be called to testify in a court of law.

Concerns regarding confidentiality may be particularly critical to traditional Asian clients with whom the stigma of mental health issues reflects unfavorably, not only on the individual client but also the family as a whole (Gaw, 1993).

Scope of Practice

Casual relationships afford the privilege to engage in a wide latitude of helpful efforts. Friends are free to mutually experiment with such practices as acupressure, hypnosis, or herbal remedies. Additionally, there are no practical limitations with respect to social contacts offering recommendations or referrals. In the realm of professional therapy, you are only sanctioned to provide services for which you have received appropriate training, certification, or licensure (*Ethical Standards of Human Service Professionals*, Statement 26; Council for Standards, 1996). This constraint to limit therapists to practice within the realm of one's training and competency cannot be superseded with the client's consent, or even pleading. In such cases, you are obliged to refuse to provide the supplemental service; if appropriate, you do, however, have the privilege to provide reputable referrals to the client.

In addition to your clinical efforts, clients may, of their own accord, choose to supplement their treatment plans by including care providers that are considered traditionally acceptable within their realm. Some African Americans may utilize folk healers for treatments involving herbs, teas, and appropriate rituals to remedy medical or mental disorders (Baker & Lightfoot, 1993; Wilkinson & Spurlock, 1986). Similarly, Latinos may confer with religious leaders to aid in the resolution of mental health issues (Dana, 1993; Ho, 1992; Martinez, 1993). American Indians may include consultations with culturally relevant figures such as tribal leaders or elders when dealing with family social issues (Paniagua, 2005).

Boundaries

Personal relationships are typically characterized by implicit boundaries, defined by social and personal norms and values. These boundaries can vary from one relationship to another. Topics discussed in one relationship may include subject matters such as politics, career issues, and media, whereas the subject matter with another person might include topics such as family functioning, details of one's sex life, and discussion of dreams. Socially, either person has the privilege to specify topics that can and cannot be discussed. Such relationships are usually not one-way. Conversations consist of mutual open self-disclosure, exchange of opinions, and advice sharing. In a therapeutic relationship, the focal point of each session remains on the client; as a therapist, your self-disclosure is typically kept to a minimum. Keep in mind that every minute spent talking about the therapist's life is a minute taken away from focusing on the client's life. As a therapist, you need not remain a complete enigma to the client. Appropriate self-disclosure typically consists of openly answering questions related to professional qualification, such as education, training, clinical experience, or experience working with a particular clinical issue. A more detailed discussion regarding the appropriate uses of therapeutic self-disclosure is presented later in this chapter.

Personal relationships can be characterized by flexibility. Over time, the contact can evolve into a variety of forms, including such venues as telephone chat friends, lunch friends, sexual partners, or business associates. The therapeutic relationship does not afford such opportunities. Your professional contact and conduct with the client should be confined to competently providing goal-directed therapeutic services at the agreed-upon time and location only and should not involve casual contact outside the therapeutic setting (*Ethical Standards of Human Service Professionals,* Statement 6; Council for Standards, 1996).

Predictability, stability and robust boundaries have been shown to be key factors, in terms of clinical effectiveness, in building and maintaining the therapeutic relationship, carefully balancing the separateness and independence of each individual within the context of a collaborative setting (Epstine, 1994).

As important as it is to set and maintain appropriate professional boundaries, flexibility is essential in order to accommodate cultural factors, particularly when working with Latino clients. The development of the therapeutic relationship may evolve from the initial formalism (*formalismo*) wherein it is appropriate to address clients in a formal manner (e.g., Mr. Garcia) to a more personal (*personalismo*) form wherein first names would be used (Bernal & Gutierrez, 1988; Ho, 1992; Martinez, 1993). Additionally, some traditional Latino clients may offer a token gift to the therapist as a sign of gratitude. Persistent refusal of such gifts could be perceived as an insulting violation of the *personalismo* practice and thereby unintentionally damage rapport (Paniagua, 2005).

Time Commitment/Responsibility

Social relationships have the advantage of time flexibility. There are no set limits on the number of contacts, frequency of contacts, type of contacts (in-person, telephone, Internet, etc.), or ultimate duration of the social relationship. Friends may be together for months, years, or a lifetime. In a psychotherapeutic setting, sessions are typically held at a fixed appointment time and duration, usually 50 minutes, and it is expected that sessions will begin and end on time (Kadushin, 1990). The number of sessions may be limited. Six to twelve sessions is not uncommon. This limitation may be a matter of financial constraints as designated by the client's managed care company or insurance provider, agency policy, or adequate resolution of the problem. Additionally, there is typically an agreement established in the initial session regarding missed or cancelled appointments. Traditionally, clients are asked to provide 24-hour notice in order to cancel an appointment. There may also be limitations regarding the total number of missed appointments.

Respect

Respect can be thought of as holding another person's feelings, beliefs, and thoughts in as high a regard as you hold your own. Although mutual respect could be considered a natural part of casual relationships, it is not necessarily mandatory. Social communication may include derogatory language such as insults, teasing, sarcasm, taunting, or mocking, which may range from playful to severe. Additionally, in casual relationships, we may not always take the other person seriously. A particular topic may be of little interest or considered trivial by one member, therefore eliciting anything from superficial listening to an abrupt change of subject. In a therapeutic relationship, it is essential to consistently convey respect for the client's dignity in order to foster a facilitative helping relationship (*Ethical Standards of Human Service Professionals,* Statement 2; Council for Standards, 1996). This is not to say that as a therapist, you are resigned to playing the role of the yes-man. The quality of the therapy largely depends on the therapist's ability to offer an honest reflection of the client's life circumstances and alternatives, but this must be delivered with respect and tact. For example, a client may choose to partake in activities that you find distasteful or do not agree with; certainly the client has the right to make his or her own decisions. Although it is your role to honor the client's right to self-determination, you need not pretend to agree nor sit silently. You would be entitled to engage the client to discuss relevant concerns or potential consequences regarding the client's decisions and actions in a purposeful manner, taking care not to degrade or shame. One of the greatest challenges that health and human service professionals face is that of honoring the client's right to self-determination, even when you do not agree with the client's decisions, actions, inactions, (potential) outcomes, or belief systems.

Nonjudgmental Attitude

As humans, it is natural that we form opinions about people, which influence our decisions about our associations, how we treat others, and our expectations of them. Socially, one has the privilege to select who will be in one's life and the nature of the relationship that we will have with another. Part of the responsibility of being a therapist is keeping one's personal biases in check. Ideally, your professional relationships need to be free of judgmental attitudes/feelings and opinions and to provide an inherently accepting stance with respect to an individual client's unique attributes (race, age, gender, sexual orientation, ideology, social class, intellect, political affiliation, religious beliefs).

Some cultures may practice rituals that are unfamiliar to you, or they may adhere to belief systems that seem foreign or implausible to you. For instance, some Latinos attribute mental or emotional disorders to evil spirits or witchcraft and may, in addition to therapy, seek help from a folk healer. In order to best serve such clients, be prepared to suspend your own judgment and work within the framework that is culturally relevant to the client (Martinez, 1986).

The value of holding a nonjudgmental attitude is twofold: By setting aside your preconceptions of the client, you are better able to comprehend who he or she genuinely is and what the actual nature of his or her problem is, as opposed to your uninformed presumptions. Also, clients are often dealing with difficult feelings that may include stress, guilt, fear, shame, or general hurt related to their problems; the last thing they need is for the therapist to put more weight on those feelings by imposing negative judgments (Ivey, 1983).

Depending on the openness or narrowness of one's perspective outside of the therapeutic environment, maintaining a nonjudgmental attitude may pose more of a challenge to some than others. There may be circumstances that may not be conducive to conducting therapy due to profound differences between you and a particular client, for instance, a minority therapist working with a client whose hallmark characteristic concurs with the principles of a hate group. In such circumstances, it is appropriate to evaluate, as honestly as possible, the extent to which you feel you can provide quality, unbiased service to this client. If after thorough consideration—which may involve conferring with peers or one's supervisor—the mismatch is not resolvable, then it may be necessary to inform the client, as blamelessly as possible, of this insurmountable roadblock and to tactfully provide the client with appropriate referrals. Alternatively, a client may express his or her own biases. For instance, a client may wish to have a therapist of the same gender or ethnic background. Certainly, you have the privilege to articulate your capacity to provide quality care; however, if after you have submitted such a proposal, the client still wishes to terminate or switch to a different therapist, the client's preference must ultimately be honored, with the exception of certain in-patient or compulsory treatment venues. The notion of a nonjudgmental attitude as a means for promoting a trusting therapeutic contact will be covered in further detail in Chapter 2.

Positive Regard

Social relationships afford substantial latitude in terms of accepting or rejecting others. Friends may express feelings toward each other ranging from pride to disappointment; heated accusations, chastising language, sarcastic retorts, and stabbing insults, though hurtful, may all have their place in such contexts. In a provocative social setting, one may proclaim the other to be a no-good failure who will never amount to anything. In your role as a therapist, you are essentially committed to fostering a perspective of positive regard, wherein the value and worth of the person remain foremost (Rogers, 1957). Although the therapeutic process inherently challenges clients to grow and change, ethical standards and research support the use of a positive, as opposed to punitive, framework. Consider a case wherein a client fails to achieve a specified goal or reverts to a dysfunctional behavior. Positive regard does not mean that you ignore it. Instead of accusing the client of laziness or failure, it would be more appropriate to engage the client in a facilitative dialogue, accentuating the client's past accomplishments, strengths, goals, and work to identify and resolve some of the factors that may have confounded or encumbered his or her progress, thereby empowering the client to lay the groundwork to try again or identify alternatives. Persistent conveyance of an attitude of positive regard toward the client promotes the therapeutic relationship (Nugent, 1992). Conveying a genuine "I'm on your side" attitude carries the positive implication that the client possesses the capacity to achieve the objectives set forth in therapy.

Self-Disclosure

Within the context of personal relationships, mutual self-disclosure is a natural part of the communication stream. In social situations, individuals typically exchange personal information about themselves in a free and spontaneous manner. Such dialogues can foster a sense of intimacy and trust between the individuals. The therapeutic relationship is different in that the focus is primarily dedicated to the story and needs of the client and not you.

In the therapeutic milieu, your self-disclosure can be thought of in two realms: professional and personal.

Suppose a client admits to a history of substance abuse and is requesting help toward achieving and maintaining recovery. In terms of making a *professional* self-disclosure, you may choose to briefly tell the client that you interned for a year as a substance abuse counselor at a chemical dependency recovery center. Such a disclosure can facilitate the therapeutic process by calling attention to the fact that you possess specialized professional experience to address such a problem. Few would argue the appropriateness of such a brief, focused, professional self-disclosure; however, opinions vary with respect to making *personal* self-disclosures. Using this example, there is an array of advantages and disadvantages to disclosing extensive details regarding your own substance abuse history and recovery to a client within a therapeutic setting.

Traditionally, as the therapist, you would presume the role of the unbiased helper; in order to accomplish this, self-disclosure, on your behalf, is typically kept to a minimum. Regardless of how little you verbally disclose about yourself, clients are privy to a multitude of other clues when it comes to formulating an impression of you. Your readily observable personal attributes, such as your gender, race, ethnicity, grooming, attire, wedding ring, mannerisms, demeanor, physicality (stride, posture, gestures), approximate age, and language characteristics (vocabulary, expressions, accent) are undeniably evident. Your working environment may provide further hints as to your tastes, personality, and education: Clients may assemble an impression of you from such common things as photos on your desk, artwork, furnishings, diplomas, licenses, certificates, and books; so even without providing extensive, detailed disclosure, the client has some basis for forming an impression as to who you are. Essentially, the principle is not necessarily for you to present as an enigma but rather to provide a neutral canvas, ready to accept the client's verbal rendering in an unbiased fashion.

There is no single right answer regarding the use of self-disclosure in the therapeutic realm; one factor that mediates the appropriateness of the therapist's use of self-disclosure is the therapist's theoretical orientation. For instance, a psychodynamically oriented therapist would consider self-disclosure inappropriate, as it could corrupt the transference potential; a humanistic therapist, however, may readily utilize self-disclosure as means to facilitate authenticity (Goldfried, Burckell, & Eubanks-Carter, 2003).

Advantages of Self-Disclosure

Self-disclosure, wherein you share with the client that you have dealt with issues similar to the client's, may facilitate a therapeutic alliance by demonstrating commonality. The client may feel that you are uniquely qualified to understand the problem from personal experience. Using your matching experience can help normalize the client's feelings by letting the client know that he or she is not the only one, that his or her experience is not one in a million. Research indicates that the therapist's use of moderate—as opposed to high or low—levels of self-disclosure in the initial interview results in higher rates of return to future appointments by clients (Simon, 1988; Simonson, 1976).

Studies also indicate that the therapist's sharing of personal thoughts and feelings provides the client the opportunity to know the therapist, thereby developing the professional relationship (Shulman, 1977). The use of focused self-disclosure may help the client perceive you as a facilitative role model, someone who has faced a relevant challenge and successfully overcome the obstacle, thereby instilling the client with a sense of hope. Successfully modeling a process or adaptation to a problem may serve as an instructive template for the client to follow (Bandura, 1986). Research suggests that the therapist's self-disclosure can result in a reciprocity effect, wherein the client, in return, engages more readily in his or her own self-disclosure, thereby advancing the therapeutic process (Doster & Nesbitt, 1979).

According to a study of clinicians, therapists tend to use self-disclosure most frequently to increase the client's awareness of options, enhance the client's self-disclosure via modeling, lower anxiety, and convey authenticity. Among the therapists studied, the most disclosed topics include the therapist's personal history and current relationship; least disclosed topics include sexuality and money (Anderson & Mandell, 1989).

Disadvantages of Self-Disclosure

When choosing to self-disclose in the therapeutic setting, you are inherently faced with the running question of to what extent do you tell your story. You must then select which personal facts to disclose, as well as the depth of detail suitable for each story.

Excessive self-disclosure may lead to the gradual development of an inappropriate bond between you and your client. Specifically, there is a risk of role reversal. In a setting wherein you regularly reveal vulnerable attributes of your life, the client may naturally develop a sense of sympathy toward you. As the client takes your personal feelings and life experiences into consideration, the client may resist burdening you with his or her own (genuine) problems. The client may feel that perhaps you are already dealing with a full load and should be spared the burden of the client's potentially critical problems. The client may resort to such strategies as withholding difficult topics, omitting details, even distorting or editing truths so as not to overtax or offend you. The client's evolving sense of compassion toward you may cause the client to feel uncomfortable discussing therapeutic roadblocks or complications in the treatment plan implementation for fear of making you feel as though you somehow failed. In such circumstances, the client is short-changed: If you are being misled into believing that the therapeutic process is working idyllically, then critical opportunities for tuning the therapy may be lost at the expense of the client.

Presenting with a genuinely friendly demeanor can be an asset in facilitating rapport; however, regularly disclosing personal information to the client may cause the client to begin to see the relationship as less a professional and more a social relationship. The risk is that the client may be misled or confused by such ambiguous boundaries. Under such circumstances, the client may desire or request that you join him or her for some social engagement. Such dual relationships are professionally contraindicated. That is to say, ethically it is inappropriate for you to serve both as a therapist and a social friend. In short, your objectivity as a therapist is compromised when a client is a friend. Additionally, expanding your professional relationships to a social realm wields an unsuitable air of authority. A client is likely to experience a sense of rejection should you fail to promote the relationship to the next level. (*"We get along so well in the sessions, I wonder why I haven't been asked to get together outside the session."*) Similarly, the client may feel as though he or she has been spurned should you decline an invitation to a social engagement.

Self-disclosure may also set off any number of unintended adverse reactions. Though well intended, your self-disclosure may not transfer to the client in the manner expected. Consider a case wherein the client raises the topic of substance abuse and you disclose that you are a recovering addict with a long history of sobriety. Depending on the drugs involved, the client may perceive you as either over- or underqualified to comprehend his or her circumstances. For instance, it is possible that a client who is a heroin addict may deem an ex–marijuana user a lightweight who cannot begin to comprehend the client's problem. Conversely, a client who is addicted to prescription pain medication may form an unfavorable opinion of you should you proclaim that you used to use illegal street drugs.

When a client presents with a problem with which you have personally dealt, it can be tempting to play the *"Oh, I've been there. . . . Here's how you handle this . . ."* card with the intention of normalizing the client's situation, instilling hope and delivering a facilitative treatment plan. Though this may initially seem the only reasonable approach, there is the potential for considerable drawbacks: Imparting the message, *"I've dealt with this, and you will too,"* naively denies the uniqueness of the client. Each individual is endowed with a unique set of talents, capabilities, and challenges. Additionally, social systems, which can include such things as family, friends, living conditions, and socioeconomic status, can vary considerably from person to person. In reality, the client and his or her circumstances are not like you and yours; hence, the solution pathway that worked for you may not transfer seamlessly to the client. Additionally, imparting your success story as it pertains to the client's problem may have an unintended negative paradoxical effect, whereby disclosing, *"I accomplished this, so you can too,"* may be received by the client with, *"Yeah, but you're a success and I'm not,"* potentially leading to a negative outcome (Mann & Murphy, 1975).

Instead of issuing fix-it directives, the derivation of which may appear elusive in nature and therefore difficult for the client to reproduce independently, consider engaging the client in a collaborative problem-solving process, thereby fostering the client's sense of skill building, empowerment, and independence. The client's participation in the solution process facilitates customized strategies that are concurrent with the client's resources and distinctive personality style, which may be different from yours. In terms of implementation, clients tend to be more likely to follow through on solution pathways that fit them, and clients more robustly embrace treatment plans that they have had a hand in assembling.

In some cases, your use of self-disclosure can potentially give the client the impression that the therapy is being guided by something less than clinically sound principles. Consider a client who discloses he or she is experiencing distress related to same-sex attraction, and the client wants to know what can be done to redirect his or her attraction toward the opposite sex. Suppose you respond by disclosing that you are lesbian, gay, or bisexual and then go on to explain to the client that attempting to alter one's sexual orientation is clinically contraindicated, and instead, the therapeutic approach involves helping the client to emotionally accept and embrace his or her orientation, not as pathological, but as a normal sexual variant. Although the clinical information given is, in fact, concurrent with the practice principles of contemporary psychotherapy, having couched this information in the context of your own sexual orientation, the client may perceive the information as personally biased, or even coercive. The client may react by seeking a more objective opinion or perhaps abandon the therapeutic process entirely.

Some forms of therapy depend on the use of *transference*. Effective transference is facilitated by you, as the therapist, persistently withholding self-disclosure, presenting as a virtually unbiased blank slate (tabula rasa), wherein the client is free to superimpose (transfer) his or her feelings for a significant person in his or her own life (a parent, spouse, sibling, peer, etc.) onto you, the neutral therapist (Breuer & Freud, 1955). From there, you and the client gain access to the client's feelings and thoughts in a controlled and facilitative manner. Excessive self-disclosure on your behalf may pollute this (unbiased) transference potential. In other words, if the client comes to know you as a unique person via your extensive self-disclosure, then it may confound the client's ability to readily transfer the emotional cloak of another onto your distinct frame (Basch, 1980).

Time is also a factor when considering self-disclosure. Simply stated, each minute that you spend talking about yourself is a minute taken away from talking about the client. The client may resent that you are consuming the client's time and money talking about yourself. Additionally, the client may not necessarily agree that your self-disclosure is relevant or even interesting; hence, self-disclosure should be done sparingly, and each self-disclosure needs to be as concise as possible.

Therapeutic work can be emotionally rigorous. As you embark on tales of self-disclosure, the client may receive this as a welcome detour from having to deal with his or her own difficult issues. In such circumstances, you may not be doing the client any favors by diverting him or her away from the challenging therapeutic work that the client is there to accomplish (Hill, Helms, Speigel, & Tichener, 1988).

It can be difficult to anticipate the effect that spontaneous self-disclosure may have on you in your capacity as a therapist. Self-disclosure can be fraught with a multitude of emotions, which may induce feelings of vulnerability, confusion, or disorganization, thereby risking destabilizing yourself, the client, and potentially the therapeutic frame(work) (Ulman, 2001).

Self-Disclosures Should Be Honest

Though at times it may be tempting to fabricate or borrow someone else's storyline and present it as your own self-disclosure, doing so has the potential for creating more complications than benefits. Fundamentally, lying breaches the ethical basis of any professional relationship. Lying also creates multiple confounds that can compromise the quality of the attention and care that you are able to provide. Even small deceptions can snowball over time (Peck, 1998). In order for a lie to present as plausible, the lie can seldom stand alone in a vacuum. To exist, it requires a contextual environment typically comprised of supplemental fabrications. For instance, suppose a client discusses stresses related to working at a radio station, and with no such background, you decide to falsely disclose that having once worked in radio, you understand how stressful that can be. Now your well-meaning statement is subject to appropriate inquiry wherein you will need supplemental false information in order to support your evolving lie. You are committed to inventing an entire fictional setting, including things such as the call letters of the station, the frequency, your job title, coworkers' names, personal characteristics and job titles, rating statistics, licensing or certifications that you held, terminology unique to that business, FCC regulations, and multidimensional characteristics of the city where you lived. Being unfamiliar with the business, you may have difficulty articulating this volume of detail on the fly. Not only must you work to conjure up this "B" storyline in real-time, it must also be accurately recalled on a consistent basis. This can be quite a volume of information to memorize and reliably recall. Composing and maintaining this false paradigm is a poor use of your cognitive capacity, as this sort of processing depletes your ability to concentrate on the client. Even if you are able to construct and sustain this fictional storyline, it cannot stand up to simple research and scrutiny. There are multiple ways in which a reasonably skeptical or curious client may discover, through outside means, that none of what you have proposed is true. Ultimately, lying risks the trust that is the very basis of the professional relationship.

Self-Disclosure Guidelines

As a general rule, selective self-disclosure is not inherently forbidden within the therapeutic setting, but it should be administered in a thoughtful and purposive manner. The following guidelines may help you regulate your use of therapeutic self-disclosure:

1. Assess how comfortable you feel disclosing this particular piece of information.

Regardless of how helpful you feel a particular piece of personal information might be to your client, if you do not feel comfortable sharing that information, then you should not. You are entitled to your feelings and sense of privacy. No matter how helpful you think a particular self-disclosure might be in serving your client, you are in no way obliged to compromise your own sense of boundaries. Above all, in a professional setting, you reserve the privilege to keep your personal life personal.

2. Reflect on how beneficial this self-disclosure would be to the client.

Your self-disclosure should only be used as a means for client growth, not to satisfy your own needs (Evans, Hearn, Uhlemann, & Ivey, 1993). Ask yourself why you are considering telling the client this information about yourself. Is your hope that the client will genuinely benefit from what you are considering disclosing, or might you be motivated by other factors (the quest for admiration, validation, the desire to get something off your chest, etc.)?

3. Keep self-disclosures genuine.

Do not borrow, embellish, or fabricate stories.

4. Consider using self-disclosure sparingly.

Should you choose to embark on therapeutic self-disclosure, identify the specific personal information that you feel is therapeutically appropriate and convey it in a succinct and purposeful manner. Avoid indulging in lengthy or tangential storytelling. Remember: The subject of the therapy is the client, not you.

As a caveat to this discussion about self-disclosure and the guidelines put forth, it is worth noting that there is no consensus among practitioners regarding the clinical use of therapist's self-disclosure. These principles are merely provided for your consideration. As an evolving practitioner, it will be up to you to determine your own parameters for embarking on self-disclosure with respect to content, depth, and frequency. Some factors that may influence your thinking may include your theoretical orientation, clinical setting, agency policies, modality (individual, couple, family, group, helpline, etc.), cultural norms, your comfort with the client, your sense of commonality with the client, your comfort with the subject matter, your comfort in your role as a therapist, your sense of privacy, and your gut feelings in the moment. As with any aspect of the therapeutic process, trust yourself to make good decisions.

Role-Play Exercise 1.1

Don't Mention It

This is Adrian's first session; Adrian reports no prior involvement in therapy. The company provides for mental health as part of the benefits package, and as such, Adrian fears what might happen if the company found out the reason for therapy.

Client

- Present as moderately guarded, as if you genuinely do not know the rules regarding confidentiality, regardless of who is paying for the therapy.

- Discuss the potential consequences should your employer find out the content of the therapy.

- When you feel the therapist has adequately addressed your concerns, reveal the reason that you are seeking therapy (possible drinking problem, anxiety related to another job offer).

Therapist

- **Respect** (p. 17)
  Acknowledge Adrian's concerns and hesitation as valid. Do not press for immediate disclosure.

- **Legal** (p. 13)
  Explain that the insurance company will be billed, but the content of the session is considered privileged information that can only be disclosed with the client's written authorization.

- **Confidentiality** (p. 14)
  Provide examples of confidentiality and mandated reporting: what can and cannot be disclosed.

Role-Play Exercise 1.2

Unpleasant Dreams

Evan is an adult who is sporadically employed and occasionally resorts to prostitution for extra income. Recently Evan has been crying and is plagued by poor sleep (nightmares, insomnia).

Client

- Speak of the prostitution in a forthright manner, as if this is old news to you.

- Discuss the crying, sleep problems, and the content of the distressing dreams.

- Tell the therapist that you would like him or her to also provide acupressure or hypnotherapy. If the therapist refuses, then offer to demonstrate how easy it is to do.

Therapist

- **Scope of practice** (p. 15)
  Tactfully refuse to provide a service that is beyond your training and competency, even if Evan authorizes it.

- **Nonjudgmental attitude** (p. 18)
  Work with the client, not on the client. It is okay to make an effort to comprehend the prostitution component of the story, but to Evan this is not the central problem.

- **Positive regard** (p. 19)
  Identify the things that you find commendable about Evan (honesty, motivation to self-improve, sense of independence).

Role-Play Exercise 1.3

My Therapist, My Friend?

Ryan has been a client for about 3 months. The therapy has primarily focused on coping with an alcoholic parent. Ryan has made good progress in therapy but today begins asking questions about the therapist and proposes that they go to lunch today after the session.

Client

- Begin by asking professionally related questions (school, specialized training, etc.).

- Ask the therapist some personal questions (where he or she grew up, family, favorite food, etc.).

- Invite the therapist to lunch; if the therapist cites scheduling conflicts, then propose rescheduling.

Therapist

- **Personal contact** (p. 11)
  Discuss the ethical principles related to dual or multiple relationships.

- **Boundaries** (p. 15)
  Tactfully reject the offer for outside contact.
  "It's flattering that you'd like to spend time with me, but that really wouldn't be appropriate."

- **Self-disclosure** (p. 20)
  Respectfully redirect the client's nonprofessional questions about you.
  "This therapy is about you, not me. Let's get back to . . ."

Role-Play Exercise 1.4

Digital Dilemma

Kyle and Toby have been involved in a close relationship for several years. Recently Kyle discovered some curious messages and pictures on Toby's computer that suggest that Toby may be interested in someone else. It is unclear if this is merely an online contact or if things have gone beyond that.

Client

- Ask for advice on to how to proceed: You want to confront Toby but that would reveal your invasion of Toby's privacy.

- Indicate that you have resisted talking to anyone else about this, fearing that news of your unauthorized computer access may leak back to Toby.

- Attempt to engage the therapist to take the lead in determining the meaning of the computer's contents. Offer to bring in evidence (the computer, printouts, photos) for the therapist's examination.

Therapist

- **Advice** (p. 7)

  Resist the client's requests regarding advice on how to proceed. Explain that at this point, the client knows the players and circumstances better than you do. Engage the client in discussing the nature of the relationship.

- **Confidentiality** (p. 14)

  If Kyle expresses concerns related to Toby finding out the content of the sessions, review the confidentiality rules.

- **Involvement** (p. 12)

  If Kyle asks you to investigate the content of Toby's materials, explain that this is not an appropriate activity for the therapist. Explain that, alternatively, you can help Kyle process feelings, thoughts, concerns, and alternatives.

Role-Play Exercise 1.5

A Lot of Class

Daryl is enrolled in 15 units at the university and is doing well with the exception of one class that is very challenging. Daryl is considering dropping this course in order to dedicate more time to the other courses but, having never dropped a course before, feels conflicted.

Client

- Present as confused about your goal: Should you put extra effort into this class or drop it to provide more time for the other classes. Are there other alternatives?

- Raise multiple topics (detailed information regarding the campus, classes, instructors, students, living conditions, friends, social organizations, entertainment).

- Express how lucky you feel that you were able to find a therapist who is so extraordinarily qualified (compassionate, attentive, well educated, dedicated, insightful).

Therapist

- **Goal** (p. 4)
  Work with Daryl to identify the primary problem. Help Daryl select appropriate therapeutic goals.

- **Topic of conversation** (p. 6)
  If numerous topics are raised, recap the topics and work with Daryl to understand how they may be related. Are all of the topics therapeutically relevant?

- **Rescind your ego** (p. 10)
  If Daryl expresses inordinate praise, graciously accept the compliment and then explain that any of your peers would essentially provide equivalent service.

2

Getting Started

This chapter provides guidance on laying the foundation for the therapeutic process: techniques for learning about the client, building a comfortable and trusting setting, and meeting the client on the client's ground.

Preappointment Review

Initially, one might think that the beginning of the therapeutic process involves warmly greeting the client and making an inquiry along the lines of *"What seems to be the problem?"* In actuality, you may have the opportunity to better prepare for this initial meeting by reviewing available collateral information pertaining to the client. Such information may include an application for service at the agency, which usually covers basic information. If the client has had an intake or assessment interview, such notes may provide valuable details that can help orient you to the client's biopsychosocial status (physical diseases; disorders; medications; medical history, which can include family medical information; disabilities; medical hospitalizations; chief complaint; provisional psychiatric diagnoses; psychotropic medications; psychiatric hospitalizations; psychotherapeutic history; living conditions; family structure; extended family; educational level; support system; employment history; legal problems; spiritual belief system; racial and ethnic identity). Familiarizing yourself with the client's available profile helps to place the client—and the client's presenting problem or problems—into a more meaningful context, thereby promoting the therapeutic process.

The facility at which the client seeks services may be a general service agency, in which case one may expect a diversity of presenting problems. Other organizations may provide a more specific service, such as substance abuse recovery, anger management, or grief therapy. Even in a clinical setting wherein a focused set of services is offered, it would be presumptuous to consider the client population as homogeneous. Each client will present with a unique history, life circumstances, belief system, set of challenges, and coping skills; hence, as the therapist, take the time to review and incorporate as much material as is legitimately available prior to meeting with a client (Lukas, 1993).

Facilitating a Conducive Environment

Rapport

Rapport involves establishing and maintaining a meaningful and trustworthy connection between you and the client. A useful definition of *rapport* is "a feeling of relationship" (Stedman, 1987). One can think of rapport as a key characteristic of the therapeutic relationship, establishing and maintaining a safe and respectful environment that is conducive to human contact wherein one can confidently and comfortably disclose and process sensitive issues (Mahoney, 1991). Bordin's model of therapeutic alliance, which is facilitated by rapport, is considered applicable to a broad array of theoretical orientations. This model consists of three collaborative components: (1) setting therapeutic goals, (2) designating the tasks that the client and the therapist will perform, and (3) professional attachment (Bordin, 1979). Research has shown a positive correlation between the quality of the therapeutic working alliance and therapeutic outcomes (Horvath & Symonds, 1991).

Rapport is an ongoing process, beginning with your first contact with a client. This may be a telephone call wherein the client will be taking note of such things as the quality of your voice, professionalism, sense of organization, patience, clarity, efficiency, attitude, attentiveness, or extraneous noises in the background. Clients' initial impressions are built on such factors. If your initial introduction is in person, the client will likely also include such factors as your general appearance, demeanor, eye contact, and facial expression. This is not intended to make you feel self-conscious. If you assume a professional stance, you will likely make an appropriate presentation.

In the role of the therapist, rapport is fostered by genuinely and consistently recognizing and respecting the principle that is the highest order of business in a therapeutic setting is the client's self-determination and perspective: The therapy is about the client—the client's feelings, thoughts, actions, inactions, and ultimately, the client's choices and outcomes. Occasionally, the client's goals or belief systems may differ substantially from your own. Does this mean that you should sit by pretending to agree with the client? No. Your job is not to be a complacent phony. You may express your clinical perspective, including relevant concerns, information, alternatives, and recommendations; however, it is also essential to consistently empower the client to understand that the final say-so about how he or she will proceed—or not proceed—is in the client's hands.

In terms of diversity among clients, it is natural that you may feel some initial discomfort when meeting clients from a racial or cultural background different from your own. The universalistic hypothesis states that the therapist's ability to provide care is more a matter of cultural sensitivity and understanding than being an actual match to the client's race and ethnicity (Baker, 1988; Tharp, 1991). Essentially, familiarity with cultural and ethnic beliefs and practices, combined with your sense of the client's level of acculturation and unique perspectives, will help to foster a sense of therapeutic rapport. If, for example, you are providing care for an American Indian and you are unfamiliar with their social norms and spiritual belief systems, consider stating this early in your first session. You may respectfully request an overview of some of their core values and ask that the client point out any errors that you may unintentionally make throughout the course of providing therapy (Richardson, 1981). This practice principle can help to build rapport with members of other unfamiliar diverse populations.

Rapport is not something that is built once; rapport is an ongoing issue. The very nature of therapy involves addressing emotionally challenging topics. To illustrate the point, a patient may hold a momentary resentment against the physician or nurse who administers a physically painful treatment such as an injection. In the same manner, a client may express harshness toward the therapist as difficult topics are appropriately exposed and explored. Even the most experienced clinicians occasionally misspeak, misunderstand, or otherwise unintentionally offend the client. This does not necessarily mark the end of the therapeutic relationship.

In the event that you begin to sense that the rapport between you and the client has been compromised, it is important to address it as promptly and openly as possible; this is referred to as "rebuilding rapport." The process is fairly straightforward: (a) If you are unclear about what the problem is, ask about it. (b) If you have made a mistake, own it and apologize one time. (c) Gather feedback from the client, and move on.

Th: It seems like you're a little withdrawn—you're usually more open. I'm wondering if something's different this week.

(a) Ask about the problem.

Cl: You could say that. I just can't believe you treated me that way on Saturday—at the restaurant. I saw you there with your friends, talking and laughing and you didn't even say hello to me. I just thought that was pretty rude. . . . I must be quite an embarrassment to you!

Th: I can see how upsetting this is for you. Considering what happened, you have every right to feel that way, and I think you're right. What happened at the restaurant was *my* fault, but please let me explain. You're right, I actually did see you there on Saturday, but as your therapist, I'm legally and ethically obligated to protect your client confidentiality, so it wouldn't have been appropriate for me to initiate contact with you in a public setting like the restaurant. Now, had you chosen to greet me, I certainly would have been pleased to say "Hello"—you see, you have the privilege to control your level of confidentiality, not me. Still, I can see how I might have seemed cold or rude. I should have explained this policy earlier. I really didn't mean to offend you. I'm truly sorry that I came off that way.

(b) If you have made a mistake, apologize for it one time.

Cl: Okay. I get it. It just didn't seem like you to ignore me; it was weird. I guess I feel better now.

Th: Okay. I can definitely see how that could throw a person. From now on, I'll make it a point to discuss this explicitly with new clients. How are you feeling right now?

(c) Gather feedback from the client and move on.

Cl: Better, I guess. It's just that it really got me mad.

Th: Sure. It makes sense that you would. [Pause] I think it took a lot of courage to raise this issue here.

Cl: Yeah, it's okay. I get it now.

Fostering Sensitive Disclosure

The role of the client is to be as honest as possible. This may not be as simple as it sounds. For instance, a client's problem may involve embarrassing details, in which case the client may feel compelled to filter or eliminate critical details.

In order to better understand the factors that may lead clients to respond deceptively, researchers have constructed models depicting the cognitive path that individuals use when asked to respond to a question (Cannell, Miller, & Oksenberg, 1981; Tourangeau & Rasinski, 1988). Principles of this model may also give us a clue as to how clients choose to disclose or withhold information in the therapeutic setting. One such model consists of a four-step process:

Step 1: *Comprehension*—understanding the instructions and question

Step 2: *Retrieval*—accessing relevant memories

Step 3: *Judgment*—organizing the retrieved information in a cohesive manner

Step 4: *Response*—selecting an appropriate answer

Despite the intuitive logical flow of this model, there is certainly no guarantee that clients will follow it reliably, particularly when it comes to sensitive questions (Tourangeau, Rips, & Rasinski, 2000). It is entirely possible that at Step 1 of this model (comprehension of the question), the client determines that the question is an inappropriate invasion of privacy. At this point, the client may covertly short-circuit this cognitive process, leap directly to Step 4, the response, and intentionally provide a misleading response.

When it comes to obtaining honest disclosure, not all questions are equivalent. Research suggests that clients are more likely to provide deceptive responses to questions that are sensitive in nature. People weigh the sensitivity of a question using three parameters:

1. *Social desirability:* "the tendency of people to say or do things that will make them or their reference group look good" (Rubin & Babbie, 1993, p. 156). Clients, out of fear of being negatively judged, may feel embarrassed to honestly disclose attitudes or conduct that departs from social norms— which may involve such things as unpopular beliefs, peculiar habits, or uncommon preferences—leading them to fabricate more acceptable mainstream responses (Rubin & Babbie, 1993).

2. *Invasion of privacy:* Questions that depart from polite daily conversation, such as inquiries regarding religion, personal finance, sex, legal issues, or certain bodily functions, are expectedly vulnerable to distortions. A client may not necessarily be embarrassed by his or her *answer* to such a question. For instance, although individuals may be very proud of their earnings,

merely asking someone how much he or she earned last year may be sensed as an unwelcome invasion of privacy (Willis, 1997).

3. *Risk of disclosure to third parties:* One may reasonably fear that one's responses may be revealed to agencies or individuals not directly related to the person asking the question (law enforcement, employer, family, community, etc.) potentially bringing about negative consequences. The client may sanitize the discussion based on a general sense of trust and confidentiality (Couper, Singer, & Kulka, 1998; Singer, Mathiowetz, & Couper, 1993).

The reasonable question stands: "How much truth will the client disclose?" A large part of the answer is dependent on the quality of the rapport that is built between you and your client. Essentially, the client will render as much information as the client feels is safe. In this respect, it is unrealistic to assume that you can just turn to the client and implicitly express: *"I'm a therapist—just tell me the truth."* Rather, part of your job as a therapist is to create and maintain an environment in which it is as emotionally safe as possible to tell such truths. To graphically conceptualize the *inverse* relationship between client honesty—in particular, disclosure of sensitive information—and the client's sense of safety, consider the fear-honesty teeter-totter in Figure 2.1.

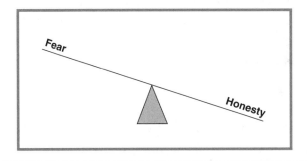

Figure 2.1   The Fear-Honesty Teeter-Totter

Fear is the controlling factor and *honesty* is the dependent factor in this model. In other words, the level of the client's fear inversely influences the level of honesty in terms of disclosure.

To exemplify this point, consider this relatively extreme confrontation: Suppose Jane points a gun at John and asks him: *"How do you like my new glasses?"*

Naturally John would say something along the lines of *"Oh, they're perfect. Very attractive. You made an excellent choice!"*

Are we convinced of John's genuineness here? Certainly not. Essentially, Jane has created a condition that is so fearful to John that he had no choice but to say that her glasses were perfect. Any response less than that and John could have faced the ultimate loss—his life. We see that fear inversely predicts honesty. As fear is high, honesty goes low.

Conversely, suppose Jane had approached John, this time unarmed. With a smile, pleasant affect, and comfortable voice tone she asks, *"Hey John, I just got these glasses; I have 30 days to return them. I'm not really sure they work with the shape of my face. What do you think?"* Clearly, this circumstance would be far less fear-laden than the initial example. Going back to the fear-honesty teeter-totter illustration, we would see that as fear drops down, honesty rides higher. Under this less threatening circumstance, John is likely to feel more comfortable in disclosing his honest impression of Jane's new glasses.

To further explore the point of fear-driven deception, consider the nature of lying. When one anticipates consequences for telling the truth, one may choose to lie in order to try to avoid such consequences. Think about any time that you lied. Now think about the consequence you were attempting to dodge had you disclosed the truth. You were afraid that something bad might happen; hence, you withheld or altered the truth in some way to reduce the risk of emotional hurt or loss. Consider this simple encounter:

Mom: *This cookie jar is half empty. Alex, did you eat all these cookies before dinner?*

Alex: *Um, no.*

Alex, sensing disapproval, lies in order to try to avoid the anticipated consequences for doing something wrong. Now consider this alternative:

Mom: *This cookie jar is half empty. I got these cookies from the health food store. I can't believe anyone would like them. Alex, did you have some cookies?*

Alex: *Yeah, they're really good. You mean they're healthy cookies?*

In this second dialogue, the implicit fear of punishment is reduced, thereby facilitating Alex's more honest disclosure.

Now, consider a therapeutic example:

Cl: *Last week, I knew I had the house to myself for about four hours. Anyway, I've never done this before, but I went through the house and closed all the doors and windows and curtains and then I just took off my clothes and just sort of strolled through the house naked.*

Th: *That's a little perverse, don't you think?*

This sort of disapproval from the therapist essentially tells the client that he or she really needs to watch what is disclosed. When a client raises a sensitive issue in therapy, it is reasonable to assume that the client assigns some emotional weight to such discussion; the last thing the client needs is you, the therapist, adding extra weight to the discussion. A judgmental reaction could understandably cause the client to feel hesitant to provide any further details regarding this story or concerns related to it. Consider again the fear-honesty teeter-totter. The client may reasonably choose to alter or abandon this line of discussion. Further, at this point, we do not know enough to determine the client's motivation in disclosing this naked alone in the house story. It is possible that this story, authentic or not, may have been a trial balloon. For instance, the client may be considering raising other sensitive issues in therapy that may or may not involve nudity or sex, but first the client wants to test the waters to see if such discussion will trigger an adverse reaction. If your response is negative or judgmental, this essentially conveys the impression that such discussions will not be easy; the client would likely conclude that such dialogues would come with costly emotional reactions and that he or she would probably be better off not pursuing this topic in therapy. This could lead to an unfortunate therapeutic paradox wherein the issues most needing to be processed are never aired.

Conversely, suppose the therapist's reaction had been different:

Th: [Smiles warmly] *People use privacy to explore lots of things. What was it like being naked in the house?*

This response implies no negative judgments on the therapist's behalf. The therapist's stance is one of normalizing and appropriate curiosity, essentially communicating: *"This sounds interesting; please tell me more."* The client can clearly sense that he or she has not rocked the boat; in fact, quite the contrary. The therapist has expressed interest and welcomes further details, thereby enabling the client to continue processing this and also other such issues. Again, referring back to the principle of the fear-honesty teeter-totter, we can see that as fear of an adverse reaction is reduced, the client is more likely to respond honestly and ultimately facilitate further sensitive disclosures and emotional processing.

Cultural or ethnic differences between the client and the therapist may also serve to inhibit sensitive self-disclosure. For example, given the African American's history of slavery and racism, such individuals may possess a healthy cultural paranoia (Ho, 1992; Smith, 1981). Similarly, considering the historic mistreatment of American Indians, White practitioners may initially be perceived in a suspicious manner (Barcus, 2003).

Until rapport is built, there may be a middle-of-the-road effect in terms of the topics discussed in therapy, wherein the client avoids discussing trivial topics that are thought to be clinically irrelevant as well as highly sensitive issues (Farber, 2003). Make an effort to be patient. Therapeutic alliance is not built overnight. Clients may have their own time frames in terms of offering sensitive disclosures. The duration and the strength of the therapeutic alliance contribute to the client's willingness to embark on the disclosure process (Farber & Hall, 2002).

Initial Contact

Introduction and Ground Rules

In the initial contact, introductions naturally come first. If the client seems amiable, a handshake can be included as part of the introduction. State your name and role clearly. The agency may have conventions regarding names. Some facilities prefer that therapists be referred to in a formal manner with titles such as miss, mister, or doctor, whereas others use the less formal first-name basis. Find out how the client would like to be addressed; a client may provide his or her full legal name on an agency application form. Make it a point to pronounce the client's name clearly and ask if that is the name the client prefers you to use. (Does the client prefer to be called Deborah, Debbie, Deb, Mrs. Doe?)

Next, clarify your role in the therapeutic relationship: Inform the client that you will be his or her therapist. In the case of an internship position, depending on the agency's policy, you may be obliged to elaborate further, disclosing that you are an intern working with a supervisor who is on the premises. You may mention the school and program with which you are affiliated, along with the name, role, academic degrees, or licensure status of your supervisor at the agency.

In addition to having new clients review and sign a treatment consent form, most agencies have a policy sheet that is issued to new clients. This sheet should indicate the date and time of a client's appointments, the length of each appointment (usually 50 minutes), telephone numbers for appointment changes and messages, fee structure, policies regarding missed or canceled appointments, and other ground rules such as no weapons in the building and no outside contact with the therapist between sessions. In addition to providing a printed copy of such a list to clients, it can be helpful to discuss each point in order to address any questions that the client might have. This helps to present the agency as a structured, professional environment, enabling the client to better comprehend and adhere to the "house rules." People tend to feel more at ease when they are explicitly told specific details as to what services they can expect to receive and what their responsibilities are.

In order to help facilitate a sense of trust, you may wish to explain to the client the extent to which you can provide confidentiality and the few legal exceptions to this principle. If such information is covered in pretreatment documentation, you may wish to ask the client if there are any questions before getting started. As mentioned earlier, rules regarding the parameters of client confidentiality and privileged communication can vary from state to state. Make it a point to clarify the legal parameters regarding confidentiality with your supervisor as promptly as possible.

Despite your benevolent mission to understand the client in a comprehensive fashion, efforts to solicit vast amounts of information in the first session can be perceived negatively (intrusive, inept, unfocused), particularly among Latinos (Seijo, Gomez, & Freidenberg, 1991). With the exception of crisis cases, allow for the possibility that more of the client's story will be revealed over the course of more than one session through the natural disclosure process and purposeful questioning.

Presenting Problem

Some beginning practitioners may be concerned about initiating the therapeutic process. Specifically, you may feel anxious about not knowing where to begin or how to identify the client's problem. It is important to recognize that psychotherapy is seldom the client's first choice when it comes to addressing a problem. Prior to entering therapy, most clients will attempt to solve the problem on their own in a variety of ways such as conferring with friends, seeking help from selected family members, or accessing relevant self-help literature. By the time a client presents for therapy, the client has usually devoted considerable thought and feelings to the problem; hence, you may be able to identify the therapeutic entry point simply by asking the client the nature of the problem. Some clients will open with cogent storytelling. The client may already know what the problem is. Alternatively, the client may only be able to provide some information as to what has been troubling him or her. The initial problem that the client discloses in therapy is referred to as the "presenting problem" (Hepworth & Larsen, 1993). A simple and direct inquiry can be used to open the therapeutic process effectively (*"How can I help you?" "Where would you like to begin?" "I understand from your file . . ."*).

Even a gentle inquiry as to the nature of the client's problem may be emotionally challenging to the client, depending on the nature of the problem, the client's cultural background, and the level of acculturation. For instance, traditional Asians do not readily disclose family problems to those outside the family (Sue & Sue, 2003). Discussion of such problems outside the family may be laced with shame or guilt (Dana, 1993). Keep in mind that although you may be genuinely relaxed, friendly, and receptive, the client will experience his or her own feelings when it comes to disclosing personal information.

Coping With Silence

After making your initial inquiry, be prepared for the possibility that there may be some silence. This is normal. The client may find him- or herself sifting through some challenging thoughts and feelings as he or she attempts to organize the discussion. Try to be patient in moments of silence. You need not fill all of the silences with words (Neukrug, 2002). When you feel it is appropriate, there are a few phrases that you can use to help get the ball rolling:

"Take a minute" suggests that you are willing to be patient. The client may be processing the facts and emotional aspects of the story. This may be the first time the client is telling the story aloud; hence, there may be a sense of fear or embarrassment. Another possibility is that the client is attempting to organize the story into a meaningful order, taking into account relevant back-story.

"How are you feeling right now?" An essential component of the psychotherapeutic process involves identifying and understanding the role that feelings play in the client's life experience. Demonstrating your awareness and sensitivity to the client's feelings facilitates rapport and discussion of emotionally charged topics. Remember, the client is not in therapy simply to convey a cold stream of data. The issues are often laced with a system of deep personal feelings as well. Inquiring about the client's feelings provides an opportunity to address emotional roadblocks (fear, embarrassment, confusion, shame) that may contribute to the client's hesitation to speak freely.

"What do you want me to know?" If a client is unable or unwilling to discuss his or her feelings, you need not press for an emotional entry point. A cognitive approach may provide a viable alternative. This direct question

permits a client to begin to talk about facts; weighty feelings may then follow as the client becomes more comfortable in the therapeutic setting.

"You're sitting on the edge of your chair." "You look tense." "You seem nervous." Address your observations regarding the client's feelings. Commenting on the client's physical stance and presenting your impression demonstrates your attentive perception of the client's emotional state. Conveying such observations in a genuinely concerned manner can help to demonstrate your sensitivity, suggesting that you have the capacity to receive the problem in an open and nonjudgmental manner, thereby facilitating the initial phase of the client's disclosure. Typically, it is appropriate to give a voice to your observations and impressions in the context of therapy.

"Start anywhere." Being unfamiliar with a client, it would be presumptuous to insist on a fixed entry point to discussing a problem. Initiating therapeutic storytelling may be quite a challenge to the client. A person under emotional stress may be considering the vastness of what he or she has experienced and how he or she feels, what he or she is thinking, what he or she does not understand, and how much he or she does or does not want you to know initially. A client may be considering such issues as *"How much back-story should I tell?" "Maybe this recent problem is related to events in my childhood—so what should I talk about first?" "Who are the relevant cast of players in this problem and in what order do I introduce them?" "How do I talk about this problem without getting myself or others into trouble?"* Additionally, a client may be hesitant to disclose sensitive or potentially embarrassing information to a total stranger. Enabling a client the privilege to start anywhere means that the client need not attempt to locate the beginning of his or her multidimensional story; the client now has permission to begin the storytelling process without having to sort events into perfect order. The client may choose to ease into the story, disclosing some neutral or moderately sensitive information, allowing him- or herself the privilege to achieve a sense of comfort by gaining a feel for your reaction and style. Other clients may choose to spontaneously blurt out the most critical point of the problem. Allowing a client to start anywhere essentially conveys the unspoken message, *"There's no wrong entry point; when you're ready, you can begin wherever you feel comfortable. You can start with whatever's most important to you, or whatever's easiest for you to talk about first. We can always pick up more back-story, fill in details, and put things in chronological order as we go along."* You may even verbalize parts of this to a hesitant client.

Alternatively, there may be cultural factors pertaining to silence. Asians may use silence as a sign of respect and conversational politeness. Not every moment needs to be filled with words (Sue & Sue, 2003). Regardless of the client's ethnicity and cultural heritage, communication styles can vary from person to person. Be prepared to adapt your style. Be patient with clients and with yourself.

Start Where the Client Is

Depending on your training, theoretical orientation, or prior clinical experience, you may have ideas about where you think a client ought to begin. For example, suppose a client presents with a depressive affect, dressed eccentrically, and wearing a foil hat and headphones connected to nothing. You may reasonably be tempted to begin probing for such things as psychotic symptoms, psychotropic medications, psychiatric history, or prior hospitalizations. Nothing is inherently wrong with that plan; however, suppose the client is determined to discuss his or her aversion to the color blue first:

Cl: *Okay, okay, I just can't take it any more—it's all the blue. Too much blue . . . dark blue, light blue, blue with yellow and blue in the sky, and then it's dark blue at night time and the stars are hard. It's just a lot.*

Th: *First of all, colors can't hurt you, so just relax. Nobody ever died of blue. Secondly, the sky does not turn dark blue at night; it turns black. Now, I need to gather some information regarding your psychiatric history . . .*

The therapist is clearly attempting to be helpful by trying to assure the client that colors are harmless and that the sky is not a threat, especially at night; however, in doing so, this therapist has essentially conveyed to the client that the therapist does not understand the client's plight and the genuine magnitude of his or her fear of blue. The therapist's effort to gather information regarding the client's psychiatric history is by no means wrong; however, curtly telling the client, *"Colors can't hurt you,"*—which is of course true—communicates to the patient that this therapist really does not understand just how terrifying a color can be to the client and may lead the client to question the therapist's qualification to provide care. In other words, without paying heed to the client's reality (his or her fear of blue), the therapist loses a valuable opportunity to establish rapport with this client. This client may feel that the therapist does not have the capacity to understand his or her circumstances. Consider this alternative response:

Th: I can see how hard this is for you. You know, everyone's afraid of something. Some people are afraid of heights; some people panic when they see blood; some people are scared of snakes. When did you start having trouble with the color blue?

This adaptation has several advantages: It respectfully acknowledges that the client is genuinely distressed by the color blue. (*"I can see how hard this is for you."*) Validating such feelings conveys to the client that you are someone who actually understands and is sensitive to the nature of the client's fears and concerns. The client's feelings are normalized. (*"Everyone's afraid of something."*) These points help to build the rapport that will facilitate the bridge toward further clinical information gathering. (*"When did you start having trouble with the color blue?"*) At this point, we neither confirm nor challenge the client's reality. We simply respectfully acknowledge that we understand that the client is genuinely afraid. Even if we consider the source of the client's fear to pose no rational threat, the client's feeling of anxiety is absolutely real (to the client); hence, it is important to proceed as you would with anyone who was in a state of fear.

Does this mean that in your role as a therapist you should passively foster such seemingly unfounded beliefs, never challenging psychotic thinking or delusional ideations? No. Such discussions would naturally be an integral part of the therapy and could even be included at this early stage:

Cl: Do you think the blue is going to get me this time?

Th: You know, I really get how scared you are. I can see that blue is very hard for you, but to answer your question, none of my clients have ever been hurt by a color. I think you're going to be safe. I think if we work together, we can get you to a better place with this.

Cl: Okay.

Th: Okay, I'm with you. We're together on this. Now, there are a few things that I'll need to know.

The therapist's response serves several purposes: Clearly the therapist does not feel that blue is a threat, per se, but acknowledges and addresses the client's feeling of fear as genuine. From his or her perspective, the fear is quite real. The therapist then suggests that forming a mutual alliance may help to reduce this fearful situation. Essentially, rapport is built by meeting the client on the client's ground, coming to understand the problem from the client's point of view. As rapport and trust are built, further critical inquiries regarding the client's psychiatric history can be gathered. Providing the client the privilege to select the entry point in his or her storytelling enables the therapeutic process to begin on the client's terms (Egan, 2006a). Remember, the client knows his or her story; you do not. Consider thinking of the client as a knowledgeable tour guide of his or her life: Listen and try to understand the client's circumstances from his or her perspective; if you require further details, you can always ask questions as the self-tour advances.

Respect the Client's Boundaries

Most theoretical orientations would agree that one of your primary roles as a therapist involves keeping the client on track, guiding the client through meaningful discussion related to the problems at hand and appropriately redirecting the client when it appears that the dialogue has departed too far from such topics. Although it is important to keep the therapy on track, it is not exclusively your job to initially *select* the track. Establishing and tuning the treatment plan must be a collaboration between you and your client. In cases of discrepancy, you certainly have the privilege to express your clinical opinion; however, it is paramount that the client's wishes be honored in terms of boundaries.

Consider a case in which your client discloses that his or her eldest child left home for a good job about a year ago.

Cl: *It's been so hard. I don't know. Something just came over me and I've been having trouble thinking straight; I can't sleep through the night; I cry for no reason at all; and I'm always just so tired.*

Th: *When did you start feeling this way?*

Cl: *About 10 months ago.*

Th: *What was going on 10 months ago?*

Cl: *Zane, my oldest child, got a good job offer in another state, and . . . well . . . just moved out.*

Th: *So this all started when Zane moved out?*

Cl: [Crying] *I don't want to talk about this.*

Th: *I understand this isn't easy for you, but it sounds like Zane's moving out might be the root of your depression.*

Cl: I can't. I'm sorry. I just can't talk about it. [Crying]

Th: Okay. We don't have to talk about Zane right now.

The therapist is reasonably proceeding along appropriate intuitive lines. From a clinical standpoint, one would reasonably consider Zane's departure to be the logical antecedent with respect to the client's array of depressive symptoms. Despite the therapist's wish to pursue this line of questioning, the therapist takes into account the client's statement, *"I can't. I'm sorry. I just can't talk about it,"* and compassionately replies, *"Okay. We don't have to talk about Zane right now."* Notice the that the therapist's use of the words *"right now"* implies that in light of the client's emotional distress at this time, it may be wise to postpone this line of inquiry—per the client's request—and revisit it in the near future, as opposed to abandoning this topic permanently. The therapist might even be more explicit: *"I can see that talking about Zane is hard for you right now, but I think it's an important issue. We can come back to it later, when you're more ready."* Although it is within your domain as a therapist to present your impression that this should be the focal point of the therapy, you are not the sole decision maker. Rather than simply *telling* the patient that he or she will be embarking on a particular therapeutic pathway, it would be more appropriate to pose such a notion as a therapeutic *recommendation*. Because you have articulated your clinical rationale for this modality, the client may tentatively agree to such a treatment plan; however, the final decision as to the treatment plan, as well as what will and will not be discussed, is ultimately the client's.

Suppose that after you have presented your recommendation for discussion involving the client's relationship with Zane, the client is only willing to agree to a treatment plan focused on improving the client's mood and sleep but explicitly refuses to discuss Zane. As the therapist, you may feel that such an intervention is off target, that you would only be addressing the symptoms and not the source of the problem. Should you refuse to work with this client? Not necessarily. One strategy could be to agree to work with the client on the client's terms; as the therapeutic alliance is built, there may be an opportunity to revisit the issues regarding the unresolved feelings related to Zane's departure. Alternatively, you may agree to work with the client as proposed, with the provision that progress will be reviewed at some specified point—perhaps after three to five sessions—at which time the effectiveness of this intervention will be evaluated. This may present another opportunity to address what appears to be the source problem. Again, in your role as the therapist, you may submit such a plan as a reasonable proposal, as opposed to a demand, subject to the client's approval. Remember, you are entitled to express your clinical opinions and recommendations; however, per the principle of client self-determination, the client is in charge of what is or is not in his or her life. With the exception of life-threatening circumstances, it is essential that you respect and accept the client's privilege to set the therapeutic boundaries (*Ethical Standards of Human Service Professionals,* Statement 2; Council for Standards, 1996).

Occasionally, clients may suggest the presence of a problem but hesitate to provide details. This may suggest a relevant (family) secret. During the early sessions with clients, pressing for such detailed disclosure may be met with substantial resistance and possibly attrition. Instead, listen carefully to the client's responses and observe the length and characteristic of the silences, observing the client's nonverbal cues. Does the client appear to be thinking or feeling something notable (Paniagua, 2005)?

Matching

As the client proceeds to communicate, in addition to taking in his or her story, make an effort to assess and match your communication style to the client's. Client's styles may range from the use of simple words and concepts to sophisticated vocabulary and the capacity for more abstract thinking. Listen to the level of language that the client uses. Matching your style to the client's helps to facilitate comfort, rapport, and comprehension. For example, persistently using multisyllable words with a client who is primarily using clear but simple language may unnecessarily confound the client's understanding of your message. Additionally, if the client senses a significant disparity in intellectual levels, the client may feel intimidated, which may result in self-censoring. Such withholding or deliberate distortions could potentially impede the therapeutic process. Consider this mismatched dialogue:

Cl: *This week my boss just dumped a ton of extra work on me, and he didn't even have the guts to do it to my face. He just left all this crap in my in-box while I was at lunch with this note that just said, "Take care of this." Yeah, like I'm supposed to just wave my magic wand and make this all just happen. It's crazy. I mean, there's six of us, and does he give anything extra to his precious favorites? No! He just dumps every-thing on me. It's like I'm the workhorse of this place and everyone else is just like decoration. I'm sick of this crap!*

Th: *It would appear that there is a significant disparity in the distribution of the workload based on a potentially unprofessional bias on your supervisor's behalf, thereby substantially exacerbating the magnitude of the job-related stress that you've been experiencing.*

Though this therapist appears to have an accurate perception of the client's problem, the therapist's language is unnecessarily clinical. This therapist would likely be perceived as cold, authoritative, and possibly judgmental. In view of the disliked boss in the story, this therapist's style of communication may lead the client to see the therapist as yet another harsh authority figure, thereby confounding the therapeutic alliance. Consider this alternate response:

Th: *Sounds pretty unfair. With that kind of thing going on at work, it makes sense that you'd be this stressed-out, even outside of work.*

This less formal response covers the same ground and comes closer to matching the client's style. This more seamless and comfortable communication contact between the client and therapist implicitly conveys the message that the client does not need to edit or upgrade his or her communication style in any way. The client is able to speak freely and spontaneously—straight from the heart. Each time a client edits his or her responses, something is lost, potentially confounding your comprehension of the client's genuine condition. Fostering an environment in which the client is able to speak as freely as possible enables you to gain a more precise image of the client's actual thought process, feelings, and experience level, thus facilitating the therapeutic process. In this case, the therapist's more casual matching language style suggests more of the role of the expert ally, rather than the cold detached scientist who may not really understand the client at the gut level.

A study of medical patients revealed that most of the patients studied preferred a patient-centered style of communication wherein the doctor took a personal interest in the patient, as opposed to doctors whose communication focused primarily on clinical attributes of the case; however, older and more educated patients tended to prefer more clinical communication with their doctors (Swenson et al., 2004). Essentially, this tells us that just as there is no single type of medical patient, there is no single type of psychotherapy client. Hence, it is important to tune your style of communication to meet the needs of each unique client.

Vocal Features

Monitor and match the volume of the client's voice: Is the client predominately soft-spoken, moderate, or loud? A client discussing a recent loss or hurtful event may speak using a lower voice tone; matching your voice tone to his or hers helps to communicate your emotional understanding and sensitivity to the issue being discussed, that you are with the client.

Another attribute of the client's communication style includes tempo. Rate of the speech may range from very slow to too fast. Again, within reason, attempt to match the pacing of your speech to the client's.

It may not always be possible or appropriate to achieve a matching communication style with your client. For instance, a client may be communicating a story at a rapid tempo, and you may be unable to speak or think meaningfully at this rate; hence, you may opt to acknowledge the differences in communication style:

Th: (Spoken with a calm voice tone and a moderate tempo) *Johanna, I'm understanding what you're saying about the important people in your life who've disappointed you—your parents, your husband, your children. I can see how stressful this is for you. Just one thing: I noticed that you're talking really fast, and that's okay; I'm understanding you. Are you okay with me talking at this slower rate?*

This demonstrates that although you may be presenting as composed, you are receiving the content and emotions of the story and you are taking the client seriously.

If the client's rapid talking tempo is making it difficult for you to comprehend the story, then you may attempt to alter the client's verbal rate by modeling the desired change. There are a couple of ways to do this: You may speak to the client in a deliberately composed, moderate to slow rate, implicitly suggesting, "Please slow down, like me." Another adaptation is to speak at a tempo that initially matches the client's and while speaking gradually reduce your rate. These techniques may involve several rounds before the client responds. This method can also be applied to raising or lowering the client's volume.

If after you have consistently modeled the desired change, the client's communication style is still preventing you from understanding him or her, then it is necessary to address the communication problem more explicitly. This consists of acknowledging the client's content and feelings in the client's story, as best you understand them, explaining that there is a communication problem and submitting the corresponding change request in a positive manner:

Th: *Jan, I can see how upset you are, and right now I'm only catching parts of what you're saying. It's very important that I understand you and I don't want to miss any of what you're saying. Please, let's take a moment . . . and slow down just a bit so that I can understand you better.*

In the interest of rapport, notice that the therapist's language plausibly frames the request as the therapist's wish to increase his or her comprehension of the patient's message, as opposed to blaming the client for communicating poorly. This request inherently tells the client that his or her words are important and that the therapist needs some assistance in comprehending.

Other vocal confounds may involve such elements as poor articulation, mumbling, speech impediments, or unfamiliar accents. In such cases, you may be able to enhance your comprehension simply by requesting a slower tempo or clearer articulation, if this is possible. You need not be embarrassed to submit such requests. The fundamental principle in any form of therapy is that in order to be helpful, you must be able to understand the client, and presumably, the client wants to be understood. It is essential that the communication be tuned in order to optimize mutual comprehension between you and the client.

Underlying Problem

As discussed earlier, the *presenting problem* is the problem that the client initially identifies as the reason for therapy, which may remain the focal point for the duration of the sessions. Other times, the client may be hesitant to discuss what is really troubling him or her until the client feels more comfortable with the therapeutic relationship, at which time, the client may disclose a more sensitive or serious *underlying problem*.

It can be difficult for clients to spontaneously discuss sensitive subjects with a stranger. A client may use the presenting problem as a means of testing the waters before spontaneously jumping all the way in with the big issue. A client who, over time, perceives your therapeutic approach with smaller issues as genuinely sensitive, concerned, and nonjudgmental is more likely to trust that you will handle heavier issues in a similar fashion.

Occasionally, clients utilize a less significant presenting problem as a means of introducing the more substantial problem. Try to remain aware, but not suspicious, of a potential underlying problem; there is not *always* an underlying problem. Make an effort to work as effectively as possible with whatever the client is giving you.

Th: *How have things been since our last session?*

Cl: *Pretty much the same. Everywhere I look, there's a mess needing to be cleaned. The living room, the attic, the yard, you name it.*

This is the client's third session; to date the client has presented with a depressive mood and spends most of the time discussing the persistent challenges of housekeeping. The therapist may be considering diagnoses along the line of a (depressive) mood disorder, or perhaps the focus on persistent cleaning may suggest obsessive compulsive disorder.

Th: *For the past few weeks, you've discussed how hard it is to keep a clean house.*

Cl: *Oh, it's not just the house. The garage and the car.* [Sigh] *It's so dirty. How does anyone keep a car clean? It makes me so tired just to think about it. I'm just so tired. So tired, and so much cleaning.* [Pause] *And now, there's just me to do it.*

The *"now, there's just me"* part is a novel departure from talk of cleaning and exhaustion.

Th: *You used to have help?*

The therapist follows the *"just me"* reference.

Cl: *Yes.*

Th: *Who used to help you?*

Cl: *Richard.*

Th: *Richard? Who's Richard?*

Cl: *My husband.*

Th: *Richard doesn't help you any more?*

Cl: [Sadly] *No.* [Silence]

Th: [Gently] *Did something happen to Richard?*

Cl: [Nods, pause] *He passed away 6 weeks ago* [Crying].

The client has utilized the initial sessions as a means for getting a feel for the therapist's sensitivity. Apparently, therapeutic rapport and trust was adequately built via the therapist's consistent respectful handling of the presenting problem involving stresses related to cleaning. This, combined with the therapist's attentiveness and focused curiosity, enabled the client to transition from the presenting problem involving persistent cleaning to the more significant underlying problem—the loss of her husband, which will now become the focal point of the therapy.

Contrary to the possible impulse to kick yourself for not having discovered the husband's death earlier, consider leaning toward patting yourself on the back for successfully creating a compassionate and safe therapeutic environment that is conducive to such sensitive disclosures. In short, you will only know as much as your clients want you to know; the safer you make the therapeutic environment, the more sensitive information you are likely to be privy to. Issues related to facilitating sensitive disclosure will be discussed further in Chapter 4.

Allow yourself to be curious beyond the stream of the words, paying heed to the subtext of the client's message. Sometimes this is referred to as "listening with the third ear" (Reik, 1948), remaining open to the presence of a potential underlying problem (Schlossberg, 1976).

Introduction of an underlying problem will naturally lead you to reconsider the initial diagnostic profile and treatment plan in light of the new information given. In this example, the therapist may now be considering diagnoses more suited to the client's loss of her husband, such as bereavement or adjustment disorder. This is not to suggest that the therapist is an indecisive or poor diagnostician; therapists make decisions based on the information that is available at each step. Psychotherapy is a dynamic process, and as such, psychodiagnostics and treatment plans are not set in stone. They appropriately evolve in accordance with the progressive revelation of new information or the resolution of problems.

Uniquely Blaine

Blaine presents in the first session dressed scantly in leather with a peculiar hat, mismatched shoes, and carrying a lunchbox decorated with tarot cards. Blaine has recently had a series of unsettling verbal confrontations with a relative who has been forcefully recommending enlistment in the armed forces.

Client

- Talk about your prior positive relationship with this relative and how things have declined over time.

- Discuss how your family has a history of misunderstanding you and does not accept your ways.

- Submit some helpful fashion tips to the therapist.

Therapist

- **Rapport** (p. 33)
  Cite the things that you genuinely admire about Blaine (sensitivity, thoughtfulness, wish to resolve this conflict, bold expression of self, etc.).

- **Presenting problem** (p. 41)
  Focus on the issue that Blaine is presenting (how hard it can be when relationships change, the challenge of dealing with judgmental or controlling people, etc.).

- **Start where the client is** (p. 44)
  Work the issue that Blaine is opening with, acknowledging Blaine's uniqueness and right to a personally satisfying perspective.

Role-Play Exercise 2.2

The Silence of the Client

Ray is quiet, presenting as depressed, predominately looking downward, and avoiding eye contact. Ray seems uncertain of what to say.

Client

- Speak slowly; use a depressive voice tone.

- Mention one or several names of people with little or no details.

- Haltingly, begin discussing a problem (abrasive peer or coworker, owing someone money, a good friend who's moved away, etc.).

Therapist

- **Fostering sensitive self-disclosure** (p. 35)
  Allow the client to select the entry point.
  "Can you tell me a little about what's going on?"
  "You can start anywhere you want."

- **Coping with silence** (p. 42)
  Be patient; respect the client's pacing.
  "Just take your time. There's no rush here."

- **Vocal features** (p. 49)
  Match your voice tone and tempo to the client's (low volume, slow pace).

Teen Tension

Drew, a teen living at home, is involved in a close relationship and admits to casual substance abuse. Drew seems fixed on discussing how unfair parents can be and how disapproving they are of premarital sex.

Client

- Openly discuss the substance use, but firmly refuse to discuss any details regarding sex.

- Use expressive language when discussing your parents (slang, profanities, funny or unflattering nicknames, etc.).

- Allude to some deeper problem that has not yet come to the parents' attention (recently dropped out of school, symptoms of what might be a sexually transmitted disease).

Therapist

- **Respecting the client's boundaries** (p. 46)
  You may make any inquiries you want, but do not press for disclosure that the client firmly chooses to keep private.

- **Matching** (p. 48)
  Tune your language style (vocabulary, voice tone) to match Drew's. Consider using some of Drew's words or expressions.

- **Underlying problem** (p. 51)
  If you are given hints regarding an underlying problem, express your curiosity; gently encourage further disclosure.

Role-Play Exercise 2.4

Insincerely Yours

Avery and Spencer have been best friends for years. Avery just found out that Spencer, who claimed to be a homeowner, is actually a tenant. Additionally, Spencer's professional credentials (attorney, health care professional) are not substantiated by the corresponding licensing public Web site. This has left you questioning if any of your relationship with Spencer has been genuine, and you are now concerned about your ability to select quality friends.

Client

- Speak slowly. Pause repeatedly as if you are in disbelief.

- Use simple but appropriate vocabulary. Consider using brief or very long sentences.

- Mention that, per what you saw on a television show, you would like to have daily appointments. Attempt to negotiate for 2-hour appointments. Ask the therapist for personal contact information (telephone number, e-mail address, etc.).

Therapist

- **Coping with silence** (p. 42)
  Be patient. Consider acknowledging the silence or providing some prompts.
  "Take your time."
  "What are you thinking (or feeling) right now?"

- **Matching** (p. 48)
  Use language that seems conducive to Avery's communication style.

- **Introduction and ground rules** (p. 40)
  Explain that the agency's policy is for weekly 50-minute appointments, but that can be expanded to twice a week if warranted. Tactfully explain that it is not customary to provide clients with your personal contact information and that, if necessary, you can be reached through the agency.

Role-Play Exercise 2.5

Loss or Gain?

Brook appears somewhat distraught over the recent death of a relative. Brook unexpectedly received a sizable inheritance from this relative and is now considering using the money to finance education but is uncertain about what career to pursue.

Client

- Initially, present as grief-stricken over the loss of your relative.

- Discuss this relative hesitantly. Consider alluding to the notion that the inheritance was likely the relative's compensation for something bad he or she did to you.

- When you feel ready, reveal your indecision about how best to use the inheritance.

Therapist

- **Presenting problem** (p. 41)
  Work with the story as it is revealed. Explore how Brook is experiencing the relative's death.

- **Respect the client's boundaries** (p. 46)
  You can ask about this relative, but if your questions are met with strong resistance, acknowledge it and be prepared to move on.

- **Underlying problem** (p. 51)
  If Brook raises another problem, identify it as such and process whatever else is included.

3

Following

Understanding the client is the basis for all helping. Understanding is accomplished by focusing your awareness on the words that the client is saying and how those words are being conveyed. This chapter includes skills for detailed listening, demonstrating your attentiveness, and validating your comprehension of the client's story.

Listening

The most basic and perhaps single most essential skill that you can possess as a therapist is the ability to listen. Your fundamental role in therapy is to try to understand the client, to deliberately and attentively listen with an open and genuinely curious ear. As discussed earlier, you must start where the client is. Your entry point is somewhere in the middle of the client's life. The client's history, current living conditions, goals, belief systems, hopes, fears, and talents are all relevant factors. In the interest of helping the client embrace and best utilize the therapeutic process, make a consistent effort to assemble a comprehensive image of the client's life system, taking into account the client's emotional and cognitive standpoint.

Initially, it can be tempting to focus exclusively on fixing or solving the client's first presented problem. As ambitious and well-meaning as this may be, what is needed first is to understand the interpersonal and intra-personal context in which the client exists: Just listen and try to understand the client's life situation. There will be plenty of opportunity to engage in facilitative therapeutic work such as goal identification, treatment planning, and interventions. In order for the therapeutic contact and interventions to be useful to the client, such processes must be tailored to each client's unique multidimensional biopsychosocial context in which the client lives. This understanding is gained by actively listening. If the client communicates a concept that is unclear or vague, or if the links between concepts, relationships, or events do not make sense to you, then ask about it. If something strikes you as interesting or unusual, ask about it. As a therapist, you will listen and build meaningful questions based not only on your thoughts and theoretical framework but also on your feelings and gut instincts.

The client can plausibly be considered to be the expert witness with respect to his or her own life and, as such, is a worthy spokesperson. The information that clients provide regarding their thoughts and feelings and their willingness to convey this information are of paramount value. Keep your role in perspective. As stated earlier, as a therapist, you serve somewhat as an emotional consultant to the client; as such, the focal point of the therapeutic contact is the client. Though well-intended, avoid the temptation to become judgmental or preachy. Lengthy lectures are likely to be ignored or even resented. Therapeutic messages are best communicated in concise and purposeful language. A common rule of thumb is that the client should be doing about two thirds of the talking, and you should be doing about one third. Certainly, there can be exceptions to this suggested ratio. For example, it would be appropriate for you to do more of the talking if the client asks you to explain a concept, answer a question, or provide the rationale for a referral. Conversely, traditional American Indian clients, particularly in their initial session, will expect to do the majority of the talking as they want the therapist to understand the basis of their problem (Barcus, 2003). A simple self-monitoring yardstick might be to ask yourself from time to time who is doing most of the talking—me or the client? If you find that you are crossing the 50% talking threshold, then it may be advisable to shorten your responses, permitting more space for your client to communicate. Remember, contemporary therapy is not about monologs; neither you nor the client should be doing all of the talking (Egan, 2006b).

Attending

Observational Cues

Attending involves being cognizant of the messages—verbal and nonverbal—that are being exchanged between you and the client. Awareness of the client's body language and facial expression may provide valuable clues as to the client's emotional state. For example, a client may be telling you a story, the nature of which seems discordant with the facial expression or posture. Useful information may be gained from tactfully and nonjudgmentally pointing out such observations:

Th: *I'm noticing something: When you talk about your aunt's death, your voice sounds solemn, but I'm also seeing a bit of a smile. I'm wondering what that smile's about?*

Cl: *Well, it's sad that she's dead, but to be quite honest, we never really got along . . . and that's putting it mildly.*

Body language may also provide clues as to the client's mood in moments of silence, but it can be difficult to know what someone's specific thoughts or feelings might be prior to asking. If you notice a change in the client's affect, consider citing your observation and inquiring about it:

Th: *A few minutes ago when you were talking about your new computer, you were so bright and excited. Now you're looking withdrawn. Your hands are folded, your legs are crossed, and you're looking down. I'm wondering what's going on.*

Cl: *I'm just thinking about my father. He likes technology too. I'm wondering if we'll ever have anything meaningful between us.*

Observe the extent to which the client makes eye contact. Eye contact may be correlated with mood. A client may spend more time looking downward or avoiding direct eye contact when depressed than when he or she is in a better mood. As with body language, eye contact—or lack thereof—can be ambiguous. In some cultures, such as that of the American Indian, it is considered disrespectful to establish or maintain direct eye contact (Thompson, Walker, & Silk-Walker, 1993). For others, looking down or away from a person may merely be a part of their communication style; it is not necessarily indicative of a psychiatric disorder or inattentiveness.

Voice tone can also be useful in conveying your meaning and better understanding the client's emotional message. While paying heed to the words, the voice tone or "song of the voice" can communicate the emotional track of what is being said (Watzlawick, 1967). When there is discordance between the actual words that are being spoken and the tone of the voice, one may sense that the voice tone carries the truer message. Saying *"I love you"* with a warm and gentle voice tone would seem to communicate genuineness, whereas saying *"I love you"* with a sullen or brusque voice tone would likely be perceived as less believable.

Consider this example in which the therapist identifies and purposefully discusses the discordances between the *words* that the client is saying and *how* those words appear to be coming across. In addition to voice tone, notice how the therapist assesses the plausibility of the client's words by observing a variety of cues such as posture, facial expression, and eye contact:

Cl: [Flatly] *I met with the vocational guidance counselor like we talked about last time. Anyway, she went through my stuff, and next semester it looks like I'm supposed to start nursing school.*

In addition to the lack of enthusiasm in the voice tone, the client uses passive or burdensome language: *"I'm supposed to . . ."* as opposed to more active or anticipatory language (e.g., *"I get to . . ."*) when describing the client's acceptance into nursing school.

Th: *Nursing school? Really?*

Noticing the lack of enthusiasm, the therapist attempts to solicit further discussion on the topic.

Cl: *Uh-huh.*

Th: *Nursing is an admirable profession; from what I know of you, I'm sure it's within your reach to graduate nursing school, but something else strikes me here: When you talk about this, you sound pretty disinterested.*

The therapist points out the client's emotional listlessness.

Cl: *What do you mean?*

Th: *For instance, near the beginning of today's session when you were talking about your plans to travel through Europe, your whole expression was up. Your voice was lively and colorful; your eyes were wide; your head was up; your posture was tall; you were gesturing expressively. Now, that's what you look like when you're discussing something that you really seem to be into. . . . . On the other hand, when you talk about nursing school, I'm not seeing any of that passion. It all just seems to lay flat with no details, no excitement, no elaboration, no pizzazz at all.*

The therapist articulates specific observations.

Cl: *Huh. You noticed that . . .*

Th: *It makes me wonder if this decision to go into nursing is something that's really important to* you, *or maybe this is* someone else's *idea . . . that maybe you don't really believe in?*

Based on the therapist's observation, the therapist submits a provisional mild confrontation.

Cl: *Well, I guess I do have the grades for it and all, but to be honest, I'm really not that into being a nurse.*

Expressing the contrast in emotional conveyance and comparing the animated affect related to discussion of the planned trip to Europe versus the unenthusiastic talk of the plan to enter nursing school, the therapist was able to help the client elicit more genuine feelings and attitudes. The therapy may then advance to address the wisdom of pursuing passionless goals and perhaps explore more suitable alternatives.

Nonverbal Attending

Though our primary communication channel is speech, nonverbal skills can provide a supplemental way of facilitating quality contact. Nonverbal techniques may be used independently, or they may be combined with verbal messages in order to further punctuate our intended meanings. Nonverbal cues constitute more than half of the emotional message (Sweeney, Cottle, & Kobayashi, 1980); hence, it is advisable to tend to both your and the client's style of conveyance, in terms of facial expressions and body language. Some cultures, in particular Asians' and American Indians', may convey more of their emotional message nonverbally via body language, eyes, and voice tone (Barcus, 2003). Nonverbally conveying your attentiveness demonstrates that you are actively absorbing and processing the client's story, and as such, your recommendations are likely to carry more weight with the client (Sue & Sue, 2003).

In terms of managing your physicality in a therapeutic setting, the acronym "SOLER" can provide some useful guidelines (Kadushin, 1990):

Straight facing the client; do not position yourself turned at an angle

Open posture; avoid crossing your arms or legs

Lean forward occasionally

Eye contact

Relaxed demeanor

Clients perceive practitioners who exhibit these attentive behaviors as having a strong sense of rapport with them (Harrigan, Osman, & Rosenthal, 1985). Conversely, folded arms, backward leaning, poor eye contact, and reduced voice dynamics are perceived as nonfacilitative behavior (Harrigan & Rosenthal, 1986). Be aware that there is no universal system of body language; cross-cultural differences exist. Although it is important to recognize cultural differences, it is equally important to avoid stereotyping. Make an effort to orient yourself to the unique nonverbal style of each client (Sue & Sue, 1990).

One can include such things as hand and arm gestures, nodding, facial expression, posture, body positioning, and other motions in a variety of meaningful ways, as in this example:

Cl: *I've been thinking of calling my brother.*

Th: [Posture: sits up. Facial expression: eyebrows up]

> The therapist nonverbally conveys, *"It sounds like this is going to be interesting. I'm ready to hear all about this."*

Cl: *The more we talk about it here, I'm starting to see that the problems between us . . . well, they're not all his fault.*

Th: [Nodding]

> The therapist nods, acknowledging the client's insight and willingness to take some responsibility, prompting the client to continue with this point.

Cl: *It's like, all I was remembering from our childhood is all the awful stupid stuff we did to each other . . . constantly.*

Th: [Leans forward. Facial expression: curiosity—head tipped, eyebrows up]

> The therapist uses an open *"I'm curious. Tell me more"* expression, as opposed to an *"I'm confused"* look.

Cl: *Like, when we were kids, he'd booby trap my closet so when I opened the door a bunch of stuff would fall down, and I'd get so mad at him. I wouldn't even think of talking to him. I'd just go and do something to his stuff, like I'd put crackers under his sheets and dance on the bed . . . stupid stuff like that.*

Th: [Facial expression: smiles warmly]

Cl: *There was a lot worse stuff. I just don't want us to be so distant any more. I'm starting to see that I was half of what was going wrong. . . . Maybe now I can be half of fixing things between us.*

Th: [Nods]

For tutorial purposes, the foregoing dialogue is somewhat atypical, in that the therapist's responses are comprised exclusively of nonverbals. Yet, even in silence, it is possible to effectively demonstrate attentiveness, prompting the client to advance the storytelling.

In terms of managing your physical presence in sessions, research suggests that the therapist who attends with a relaxed posture, sitting back in the seat as opposed to leaning forward, presents as having a more robust interest, empathy, and respect for the client (Hermansson, Webster, & McFarland, 1988). As you communicate, you need not remain rigidly parked in your seat. Consider using body empathy wherein you intuitively utilize your posture, head position, nods, body movements, and gestures in concert with your words (Jacobs, 1973). Therapists who provide positive eye contact and meaningful nonverbal cues are perceived as providing a stronger sense of empathy, warmth, genuineness, and effectiveness, thereby facilitating the therapeutic process. One is more likely to disclose sensitive information to someone who demonstrates compassionate competency (Sherer & Rogers, 1980).

Brief Verbals

The strategic use of brief verbal responses (*"mm-hmm," "hmm," "gotcha," "okay," "right," "I get it," "I see," "go on"*—selectively repeating key words that the client has said) can facilitate communication in a number of ways: You are following the story; request clarification or elaboration of a particular point; challenge the client; prompt the advancement of the story; or request further details. The compact nature of brief verbal responses provides the advantage of not bogging down or derailing the client's stream of thought or feelings (Knippen & Green, 1994).

Cl: *I've finally decided to do something.*

Th: *Something?*

Repeating a single word suggests that the therapist wants elaboration or clarification: What does this *"something"* entail?

Cl: *We've talked for a long time about me being such a workaholic, and how I've been depriving myself and how I work like a dog, heading for burn-out, just going nonstop without a vacation for years.*

Th: *Mm-hmm . . . six years.*

Accessing prior information to further clarify a point provides a sense of continuity to the therapy and also demonstrates acute attentiveness.

Cl: *Six long years. Anyway, I'm going to Alaska!*

Th: *Really? Alaska?*

Prompting the client to talk about this further, *"How did you come to select Alaska?"*

Cl: *Yeah. Ever since I was a kid, I've wanted to see the aurora borealis. I mean, I've seen it on TV, but that's like watching fireworks on TV. That doesn't really count. I have a travel agent hunting for travel packages right now. I have so much to do before I go: I need to get warm clothes, hire a temp, get a new battery for my laptop, get someone to take care of my plants . . .*

Th: *Your laptop?*

Knowing of the client's overworking propensity, the therapist challenges the client to consider the impact that taking a computer might have on a vacation.

Cl: *Oh, you're right. I'd just work. See how I think! Right, . . . definitely no laptop.*

Sometimes, the temptation in therapy is to do or say too much. This case demonstrates the power and diversity of what can be accomplished using a minimum of thoughtfully selected words.

Pausing

Pausing involves leaving some space, several seconds, before responding to the client's message. Most conversations that people have do not involve discussing difficult personal issues, such as emotional vulnerabilities, or confronting dysfunctional behavior patterns; hence, they tend to flow smoothly without many pauses. This is not to imply that such social conversations are unimportant, but they tend to involve topics that are easier to discuss.

Engaging in psychotherapy challenges both you and the client to expend considerably more cognitive and emotional energy to process a potentially complex array of sensitive personal facts and feelings.

Pausing can facilitate the therapeutic process in a variety of ways: Although a client may have spent considerable time *thinking* about a problem prior to entering therapy, it is possible that difficult feelings such as hurt, embarrassment, fear, or confusion may have inhibited the client from actually *discussing* the problem with anyone, including him- or herself. The therapeutic setting may be the first time that a client partakes in actual out-loud discussion of the problem, which can present challenges in the storytelling. When we *think* about a problem, our thoughts do not always occur in the sequence in which they happened in real life. The ordering of emotionally laden events can be heavily influenced by the weight of our feelings, which to an outsider may seem somewhat scattered. When thinking about a problem, one might begin somewhere in the middle, with the most prominent, hurtful point coming first. One's thoughts may then jump to the ending, considering how one feels right now. The next thought may revert back to the beginning of the story, considering among other things what might have been done to prevent this problem.

There is nothing inherently wrong with this skipping-about thought process; however, when it comes to actually *telling* this story aloud to another person, the client may appropriately feel compelled to convey the story in a more chronological order. This sorting process may take some time because the pieces of this story are probably not all homogeneous in terms of emotional significance: Some of these story pieces may be more intense or burdensome than others. Pausing provides the client the opportunity to sort and resequence the components of the story and can also provide some useful emotional space as the client discusses the details of a feeling-laden story.

Pausing enables both you and the client the opportunity to reflect on what is being discussed. The client has the chance to hear him- or herself. Remember, this may be the first time that the client has moved through the story in a comprehensive, sequential order. Pauses may afford the client the chance to correlate the factors within the story or to relate components of the current circumstances to relevant aspects of the client's life history, thereby facilitating potentially valuable insight. Pausing also provides the client the opportunity to recall and articulate further information associated with the story.

One can think of the therapeutic storytelling as a stereo system consisting of two tracks: data and emotions. The data track consists of the facts or content of the story: What happened? Who did what to whom? The emotional track consists of the feelings associated with the data: How do you feel about the individuals involved? How do you feel about what happened? The client may experience heavy feelings while telling the story. Just as the weight of toting a heavy backpack may slow the stride of a hiker, the weight of intense feelings may reasonably slow down the storytelling. If the client begins to seem overwhelmed, then you can gently suggest that he or she pause. Pausing affords the client space to feel and process the emotional track of the story. In your wish to be helpful, it can be tempting to promptly speak your mind, thereby closing up potentially uncomfortable gaps of silence; this may unintentionally derail or cut short critical cognitive or emotional processing or curtail portions of the story that may be forthcoming. Try to monitor and manage your sense of impatience or discomfort with what appears to be sluggish pacing. Instead of attempting to accelerate the dialogue, consider going in the other direction by granting the client the opportunity to take the extra time necessary to experience the feelings associated with the story. You might even express this verbally: *"I can see this is difficult for you. . . . Take your time with this."* Not only is it essential to start where the client is, but it is equally important to move at the client's pace. Pausing can convey patience, thoughtful attentiveness, and sensitivity.

Taking a moment before responding to a client provides an opportunity for you and the client to reflect on what was just said. Slowing things down gives you more time to thoroughly assess both the client's feelings and yours and to consider how what the client just said fits into the assembling image of the client's life story. Pausing affords you the chance to listen and respond more thoroughly. It can be difficult to listen while simultaneously attempting to formulate a complex response. Pausing grants you some time to think about what you want to say or ask next. In fact, there is nothing wrong with occasionally requesting some extra time before responding to a client; you might say *"This is interesting. . . . Let me think about this for a moment."* This lets the client know that your silence is not due to inattentiveness, disinterest, or boredom. Rather, the client can see that you are, in fact, acutely engaged and taking the time necessary to construct the best, most meaningful response.

Cl: *Two days ago, I was on my way to work.* [Pause] *I left on time, but I didn't get there on time.* [Pause] *I saw something.* [Pause] *I've never seen this before.* [Pause] *It was so awful. So awful.* [Pause]

You may provide nonverbal responses (nodding gently, softened facial expression) in order to demonstrate your understanding of the story and the feelings without hindering the stream of the storytelling.

Th: *Take your time.*

The client appears to be experiencing weighty emotions related to the event. It is appropriate for the therapist to identify this challenge and normalize this part of the storytelling as a "reduced speed zone."

Cl: *Okay, I was at this red light, and I was listening to the radio, ya know, just like always. Anyway, there was this guy. [Pause] He was in this white suit, up on one of those window washing things up on the side of this building. [Pause] He was up high. I mean really high. [Pause] Damn!*

Th: *It's okay. Just go slow.*

The therapist helps the client feel comfortable with a slower tempo, thereby facilitating storytelling that is factually and emotionally rich.

Cl: *Okay. There was this rope . . . one of the ropes on the side of this thing that he was standing on . . . one side of the platform just tipped really fast and everything just fell off [Pause$_1$] except for the guy. He was on some other like safety rope, so he was just left there hanging and waving. [Pause$_2$] I was so scared for him. . . . I was so scared, and I couldn't do anything to help him. [Pause$_3$] I started digging for my cell phone so I could call 911, which I did. [Pause$_4$] Anyway, it turns out the guy was okay. . . . I watched while they got him off the building. . . . He didn't fall, but I just can't stop thinking about it.*

Through the therapist's patience, resisting the impulse to speak prematurely, the client effectively benefits from the pauses in multiple ways: Before the first pause, the therapist may be anticipating that the worker on the scaffolding fell. After the pause, the client continues to provide the next vital details of the story. We see that the worker did not fall. After the second pause, the client has the opportunity to articulate (in words) feelings of fear, concern, and perceived helplessness. After the third pause, we see that the client was actually not so helpless. The call to 911 demonstrates active and effective helping efforts. After the fourth pause, we gain further cognitive and emotional information, suggesting an appropriate posttraumatic reaction to the event.

Anyone performing a detailed or complex task, either physical or cognitive, must be given adequate time and workspace, including elbow room to accomplish the objective. This story is rich in events and feelings. Exercising patience by allowing for a more gradual tempo, which includes pauses, allows for more thorough elaboration of both facts and feelings, thereby facilitating the quality of the client's storytelling. The better you understand your clients, the more effective your interventions can be.

Verifying Perception

Therapy involves the exchange of complex concepts involving not only a detailed set of facts but also the associated feelings. The combination of intense emotions and potentially multifaceted storytelling may confound the communication path, leading to one or more misconceptions. Therapeutic productivity depends on the quality of the two-way understanding between you and the client. As such, it is essential to progressively verify the quality of the communication to actively confirm that each member is understanding the other. Your effectiveness extends only to the point of your comprehension of the client's life condition; furthermore, your efforts are only useful to the extent that your client understands your message. There are specific skills that can be employed to evaluate and enhance the accuracy of this two-way comprehension, specifically reflection of content and feelings, reverse reflection, summarizing, and clarification (of content and feelings).

Reflection/Paraphrasing

Reflection, also known as "paraphrasing," involves selectively stating your understanding of the information that you are gathering from the client in a provisional manner, implying *"This is what I'm getting. . . . Is that right?"* This is typically done in the form of rephrasing the client's message in an abbreviated fashion, which may include some of the client's own words or phrases played back verbatim. Exclusively echoing back the client's words can sound thoughtless and redundant. The client's words and expressions are by no means off limits, but make an effort to assemble your reflective constructs using mostly your own words—your provisional understanding of what you are hearing.

Reflecting demonstrates that you are genuinely attending to the details of the evolution of the story by progressively checking your perception of what the client is telling you. Occasionally, the client may point out your misconceptions; this is not inherently bad. Consider using such corrections as opportunities to gather further details regarding the client's story. Misunderstandings may be due to a variety of factors such as the client's emotional conveyance, incomplete or distorted information, the use of vague or inexact language, unique use of language, or novel expressions. Reflection can be useful in pointing out and soliciting details that may have been understated or skipped in the storytelling. In addition to aiding the therapist in comprehending the storyline, reflection helps the client hear what he or she is saying to you, which may facilitate introspection and self-understanding.

Reflection can be used to clarify both the content (the data) and feelings (the emotional track) of the story.

Cl: *So, my mom and dad have this curfew rule about me having to be in by 10:00, which I think is totally stupid. Anyway, on Saturday, I got in at midnight.*

Th: *After 10:00.*

The therapist reflects a salient point of the content: that the client returned home after the curfew.

Cl: *Right. So my mom starts yelling at me and wakes up everyone in the house and stands there spouting-off this whole thing about how I could have been killed or dragged off somewhere by some maniac with a gun or a knife or something completely insane like that.*

The client confirms the therapist's commentary and advances to the next point.

Th: *Sounds like you were both pretty mad at each other.*

The therapist reflects the feelings, presuming that both the mother and the client experienced the same (mad) feeling.

Cl: *Mad? Yeah, she was mad. I was more like scared.*

The client accepts the therapist's assessment of the mother's (mad) feeling but clarifies the client's own feeling as different: scared.

Th: *Okay. Got it. . . . So, your mom was mad and you were scared.*

The therapist implicitly thanks the client for making the correction (*"Okay. Got it."*) and reflects the feelings that the client has conveyed.

Cl: *Scared. Yeah, scared . . . more like terrified. See, when my mom gets like this, she usually throws things. Last time she got me with the remote. It didn't really hurt, but on top of the yelling, it's just too much.*

Th: *I see. So your mom catastrophizes about you breaking curfew?*

The therapist makes a tentative effort to focus on what appears to be a problematic behavior.

Cl: *No. You don't get it. See, she's like that on everything: grades, work-ing, not working, going out, staying in my room, doing chores around the house. Just everything. Like just last week, I just finished vacuum-ing, and there was a part of the rug that apparently wasn't vacuumed completely perfectly. She found a staple in the carpet and she was wav-ing this mutilated staple in my face and just yelling and screaming like someone was stabbing her.*

The client makes a correction: The mother's extreme behavior is not limited to just this one circumstance; according to the client, the mother's reaction is more generalized. This clarification suggests that not only is the client feeling stress from the mother's efforts to enforce the curfew (which may or may not be appropriate) but also that the overall parent-child relationship may be stressed from similar such incidents.

Th: *So when your mom spots something she doesn't like, no matter how small, her thing is to do a lot of yelling and accusing?*

The therapist reflects the new (broader) findings, presenting a provi-sional summary of the stressful communication pattern described by the client, again, giving the client an opportunity to comment on the accu-racy of the therapist's refined perception.

Cl: *Pretty much.*

In this example, the therapist plays back parts of the story as it is being told. The client can clearly see that the therapist is listening critically to the story and making a serious effort to understand the details of the situation as the client experienced it. The client has multiple opportunities to affirm or cor-rect the accuracy of the therapist's perception. When the client rejects the therapist's reflection, *"No. You don't get it, . . ."* this should not be seen as a failure on the therapist's part. On the contrary, the client responds by pro-viding valuable elaboration that offers the therapist a more detailed picture of the client's stressful circumstances.

Reverse Reflection

In addition to using reflection to check *your* comprehension of the *client's* message, the process can be reversed: You may employ *reverse reflection* to check the client's comprehension of your message.

For instance, suppose you just explained a critical or complex concept to a client. Despite the fact that the client may nod affirmatively or even say,

"Okay, I get it," this is no guarantee that your message actually got through. When people do not fully understand a concept, especially when it is conveyed by an authority figure, they may resort to *acquiescent responding,* wherein they may pretend to understand (replying affirmatively) when they really do not understand (Rubin & Babbie, 1993). Acquiescent responding can happen for a variety of reasons: The client may not want to appear unintelligent; he or she may feel embarrassed about not understanding; or the client may just assume that because you as the therapist, a perceived authority figure, raised the issue, then it must be right.

Your words and your efforts are essentially useless if you are not understood. When using reverse reflection, ask the client to play back, in the client's own words, his or her understanding of what you just said. Be aware that the act of simply echoing back your own words does not necessarily verify comprehension; if the client merely parrots your words, then acknowledge the accuracy of the words but also ask the client to reiterate the concept using the client's own words. As with reflection, reverse reflection provides the opportunity to confirm or tactfully provide corrective feedback to enhance the client's comprehension. The client need not necessarily agree with everything you say, but it is essential to verify the quality of his or her understanding.

Cl: *For about the last 4 or 5 days, a couple of times a week, I've been getting this really flushed feeling, and then my arms and hands start to tremble. Sometimes it feels like my whole body is dropping, like I'm on some platform that's going down fast, like a really fast elevator. It goes for about 10 seconds, and then I get all sweaty and nervous, and my heart races, and it really scares me. It happens mostly at school, but it's happened a couple of times when I'm home at nighttime. I don't know what's going on. Why is this happening to me?*

The phenomena that the client is describing may be associated with an anxiety disorder; however, the symptoms are predominantly physical in nature. The therapist's primary responsibility is to refer the client to a physician for a checkup to diagnose and treat or rule out any physical problems or diseases.

Th: *I'm glad you told me about this; I'll continue to work with you, but you need to schedule an appointment to see your doctor for a checkup to rule out any physical problems. With your permission, I'll confer with your doctor to discuss how much of this might be due to a physical problem and how much of this might be related to emotional stress. We might even consider conferring with a psychiatrist. There may be medications that could be helpful.*

The therapist proposes an appropriate treatment plan, which contains a lot of information involving several players.

Cl: Okay.

It sounds like the client understands and accepts this plan.

Th: What I just said involves a lot of details. I just want to make sure I was clear enough. Could you please tell me, in your own words, what I just said?

Because reverse reflection is not usually part of our casual conversation, this may initially sound like an awkward or nonproductive request. Notice that the therapist does not imply that the client does not have the capacity to understand; rather, the therapist identifies him- or herself as the potential source of the misconception by saying, "*I just want to make sure I was clear enough,*" thereby facilitating rapport.

Cl: You want me to see my doctor, and she'll tell me which psychiatrist to go to.

Clearly, there is a misconception here. The therapist needs to make a second pass at providing this information. One strategy is to simplify or restate the information or to break the message into smaller pieces.

Th: Close. I'll keep working with you, and here's how I think we should proceed: Number one, get a doctor's appointment to see if there's a physical problem. Number two, based on your doctor's findings, we— meaning you, me, and your doctor—might consider including a psychiatric evaluation.

The therapist uses concise language to identify and enumerate each discrete task.

Cl: Okay, I get it.

Again, the client says that he or she understands; it is time to verify this.

Th: Okay. This is important; I just want to double-check this. Tell me back what I just said.

The therapist requests the next reverse reflection.

Cl: First, I go to my doctor to let her check me out and see if this stuff that's happening is because I'm sick. And then we'll all figure out if

*I should go to a psychiatrist, but I'll keep on working with you.
Right?*

The client reflects his or her refined comprehension to the therapist.

Th: *Exactly.*

The therapist validates the client's more accurate reflection.

This cycle of clarifying and then requesting reverse reflection should continue until the accuracy of the communication is confirmed. Naturally, you will tune the frequency of this skill depending on your familiarity with each client, taking into account such factors as the complexity of the information and the client's mood, level of attentiveness, intelligence, and self-advocacy. It follows that you may find yourself using reverse reflection less often with clients who have a reputation of actively identifying their misunderstandings or disagreements with the notions that you put forth, whereas reverse reflection may be used more often to elicit the level of comprehension among less articulate clients.

Reverse reflection should be used progressively in sessions. Waiting until the end of the session to verify comprehension may leave little time to provide effective clarification. Additionally, therapeutic concepts may be cumulative. Failing to confirm comprehension in a progressive fashion may confound the client's ability to understand and effectively partake in the path of the therapy. Persistent confusion on the client's behalf is likely to lead to frustration and possible premature termination; therefore, progressive verification of the client's comprehension should be an ongoing process.

Summarizing

Summarizing is similar to reflecting; however, it covers a little more ground. *Summarizing* entails reflecting a brief synthesis of the client's story. This playback helps to keep you in synch with the client's storytelling, allowing the client to offer corrections, enhancements, or supplements to your accumulating image of the client's scenario. Summarizing also serves to confirm that you understand what the client is saying, that you are really hearing the client.

Summarizing is a verification skill. Think of the client as the expert witness in his or her life, and as such, the therapist's summarizations should be phrased provisionally, as opposed to authoritatively. When summarizing, essentially you are implicitly asking, *"This is what I'm understanding from you. . . . Is that right?"*

An authoritative summary might sound like this: *"You always quit just before you complete a project."* Although this may be an accurate summary, it uses the word *"always."* Because you do not have access to the client's full life history, semantically it would be inappropriate to use the word *"always."* The use of the word *"always"* also suggests that there is no chance for growth or change in the future, that things will *"always"* be this way. A more facilitative summarization might be, *"It sounds like there's a pattern of stopping before you're done."* This phrasing essentially covers the same ground; however, it is neither accusatory nor judgmental. The tentative phrasing suggests that your conception of the problem is malleable, open to further information and further growth. For example, the client might identify prior successes that could suggest strengths or other resources that might be useful in the therapeutic process.

When proposing a summary to the client, you need not be timid, but consider using tentative language (*"typically," "usually," "tend to," "sounds like," "seems that," "there's a history of"*) as opposed to more definitive language (*"always," "never"*). Remember, summarizing involves proposing and then verifying your overall impression, not unilaterally imposing your perception of the client's story.

If the storyline starts becoming complicated or difficult to follow (extensive details, scenarios, time lines, multiple characters), it is advisable to summarize your understanding of the story up to that point and then incrementally as the story advances.

Summarizing enables the client to hear what the story sounds like from another point of view. Providing an opportunity to gain a different perspective on his or her story may facilitate insights that may serve to advance the mutual understanding of the problem and suggest possible solutions.

In a broader sense, summarizing may also span several stories or even sessions; feel free to think broadly. You may be able to plausibly link events together. Correlations among related events in the client's life may reveal key patterns in the client's behavior, thought process, or feelings, which may become the focus of therapy.

Cl: *Yesterday I was at Justin's house, and there were some pictures lying on the counter, so when he went to go answer the phone, I just started looking through them, and there was shot after shot of Megan and Justin at our favorite restaurant.*

Th: *You mentioned Megan and Justin before—your two best friends . . . the "Triple Threat"?*

Summarizing acknowledges that the therapist is familiar with the characters in the client's life. This is emphasized by the therapist including the client's nickname for the threesome: *"Triple Threat."*

Cl: *Right. We do* everything *together. I was looking at the pictures.*
I noticed that in the corner of the picture, it has the date, and those
pictures were taken just this last weekend and 2 weeks before that. So
I don't get it. Why would they leave me out? I was so mad when I saw
those pictures.

The client provides further emotional storytelling spanning several events.

Th: *So you typically think of yourself and Megan and Justin as a trio . . .*

The therapist begins to summarize.

Cl: *Right—best friends.*

The client confirms this part of the summary.

Th: *. . . best friends, so you felt bad when you found out that Justin and*
Megan were spending some time without you?

The therapist continues the summary, citing facts and feelings.

Cl: *Exactly. I felt totally betrayed.*

The client acknowledges the accuracy of the therapist's recap and also
appends further (emotional) expression.

As with reflection, summarizing demonstrates that the facts and feelings of
the client's story are being received accurately. In listening to the therapist's
recap of the story, the client has the opportunity to correct any misconceptions and provide supplements to the story.

In addition to recapping the basic story, the therapist begins to (speculatively) identify the feelings and put them in synch with the events. (*"So you
felt bad when you found out that Justin and Megan were spending some time
without you."*)

Summarizing may be confined to recapping one or several events *within*
a session, or it may involve linking similar sounding story segments together
that may span multiple prior sessions. Such summarizing may congeal in a
meaningful manner; these correlations may point the way to identifying a
source problem that may become the focus of the therapeutic intervention.
Similarly, recurring strengths and positive adaptations may also emerge.

Clarification

Clarification takes summarizing to the next level. *Clarification* entails
requests for further details to address vague, confusing, or discontinuous storytelling. Occasionally, the client may use an expression or even an isolated

word with which you are unfamiliar. This may be a phrase, expression, or syntax (the arrangement of words within a sentence) that is unique to a particular cultural background (Wilkinson & Spurlock, 1986). If it is not immediately clear from the context precisely what the client means, then request clarification promptly. Remember, your fundamental goal is to understand the client.

Cl: *So I was half asleep when I got a call from my best friend at 11:30 last night. Get this: We wound up going for a moonlight hike until around 2:00 a.m. It was completely klooby!*

Th: *It was "completely klooby"? How do you mean? . . . What made it so klooby?*

At this point, the word *klooby* is unclear; we do not know if the oddly timed hike was good, bad, peculiar, dangerous, or boring. The therapist immediately requests clarification.

Cl: *It was the most amazing thing ever! I've never heard an owl hoot until that night. It sounds totally different than it does in movies. And the moonlight and shadows and the air was so soft. The crickets were chirping. . . . It's like these amazing sounds were just coming from everywhere. It was just one of those times when you see and hear and feel this incredible combination of stuff that you've never seen before. Something that I just never really knew was there.*

Further detail is provided.

Th: *So being "klooby," this was a unique and wondrous experience?*

The therapist pitches his or her understanding of what "klooby" appears to mean.

Cl: *. . . that I never knew was possible! Yes. Yes. Totally klooby!*

The client provides further elaboration.

Another technique to achieve clarification when the storytelling becomes unclear is to recap the parts of the story that you do understand and then ask about the elements of the story that are unclear to you. It is possible that the client may have a well-organized mental image of the story: A → B → C → D, but when converting the story from a mental image to verbalization, the client may unintentionally skip from point B to point D. The client already knows all about point C, so the skip may appear seamless to the client, but this leap may leave you feeling lost. In such a case, it is appropriate to pause the storytelling, summarize your understanding of the story thus far, and then request clarification regarding the missing link in the chain of events. (*"I understand that first A happened, which led to B, . . . but I'm not getting how you got from B to D.*)

Clarification can also be used to gather further details about critical sounding points that may have gone by too fast or seem under- or overstated in the storytelling.

Details gathered from clarifications help to reduce the likelihood of inaccurate assumptions that may unintentionally mislead the course of the therapy.

Th: *Tell me about your living conditions at this time.*

Cl: *Right now, I'm living with my Aunt Reva.*

Th: *Was there a problem at home?*

The therapist requests clarification as to what brought about this move.

Cl: *Oh no, nothing like that. I always stay with Aunt Reva on school breaks.*

Th: *Your Aunt Reva, is she your mother's sister or your father's sister?*

The therapist requests clarification regarding the family structure.

Cl: *Well she's kind of from my mom's side of the family. I mean, techni-cally, she's not really my aunt; but Aunt Reva and my mom met in the third grade and they've always been best friends together, so she's pretty much family to me. I mean, I've known her all my life. It's kind of like having a second mother.*

The therapist now sees that Aunt Reva is not a blood relative but a key player in the client's life nonetheless.

Th: *What do you mean "a second mother"?*

The therapist seeks clarification on what the client means. Is having a second mother a good thing or a bad thing?

Cl: *Well, it's like I love my mom, but I really have to watch what I say to her or even ask her. She's mostly okay, but on some stuff, she can go off like a bomb! Like with the bass guitar, that was definitely an Aunt Reva thing.*

Th: The bass guitar? What makes that an "Aunt Reva thing"?

The therapist asks for clarification regarding the guitar that was mentioned briefly. This real-life example may help to illuminate the contrast between the client's relationship to the mother and the client's relationship to Aunt Reva.

Cl: Okay, I've always loved the sound of the bass. The bass on my stereo is always turned all the way up. I love how when the music is turned up good and loud, you can feel a good clean bass like right in the gut. Anyway, about 3 years ago, I decided I wanted to learn to play the bass. Now my mom thinks that the bass guitar is a rock instrument that leads straight to death.

Th: Rock music leads to death?

The therapist requests clarification regarding the client's mother's thought process: How does rock music lead to death (A → D)?

Cl: My mom thinks that basses are only in rock bands; rockers do drugs; then they overdose; then they die. I know . . . it's stupid. Anyway, about 3 years ago, I went to a pawn shop and I picked up a bass and amp and ever since then, I've been taking lessons and practicing and loving it. Of course, all of this is at Aunt Reva's house, and fortunately, my mom hasn't got a clue!

The client elucidates the sequence of the mother's fearful thought process (A → B → C → D). Additionally, the therapist gains valuable information regarding the different types of relationships in the client's life (client: mother; client: Aunt Reva).

This type of progressive clarification serves to paint a richer, more detailed picture. Through clarification, the therapist gains a more comprehensive image of the people in the client's life and the nature of their roles and relationships.

Clarification can be used to gather further detail on many levels, such as thought processes, feelings, priorities, tastes, preferences, life condition, and key players in the client's life, including their roles and relationships. Therapeutically, such detailed information may be used to identify such things as sources of stress, roadblocks, facilitative resources, significant relationships, or meaningful goals for the client.

Clarification can also be used in cases when the client's storytelling is comprised of too many pronouns (she, he, her, him, they, them). Overuse of such pronouns can lead to confusion as to who's who in a shifting storyline.

In such cases, openly cite this confound and recommend that the client use people's first names. If the client does not know the names or is hesitant to disclose actual names, then you may suggest that the client assign fictitious names. Alternatively, you may consider taking the lead in helping the client to attach respectable monikers to identify the people described in the story (*"the white shoe girl," "the gold tooth guy,"* etc.). This helps to keep each character's role in the storyline straight.

Car Crash Conundrum

Erin was recently involved in a serious automobile accident involving two other cars. Several people, including Erin, sustained various levels of injuries. Since then, there have been multiple stressors involving complications with insurance companies, doctors, attorneys, auto mechanics, and the other parties.

Client

- Provide a detailed description of the accident and whose fault you think it was.

- Convey that as a private person, it is hard dealing with the repercussions of the accident (physical therapy, paperwork, phone calls, appointments, etc.).

- Refer to several people in pronoun form (she, he, her, him, they, them, etc.).

Therapist

- **Nonverbal attending** (p. 63)
  Use appropriate nonverbals such as facial expression and body language to express your attentiveness (compassion, comprehension, confusion, curiosity, etc.).

- **Summarizing** (p. 75)
  Periodically, summarize your understanding of the story.
  "Let me see if I'm getting all this . . ."

- **Clarification** (p. 77)
  If Erin's use of pronouns causes you to lose track of who's who, request clarification.

Role-Play Exercise 3.2

A Lot to Kerry

Sean has been involved in a close relationship with Kerry for about 6 months. Sean comes to the session alone, discussing how over the past several months Kerry has become depressive and persistently needy. There is little joy left in the relationship. Sean is beginning to suspect that this is Kerry's genuine personality and is now wondering if the first few months of their relationship might have just been "good behavior."

Client

- Present as torn between wanting to cut the relationship and concern that Kerry may be too vulnerable to handle the break-up at this time.

- Spend most of your time talking about your recent dissatisfaction but also include some of the good things that the relationship used to provide.

- Mention that this is not the first time this has happened to you.

Therapist

- **Observational cues** (p. 60)
  Provide observational commentary.
  "I notice when you say Kerry's name, you look (or sound, seem) . . .

- **Brief verbals** (p. 65)
  Use brief verbals to advance the storytelling.
  "Mm-hmm."
  "Yeah."

- **Reflection/Paraphrasing** (content and feelings) (p. 70)
  Ask about what the relationship was like initially and reflect the contents and feelings.
  [Content] *"You used to go camping?"*
  [Feelings] *"It sounds like you really enjoyed your time together."*

Role-Play Exercise 3.3

Family Funeral

Dale initially entered into therapy about 3 months ago to address stress related to an uncle's struggle with cancer. This week, Dale's uncle passed away. Dale is appropriately saddened by the loss and is dreading seeing certain family members at the funeral.

Client

- Speak at a moderately slow tempo.

- Request assistance on how to deal with contentious people in a funeral setting.

- When the therapist provides you with step-by-step assistance, repeat it back with some parts missing or distorted (once).

Therapist

- **Pausing** (p. 66)
  Pause, leaving some space, about 3–5 seconds, before responding to Dale. If Dale has more to say, then listen; do not interrupt. You may use nonverbal skills (nodding gently, etc.) during pauses to demonstrate attentiveness in your silence.

- **Reverse reflection** (p. 72)
  If Dale requests guidance in dealing with difficult relatives, provide several simple steps:
  1. Greet them in a civil manner.

  2. If they insist on a confrontation, tell them you're there to pay your final respects and that you would be willing to discuss your differences some other time.

  3. Walk away.

  Next, request reverse reflection to verify comprehension.

- **Clarification** (p. 77)
  Request clarification as to the problem between Dale and the relatives.

Role-Play Exercise 3.4

Riley to the Rescue

Over the past few months, Riley's mother has been experiencing what seems to be a cognitive decline (wandering and getting lost, leaving the stove on, losing things, memory problems, etc.). Riley feels that something must be done to compensate for her deficits.

Client

- Present with some reasonable ideas (hire an in-home sitter, transfer to an assisted living facility, have her move in with you, etc.), but be indecisive.

- Discuss your mixed feelings: You want your mother to have her independence, but you are also concerned about her safety and well-being.

- Solicit recommendations from the therapist. If the therapist uses reverse reflection, consider distorting your playback once.

Therapist

- **Summarizing** (p. 75)
  Review Riley's story: mother's condition, Riley's feelings, and options.

- **Nonverbal attending** (p. 63)
  Use appropriate variations in facial expressions, nodding, gestures, and posture to unobtrusively demonstrate your attentiveness.

- **Reverse reflection** (p. 72)
  Provide some recommendations:
  1. Riley's mother should be assessed by a geriatric psychiatrist.

  2. Based on the findings and recommendations of the psychiatric evaluation, we can discuss options.

  3. We should also address the emotional impact that each option will have on Riley, Riley's mother, and other family members.

     Next, request Riley to replay your recommendations to verify comprehension.

Role-Play Exercise 3.5

Lay Off

Corey has been at the same job for the past 5 years and has been advancing nicely. Corey is professionally competent and well liked at work. Three weeks ago, Corey's boss and two colleagues were laid off with no notice. Corey has been reassigned to a supervisor who has a reputation for being incompetent and unreasonable.

Client

- Discuss how well you got along with your laid off peers and how the day-to-day experience at work has changed for the worse.

- When talking about your new supervisor, show your anger physically (make a fist, pound the chair, fold your arms, alter your voice tone, etc.).

- Talk about steps that you are taking to look for employment elsewhere, although you know you will miss some of your coworkers.

Therapist

- **Brief verbals** (p. 65)
  Provide concise comments as Corey conveys the unfortunate story.
  "Mm-hmm."
  "Sounds unfair."

- **Observational cues** (p. 60)
  Comment on any physical changes that you observe. Relate your observations to specific components in Corey's storytelling.
  "When you talk about your laid off coworkers, you seem . . ."
  "As you tell me about your new supervisor, you look/sound . . ."

- **Reflection/Paraphrasing** (content and feelings) (p. 70)
  Discuss your perception of Corey's circumstances and emotional reaction concerning the recent events at work.

4

Emotional Communication

T he therapeutic realm provides a forum for the expression of one's thoughts and life experiences, including articulating and processing the accompanying feelings. This chapter discusses techniques for identifying and addressing the client's feelings in a compassionate and professional manner, as well as skills for monitoring and effectively dealing with your own emotions as they emerge throughout the course of providing therapy.

Emotional Language

So far, much of what has been discussed has involved skills to promote *content* exchanges—techniques for eliciting and understanding the *facts* of the client's story. Along with the content, it is essential to effectively recognize and work with the feelings that run parallel to the facts.

Numerous words can be used to describe emotions, each carrying its own nuance and magnitude; however, an emotional word in isolation, can be ambiguous, as in this brief dialogue:

Th: How are you feeling?

Cl: Great.

Without the benefit of knowing the context of this word, *"Great,"* or hearing the verbal inflection, it can be difficult to know precisely what the client means. The client may be using the word *great* in a genuinely positive fashion, or the client may be speaking sarcastically, thereby implying the opposite. Observing the style of the conveyance, such as vocal characteristics, body language, and facial expression, can provide further clues as to the strength and meaning of the client's emotional message. Because the emotional meaning of a word is so strongly influenced by context and conveyance style, it would be presumptuous to attempt to arrange the feelings lexicon in Table 4.1 by magnitude; hence, they are simply sorted alphabetically.

Familiarity with feelings synonyms can enhance your perception of the client's emotional state, thereby advancing the therapeutic process. For example, suppose a client mentions feeling "nervous" and only provides vague details. *Nervous* is a synonym for *anxiety*, a category on the feelings table. Because anxiety is fear about an anticipated loss or hurt, you may form a question based on this definition to elicit further details: *"You mentioned feeling nervous. It sounds like you're expecting something bad might happen. What are you afraid might happen?"*

Table 4.1 is divided into two domains: positive feelings and negative feelings.

Positive Feelings

The positive feelings are organized into two categories: strength and happiness.

Strength: A sense of personal surety and solidity

Happiness: A state of personal satisfaction and contentment resulting from one's needs being met

Negative Feelings

The negative feelings are arranged in five categories: frustration, anger, depression, anxiety, and guilt.

Frustration is experienced when one is unable to gratify a desire or to satisfy an urge or need (Stedman, 1987). Essentially, when the accomplishment of a goal is encumbered, one feels frustrated.

Psychiatrist David Viscott (1976) provides a practical framework for comprehending a continuum of negative feelings—anger, depression, anxiety, and guilt—as a function of how one processes, or fails to process, hurt and loss.

Anger is the natural emotional reaction to hurt, loss, or disappointment. Anger can manifest from extreme rage to mild annoyance or irritation. Although it can be tempting to think that anger is easily detectable, particularly in a therapeutic environment, in many cultures, anger is considered to be uncivilized

Table 4.1   Feelings List

Positive Feelings

Strength—*Feeling positive about oneself and circumstances*

Aggressive, Attracted, Capable, Certain, Charged, Competent, Confident, Determined, Durable, Energetic, Forceful, Hopeful, In charge, Independent, Motivated, Powerful, Proud, Safe, Secure, Solid, Super, Sure, Tough, Trusting

Happiness—*Feeling that one's needs and desires have been met*

Accepted, Affectionate, Amused, Belonging, Calm, Cheerful, Clear, Comfortable, Complete, Composed, Content, Delighted, Ecstatic, Elated, Excited, Exhilarated, Exuberant, Fantastic, Fine, Free, Fun, Glad, Good, Great, Hopeful, Joyous, Loving, Overjoyed, Peaceful, Playful, Pleased, Positive, Proud, Ready, Refreshed, Relaxed, Relieved, Respected, Rested, Safe, Satisfied, Secure, Thrilled, Together, Up, Warm, Wonderful

Negative Feelings

Frustration—*Feeling that a goal is delayed or encumbered*

Baffled, Bewildered, Blocked, Bothered, Confused, Disorganized, Disoriented, Displaced, Divided, Foggy, Impatient, Insecure, Lost, Misplaced, Mixed up, Perplexed, Puzzled, Split, Torn, Trapped, Troubled, Uncertain, Unclear, Undecided, Unsure, Weird

Anger—*Initial reaction to hurt, loss or disappointment*

Aggravated, Aggressive, Agitated, Annoyed, Betrayed, Defensive, Disappointed, Disgusted, Dismayed, Enraged, Fed up, Fuming, Furious, Hateful, Incensed, Inconvenienced, Irate, Irritated, Jealous, Mad, Mean, Nervous, Outraged, Put out, Put upon, Repulsed, Resentful, Sick of, Spiteful, Strained, Suspicious, Tense, Tired of, Upset, Uptight, Vengeful

Depression—*Anger that is trapped or held in*

Abandoned, Apathetic, Bad, Beaten, Blah, Blue, Bored, Crushed, Defeated, Dependent, Desperate, Disappointed, Discontent, Dissatisfied, Distressed, Down, Drained, Exhausted, Grief-stricken, Heartbroken, Helpless, Hopeless, Hurt, Ignored, Incapable, Inferior, Lazy, Left out, Lifeless, Listless, Lonely, Lost, Low, Miserable, Numb, Overwhelmed, Rejected, Rotten, Run down, Sad, Shaky, Sick, Sleepy, Sorrowful, Tired, Trapped, Troubled, Uncomfortable, Unhappy, Unwanted, Upset, Useless, Vulnerable, Worthless

Anxiety—*Feeling that hurt or loss is looming*

Afraid, Apprehensive, Cautious, Concerned, Distraught, Dreading, Edgy, Fearful, Frightened, Horrified, Hysterical, Insecure, Jittery, Miserable, Nervous, Panicky, Pensive, Petrified, Reluctant, Scared, Shaken, Shocked, Shy, Tense, Terrified, Threatened, Timid, Uncertain, Uncomfortable, Uneasy, Unsettled, Unsure, Uptight, Worried

Guilt—*Feeling a discrepancy between how one is and what one conceives as acceptable*

Embarrassed, Humiliated, Regretful, Remorseful, Shameful, Sorrowful

and must be quelled in order to get along in society. Clients may resist recognizing or expressing their anger, fearing that they may appear vulnerable, unlovable, out of control, or undeserving of respect.

Depression is anger trapped and turned inward. Clients who are depressed are fearful of what might happen if they were to let their hurt (anger) leak out and be expressed.

Sadness is not depression. *Sadness* is an active emotional expression associated with a recent hurt or loss, whereas depression is an *interruption* of the flow of feelings. When hurt or loss is experienced openly as sadness, the client has the opportunity to resolve his or her feelings by processing the emotions or actively addressing the source of the sadness in an effort to reduce or eliminate it. Because depression consists of concealing anger, it is less likely that the hurt feelings will be addressed openly, thereby extending the duration of the persisting hurtful conditions and the depression.

In terms of emotional energy dynamics, depressed people expend a lot of energy to suppress their hurt feelings, leaving less energy to go about their daily activities; hence, depressed people tend to feel tired, listless, and depleted.

Anxiety is an anticipated loss or hurt. Clients who are anxious feel as if there is a threat to their safety or well-being, as if they are on the verge of being hurt or losing something. Not knowing the precise moment or nature of the expected event, they feel uncertain about the future. The more significant the expected loss or hurt, the higher the anxiety level.

Guilt: Clients who believe their thoughts, feelings, lack of feelings, actions, or inactions are unacceptable—or unacceptable to others considered significant—experience a sense of guilt. They feel as if they have done something wrong or failed to do something that they should have done. Feeling guilty makes them feel as if they are bad and deserve punishment. This may result in self-punishment or behaving in such a way as to trigger others to administer punishment. The most common form of guilt involves feeling that they have done something harmful to themselves or another person.

Therapeutically, guilt can be challenging to elicit. A client who feels guilty may resist voicing precisely what he or she feels bad about in order to avoid the possibility of someone confirming that he or she is indeed bad.

Emotional Communication

The preferred skills for therapeutically addressing and processing emotional issues are empathy, validation, and normalizing.

Empathy

Whereas skills such as summarizing and reflection are used to demonstrate and verify your perception of the facts of the client's story, empathy is used to identify and articulate your awareness of the client's feelings. *Empathy*, derived from the Greek word *empatheia* meaning "in feeling" is defined as "the ability to understand and share the feelings of another" (Jewell & Abate, 2001). Similar to summarizing and reflection, appropriate use of empathy demonstrates to the client that his or her feelings are being perceived and taken into account as an essential component of his or her condition. As with summarizing and reflection, empathic expressions are typically proposed in a provisional manner, pending the client's confirmation or correction of your perceptions. Empathy does not require or imply that you are committed to actually reproduce the client's feelings within yourself but rather that you understand and are sensitive to the nature of what the client is feeling. Essentially, empathy is about trying to comprehend the client's experience from the client's emotional standpoint, in essence seeing or feeling through the client's eyes and conveying your perception to the client (Bohart & Greenberg, 1997). Communicating such comprehension demonstrates that you are acutely tuned in to the richness of the client's experience. Demonstrating such attentiveness helps to assure the client that he or she is being taken seriously, thereby further developing a sense of rapport. Effective use of empathy has been shown to facilitate the therapeutic relationship, helping to bridge gaps among clients and therapists from different ethnicities (Carkhuff & Berenson, 1977; Traux & Mitchell, 1971). Empathetic communication has also been noted to reduce premature therapeutic termination (Bohart, Elliott, Greenberg, & Waston, 2002).

Empathy differs from sympathy. Sympathy essentially conveys that you feel sorry for or pity the client and implicitly communicates that the client should feel bad (or worse) too, thereby encouraging the client to assume the helpless victim role. Empathy, however, demonstrates that you perceive and respectfully acknowledge the client's (hurt) feelings, leaving the door open to identifying and more actively dealing with the troublesome issues (Egan, 1994).

Consider this brief dialogue wherein Therapist 1 responds sympathetically and Therapist 2 responds empathetically:

Cl: *Two days ago, my cat Pixel passed away.*

Th_1:   *Awww, the poor cat—gone forever. What a terrible thing. That's so sad.*
        Sympathy
        Sympathy extenuates the client's sense of hopelessness and loss.

Th₂: You seem pretty distressed today.

> Empathy
> Empathy compassionately identifies and acknowledges the client's sense of loss.

At first glance, Therapist 1's sympathetic response presents as goodhearted. The therapist is expressing sorrow for the deceased cat; however, on closer inspection, we see that it is comprised of more than one faulty message: The statement, *"Awww, the poor cat—gone forever,"* inadvertently compromises the focus of the session by discussing the cat's experience. With all due respect to the cat, the cat is not the client. Instead, the dialogue should address the client's reaction to the cat's death. The therapist's next sentence, *"What a terrible thing,"* may serve to inflate the problem. At this point, we do not yet know the precise nature of the client's feelings; it is wrong to automatically assume that the client senses the cat's death as a *"terrible thing."* Specifically, the circumstances of the cat's death have not been clarified. Perhaps the cat had a long bout with a difficult, debilitating disease, in which case death may be seen as a welcome alternative to prolonged suffering. Finally, saying, *"That's so sad,"* prematurely prescribes a feeling to the client. Without further inquiry, there is not enough information to know how the client actually feels. The client may be experiencing any number of feelings, which may involve anger, relief, sadness, guilt, loneliness, numbness, or confusion. The client may appropriately resent the inaccuracy of the therapist's unfounded assumptions.

Telling the client, *"That's so sad,"* may unintentionally evoke a sense of guilt. The client may not necessarily be feeling intense sadness at this time; however, the therapist's assertion, *"That's so sad,"* may cause the client to become emotionally confused and inappropriately feel that he or she somehow needs to set aside *actual* feelings and attempt to feel sad or sadder in order to meet the emotional expectations of the therapist (a presumed expert).

Now consider Therapist 2's empathetic response: *"You seem pretty distressed today."* This statement achieves more facilitative functions: Compassion is expressed without implying pity. Additionally, the therapist's acknowledgment of the client's affect communicates that the client's feelings have not gone unnoticed and that further dialogue will proceed with appropriate sensitivity.

Notice that the therapist phrases the empathetic expression speculatively: *"You seem . . ."* as opposed to prescriptively saying, *"You are . . ."* Expressing empathy in a speculative manner indicates that this is your *impression* of the client's emotional state, subject to the client's acceptance, correction, or elaboration. Remember, only the client knows precisely how he or she feels; it is your job to try to understand the client.

The following dialogue further exemplifies uses of empathy:

Cl: [Subdued affect] *I got an invitation to a family reunion, but I don't know if I want to see my parents.*

Th: *You have some heavy feelings regarding your parents?*

Empathy: The client's feelings toward the client's parents are unspecific at this time; nevertheless, the therapist mentions the observation of the client's change in emotional conveyance.

Cl: *They always just pretend like everything's fine. They act like everything was always fine, and it's not. It never has been. Never!*

Th: *It sounds like your parents make you angry.*

Empathy: Provisional emotional feedback is pitched.

Cl: *See, my dad drinks. He always has. When I was a kid, he used to come home drunk and yell at us. Sometimes he'd hit us or throw stuff at us. I once got hit in the head with this stupid solid glass dog figure that we used to have on the coffee table. Sometimes he'd come home like that. Other times, he'd come home, and he'd be like this ideal TV dad, like to make it up to us.*

The client may not always explicitly confirm the therapist's emotional commentary, but notice that the empathetic response is neither rejected nor corrected, suggesting that the therapist's assessment was adequately on target.

Th: *I imagine it was hard for you, not knowing if your dad was going to come home as Jekyll or Hyde. That can be scary . . . confusing . . . maybe anxiety-making.*

Empathy

Cl: *That's kind of how it was. And on the nights when he got mad, there was no way of knowing what he might do: He could throw things, break stuff, hit us, yell at us, throw up, pass out. . . . You'd just never know. What a way to live! . . . I hated living like that.*

The client confirms the therapist's empathetic expression and provides further (emotional) details.

Th: *It sounds like you've got a lot of anger at your dad for what he did to you.*

The therapist uses empathy to address the client's emotional reaction to the father's unpredictable rampages.

Cl: *A lot. And then there's my mom. She was okay during regular times, but whenever my dad got out of control, she'd run to her bedroom and lock the door. She just bailed on us. Every time. That was her thing. How could she do that?*

Th: *You were disappointed in your mother for not intervening?*
Speculative empathy

Cl: *Ya know, sometimes I can't figure out who I'm madder at: my dad for what he did to us or my mom for not stopping him or throwing him out or divorcing him or just getting us the hell out of there.*

Th: *Yeah. As kids, we'd like to think of parents as the ones who are there to protect us. It's a pretty scary scene when just the opposite happens.*
Empathetically summarizes events and emotions

Notice that in responding empathetically, the therapist neither says nor implies, *"Oh, I know just how you feel."* It is certainly within the realm of professionalism that you may, on occasion, feel emotionally moved by a client's story or condition; however, effective use of empathy does not necessarily mean that you must find a matching feeling or emotional experience within yourself, nor does it require you to spontaneously conjure up a genuine matching feeling, though this can happen. Essentially, empathetic responses involve provisionally submitting your perception of the client's emotional conveyance for the client's confirmation or correction and respectfully proceeding in a manner that sensitively honors the client's feelings.

To frame empathy in more concrete terms, imagine a physician examining a patient who appears to have a broken arm. The doctor may use empathy as such:

Dr: *It looks like you're in some pain here. . . . You may have a fracture. I need to examine your arm, but I'm going to handle you as gently as possible.*

Such an expression conveys that the doctor need not be experiencing concurrent physical pain within him- or herself in order to express an empathetic appreciation for the patient's discomfort and, as such, assure the patient that this will be taken into account as the necessary care is provided in a sensitive manner.

Validation

Occasionally a client may have, implicitly or explicitly, concerns that his or her attitudes, beliefs, thoughts, feelings, or actions (or lack thereof) may in some way be wrong, lacking, or not make sense. Validation serves to support the client by providing positive assurance that the client's feelings, actions, and thoughts are appropriate per the client's unique situation and perspective.

Cl: *This last weekend, my cousin Troy got into this car wreck. He's in the hospital, unconscious, on life support with some major head injury. The doctors said that they can't operate, and it doesn't look good. Everyone was around his bed just crying and crying.*

Th: *It's not easy to see someone you care about in that sort of condition. The tears make sense.*

The therapist validates the feelings: Tears can go together with tragedy.

Cl: *Yeah, but here's the thing: I just stood there thinking, Well, it's too bad that this happened, but this guy has always driven like a maniac—never pays attention, speeds, has major road rage. He's totaled tons of cars ... literally! I always knew something like this would happen eventually. I'm just glad he ran his car into a tree instead of killing some innocent kid or something. I don't know. . . . I tried, but I just couldn't find a way to cry. I think it made me look bad.*

The client expresses dissatisfaction with his or her emotional response.

Th: *You know, people see things in different ways, sometimes more emotional, sometimes more logical. It sounds like right now, you're coming at this in a very realistic way, that essentially he brought this on himself. As you say, it's too bad that this happened, but reasonably knowing what you know about his driving habits and his ways, it makes sense that tears didn't come for you at this time.*

The therapist uses the components of the story to support a reasonable context for the client's inability to cry. Notice that the therapist avoids directly blaming the cousin. This could set off a defensive reaction in the client. Instead, the therapist purposefully attributes his or her paraphrasing, *"As you say, it's too bad this happened, ..."* to the client. Also, the therapist uses tentative language: *"It sounds like right now, ..." "It makes sense that tears don't come for you at this time."* This suggests that there may or may not be a change in the client's feelings over time and that this would be valid too.

Cl: *Maybe. But I mean, even when I'm alone, and I really try to feel something, I just keep thinking: "What a jerk. Why didn't he just take some anger management class or something?" It's like I feel mad at him, and everyone else feels sad.*

The client expresses dissatisfaction that his or her feelings diverge from those of others involved.

Th: *Well, everyone's got their own feelings. Right now, coming from your reasonable perspective, your anger makes perfect sense. Now, this isn't over. As you move through this, it's possible that at some point, you may begin to have some other feelings too, but right now, this is where you are, and the way you're experiencing this is completely appropriate.*

The therapist validates the client's current feelings and thoughts but also leaves the door open for the possibility that the client may experience additional valid feelings.

Validation essentially honors and supports the client's uniqueness: No two people have the same history, perspective, experience level, or emotional constitution. Hence, it follows that their actions and reactions may be appropriately unique. As each client progressively discloses more details about him- or herself, the client's feelings, actions, and thoughts will likely make more sense within the client's unique context. As such, plausible and supportive validations can be more readily submitted.

Normalizing

Normalizing is similar to validation. Whereas the purpose of validation is to honor the client's perspective as appropriate for the client, normalizing can be useful in instances when the client considers his or her condition or symptoms as unique, atypical, or perhaps distressingly abnormal. As the therapist, you have the opportunity to provide a broader, more objective context, suggesting that although the client's situation seems exceptional—perhaps in a negative sense—such conditions are considered within the boundaries of normality, that many others have similar experiences (Sue & Zane, 1987). Normalizing can be a particularly effective skill, especially when dealing with covert symptoms that may be nonvisual or that may seem odd or embarrassing, wherein one cannot readily observe just how common such a phenomenon actually is.

Cl: *I'm a failure. I have to be honest: Two days ago, I had a drink.*

The client pairs relapse with failure.

Th: *You've been sober for about 4 months now?*

The therapist recaps and gathers some information to set the stage for normalizing the client's condition.

Cl: *122 days.*

Th: *What's your drinking like now?*

Cl: *It was just the one drink. Right after I finished it, I knew I wanted more—way more. I got so scared that I just got the hell out of there. But now I don't know what to do. I'm afraid if I don't go to the meetings, I'll drink again, but I'm afraid if I go back to the meetings, they'll be mad at me. It'll be so embarrassing. I don't know what to do. . . . It's like now I have no place to go.*

Th: *I know this isn't the way you wanted your recovery to go, but you know, everything that you've described is really quite normal.*

This reply lays the groundwork for redefining the client's relapse as normal; although relapse is certainly not preferred, it is by no means uncommon and can be dealt with.

Cl: *What do you mean?*

Th: *Certainly you've heard the stories in the meetings. Yes, there are some people who achieve sobriety and never relapse; others have a slip or relapse and then resume their program, sometimes stronger than ever.*

The therapist encourages the client to recall genuine stories of recovery that involve a relapse, thereby challenging the client's assertion that he or she is uniquely inadequate. The therapist discusses that it is normal and acceptable to return to recovery after relapsing.

Cl: *I know. I guess I have heard stuff like that before, but I just didn't want that to be me.*

Th: I think I understand. You wanted an uninterrupted recovery, and that's a virtuous goal, but I assure you, your experience is by no means a one-in-a-million thing. You know that. Relapses do happen from time to time, and people can and do come back from them, and it sounds like that's where you might be headed now.

The therapist further supports the notion that the client is not alone in his or her experience, that this is an expected phenomenon: It happens all the time, and there is hope.

In this example, the therapist neither denies nor minimizes the client's relapse. Rather, the therapist applies his or her clinical knowledge of addiction and recovery to the problem, thereby educating the client that the experience, though distressing, is by no means uncommon, nor unrecoverable. Appropriate use of normalizing can help people to see their experiences as less aberrant than they initially thought. Such emotional support has the potential to reduce their adverse self-opinions, which may involve a sense of isolation, poor self-image, self-consciousness, inferiority, guilt, or anxiety, clearing the pathway to taking further facilitative action.

Self-Awareness

As important as it is to perceive and process the client's feelings and thoughts, it is equally essential to acknowledge that as a therapist, you use yourself as a feeling and thinking instrument to perceive the client. Though the focus of each session is on the client, it is important to acknowledge that you carry your life history with you at all times. Self-awareness involves actively monitoring the dynamics of how you are receiving, processing, and responding to clients in light of your cognitive and emotional history. In your role as a therapist, it is important to embrace your sense of self-awareness and seek out relevant opportunities to promote self-growth (*Ethical Standards of Human Service Professionals,* Statement 36; Council for Standards, 1996).

Recognizing Your Perspective

It may seem overly simplistic to say, "The only thing you can make a therapist out of is a person," but this is a point worth addressing. As a person, you ultimately are not an objective being. You have your own thoughts, opinions, beliefs, and feelings. Your experiences in life have led you to form a self-identity: You have a sense of who you are and what you are about. You know what is and is not important to you, what you do and do not care about, what you like and dislike, and what qualities you like and dislike in others. Because your feelings are always turned on, the role of the therapist can, at times, seem like a delicate balancing act: trying to keep your personal feelings in check while effectively using your "emotional antenna" to function empathetically (Brammer, 1993).

Monitoring Your Feelings

Throughout the process of providing therapy, in addition to tending to the client's expressions, make an effort to monitor your reactions to the content of the sessions. Take special care to recognize your strong reactions to clients, both positive and negative; this is an opportunity to ask yourself how much of what the client is processing matches your prior experiences or preexisting opinions. Simply stated, *transference* occurs when the client superimposes prior emotional experiences on the therapist. The client may perceive something about your personality, style, demeanor, or appearance that may remind him or her of a significant person in the client's past, such as a parent; hence, the client may begin to respond to you as the client would that parent. *Countertransference* occurs when the therapist does this to the client. Suppose you were brought up with a sibling who had strong dependent characteristics. When dealing with an otherwise able-bodied client who exhibits a persistent sense of helplessness, as his or her therapist, you may begin to emotionally interact with this client in the same manner as you would your sibling.

As you monitor your (positive and negative) feelings, be aware of some reactions that therapists commonly experience:

- Dreading or happily anticipating sessions with a client
- Having exceptionally strong hateful or loving feelings toward a client
- Wanting to end sessions early or extend sessions
- Strongly wishing for or dreading termination

Managing Countertransference

The first step in managing countertransference is recognizing that your feelings toward a client are unusually strong, either positive or negative. Monitor your own emotional reactions and behaviors during sessions in order to determine what the client said or did to bring about that reaction (Goldfried & Davison, 1994). Take some time, perhaps outside the therapeutic environment, to patiently ask yourself some introspective questions:

- What is making me like or dislike this client?
- What issues do I want or not want to discuss with this client?
- What is making me feel uncomfortable?

Such self-questioning may provide insight as to the unresolved feelings or experiences from your past that may be resonating within you as you have contact with particular clients or issues. This may be sufficient to enable you to achieve a more objective perspective.

A second step may involve seeking out consultation with a colleague, an instructor, a supervisor, or another health care professional to help you delve deeper into addressing and potentially resolving the source of your strong feelings.

Ultimately, if you find that there is a particular population, clinical problem, or diagnosis with which you are unable to work effectively, then it is advisable that you provide the client with an appropriate referral, along with your rationale, rather than provide substandard or biased therapy (Hepworth & Larsen, 1993).

Coping With Prejudices

Regardless of the code of ethics to which one adheres, each person holds his or her own set of preferences and biases. Such preconceptions, both negative and positive, are virtually unlimited in terms of scope. They may pertain to one or more characteristics, such as gender, age, geographical location, socioeconomic class, marital status, race, color, or educational level. Hence, the question then stands: "How does one undo such prejudicial attitudes?" A study investigating homophobic attitudes among psychotherapy practitioners may hold a clue: The study revealed that regardless of educational levels, homophobic attitudes were inversely correlated to the therapist level of personal contact with homosexuals, such as acquaintances, family members, peers, coworkers, or supervisors. In other words, the more significant contact the therapist had with homosexuals, the lower the likelihood of holding a negative opinion of them. The study also showed lower levels of homophobia among practitioners who had undergone prior psychotherapy (Berkman & Zinberg, 1997). This suggests that one strategy for overcoming prejudices toward specific client populations may be to find an opportunity to establish meaningful, ongoing personal contact with such individuals (Cook, 1978). Brief, impersonal, or infrequent contact is unlikely to achieve the desired effect (Brewer & Brown, 1998).

Ultimately, actively working to recognize and reduce your levels of prejudices can serve to broaden your potential as a therapist in terms of the diversity of individuals and clinical issues with which you can comfortably and effectively work.

Role-Play Exercise 4.1

The Barking Lot

Val's dog just had a litter of seven puppies; one is doing poorly. Val works full-time, lives alone, and is feeling overwhelmed with the responsibility of tending to the multiple needs of the eight animals (health care expenses, finding homes for the puppies, feeding, the noise, the mess).

Client

- Express regret for not having had your dog spayed.

- Discuss your mixed feelings toward the animals (guilt about resenting your dog, dislike and also compassion toward the ill puppy, stress regarding having to find homes for the puppies).

- Talk about how you are feeling isolated because the animals require so much attention during nonworking hours.

Therapist

- **Empathy** (p. 91)
  Express your comprehension of Val's feelings.
  "I can see how the responsibility of tending to all of these lives alone is stressful to you."

- **Validation** (p. 95)
  Confirm that Val's feelings are justified per the circumstances at hand.
  "It makes sense that you have mixed feelings toward your pets and yourself. There's a lot going on here."

- **Normalizing** (p. 96)
  Discuss how anyone faced with these multidimensional stressors would have a variety of possibly conflicted feelings.

Role-Play Exercise 4.2

Back to the Books

Brett is a student returning to college after some time away. In addition to the usual life commitments (family, financial concerns, etc.), Brett is feeling the burden of adjusting to student life again (attending challenging courses, reading load, studying, homework, administrative bureaucracy, etc.).

Client

- Comment on your rationale for returning to college.

- Discuss how one of your courses consumes 50% of your time (difficult instructor, unfamiliar or complex material, heavy reading load, assignments, etc.).

- Identify some sacrifices that you had to make in order to return to school (quit work or reduce work hours, less social or leisure time, relocation, etc.).

Therapist

- **Empathy** (p. 91)
  Express your comprehension of these feelings.
  "You seem really stressed when you talk about that course."

- **Validation** (p. 95)
  Provide support for Brett's feelings.
  "Those aren't easy courses, and those deadlines are very real. Your feelings sure make sense to me."

- **Normalizing** (p. 96)
  Discuss how stress is a normal reaction to virtually any change.
  "It's normal to have a stressful reaction to any life change, especially something as demanding as college."

Role-Play Exercise 4.3

How Sweet It Isn't

Dean has recently been diagnosed as diabetic and has been having difficulties adapting to the new diet, stocking and carrying supplies (insulin, hypodermics, etc.), and administering the dosages.

Client

- Mention how you feel defective. Everyone else can eat or drink whatever and whenever they want, whereas you need medical supplies just to get through the day.

- Discuss how hard it is emotionally and physically giving yourself the injections.

- Talk about how you wish you could just throw away all the diabetic care stuff (medication, literature, etc.), but you are not going to.

Therapist

- **Empathy** (p. 91)
  Demonstrate your understanding of Dean's emotions.
  "I can see how hard this is for you, especially when you talk about having to inject yourself."

- **Validation** (p. 95)
  Affirm that Dean's feelings are reasonable.
  "Your feelings make perfect sense. This is a pretty big change in your life and also a real inconvenience. Of course you resent this."

- **Normalizing** (p. 96)
  Point out that Dean's perspective is not atypical.
  "Diabetic care is very involved and there's a lot to get used to. I expect it'd take anyone some time to adapt to this change."

Role-Play Exercise 4.4

Up in Smoke

Jessie's apartment was destroyed by fire. Although there were no injuries, all of Jessie's property was lost. Jessie is temporarily living with family until the insurance company settles the loss.

Client

- Discuss your feelings about the things that can be replaced (clothes, furnishings, artwork, music, movies, etc.) and the things that cannot be replaced (an antique family clock, photographs, writings, etc.).

- Talk about the advantages and disadvantages of living with family.

- Mention your concern about a neighbor that you and the other tenants collectively looked after.

Therapist

- **Empathy** (p. 91)
  Present your perception of Jessie's feelings.
  "When you talk about the fire, I can hear the sadness and disbelief in your voice."
  "It sounds like you really care about what happens to your neighbors."

- **Validation** (p. 95)
  Support Jessie's (mixed) feelings.
  "I can see how staying with family, even temporarily, can have some real plusses and minuses."
  "Based on what's happened, it makes sense that you'd feel . . ."

- **Normalizing** (p. 96)
  Point out that Jessie's reaction to the loss is appropriate.
  "Considering that nobody anticipates having their place burn down, I think you're coping as well as anyone could be expected to."

Role-Play Exercise 4.5

Business or Pleasure?

Taylor and Morgan's relationship has been satisfying and stable over time. They are both kind people and mutually supportive. About a year ago, the company that Taylor worked for went out of business. Per Morgan's encouragement, Taylor started an independent business that has thrived. Unfortunately, this has left little time for the couple to be together.

Client

- Express your joy that Taylor's business is successful but that you are concerned about the impact of the stress and long hours.

- Mention that you sometimes wish you had never encouraged Taylor to build a business, despite the success.

- Discuss that you find your mixed feelings (jealousy, pride, loneliness, etc.) confusing and unsettling.

Therapist

- **Empathy** (p. 91)
  Demonstrate your comprehension of Morgan's experience.
  "When you talk about Taylor, I can see how proud you are. . . . I can also understand how lonely you're feeling."

- **Validation** (p. 95)
  Talk about the appropriateness of each of Morgan's feelings.
  "Your concerns about Taylor working such long hours are certainly well-founded."
  "With Taylor less available, it follows that you'd feel lonely."

- **Normalizing** (p. 96)
  Discuss that it is not atypical to have conflicted feelings.
  "It's normal to have mixed feelings because there's more than one thing going on: Taylor's success is a good thing, but Taylor's unavailability, right now, is something of a loss."

5

Leading

As important as it is to provide space for clients to tell their stories as they see them, it is equally important that you are equipped with skills for guiding sessions in a meaningful manner. In this chapter, techniques are covered for effectively collecting supplemental information, keeping sessions on track, proposing alternate perspectives, identifying and resolving discrepancies, and educating.

Gathering Details

As important as it is to follow attentively, catching and processing the client's data and feelings, it is equally important to be skillful in leading. *Leading* involves guiding the discussion in a therapeutically meaningful direction. Purposeful leading can advance the therapy by eliciting further information and feelings, bringing focus to a seemingly meandering session, or even prompting a client to think about a problem in a different way.

Furthering

Furthering involves requesting that the client provide additional details regarding a point that has already been mentioned or spurring the client to advance to the next step in the storytelling. Furthering is a versatile skill that can be used to gather more detailed information when the client has skimmed quickly past a relevant or curious-sounding point (*"Tell me a little more about your relationship with your twin."* *"You said that you used to be an artist."* *"I'm curious about this 'weird boss' that you mentioned."*) Additionally, furthering can be employed to advance the therapy when the dialogue stalls or when the client begins repeating him- or herself (*"And then what happened?"* *"What happened next?"* *"What happened before [or after]?"*).

Cl: *So on Thursday, I wasn't feeling well. My boss said I could go home early. That was about 1:00—about 4 hours early. I got home around 1:30 and there was this car in the driveway. I didn't know whose car it was, so I just parked on the street. Anyway, I walked into the house, and I heard these muted noises—like someone talking—but I didn't recognize the voice and I couldn't really hear what they were saying. I just stood there, thinking, "Who is that and what are they saying and what's going on in my house?" It was just confusing. I didn't really know what to think.*

> The client is providing a lot of details regarding an unexpected person in the house.

Th: *What happened next?*

> The client has provided very clear details regarding the events thus far; the therapist asks the client to advance the storytelling.

Cl: *Well, I followed the sound of the voice to the bedroom. I tried to listen for a while longer, but the voice was still muffled. So, after about a minute I opened the door and there was this guy sitting on the bed. He looked pretty surprised to see me. Okay, so I walked in the room and there was my girlfriend, just coming out of the bathroom.*

Th: *And this guy was . . . ?*

> The therapist requests more information on the stranger.

Cl: *I'd never seen him before. At first I was really mad. I thought he was fooling around with my girlfriend. Then she told me he was her step-brother.*

Th: *And did you find out what he was doing there?*

> It seems as if the storytelling has dead-ended. The therapist asks the client to continue.

Cl: Yeah. Apparently he just got laid off from his job and he came over to have Kris help him fix up his résumé. She's really great with that sort of stuff. She does everyone's résumés. But like I said, the whole thing just sort of threw me at first.

In this example, the therapist uses various forms of furthering to help advance the storytelling and elicit useful information. Keep in mind, the client is already familiar with his or her story. It is your job to try to understand the image that the client has in mind. If things seem incomplete, unclear, or shallow, skills such as furthering can be valuable in helping you to gather useful details to fill in the picture.

Prompting

Prompting is similar to furthering in that it serves to cue the client to advance his or her storytelling. Whereas furthering involves full-sentence requests (*"And what happened when the elevator doors opened?"*), prompting consists of a brief verbalization (*"And . . . ?" "Go on. . . ."* *"Then what?"*). Prompting may also consist of nonverbal cues such as a hand gesture, nod, or a facial expression suggesting that you understand the point that the client was conveying and that you are ready for the next piece of the story.

Cl: This happened 2 days ago. I was at work in the middle of a phone call and the fire alarm started going off.

Th: [Facial expression: surprised or attentive]
Nonverbal prompting

Cl: We have an emergency preparedness drill the first Friday morning of every month, but this was Tuesday and it was after lunch and there were no drill captains walking around, so at first, I didn't know exactly what to make of it. I mean, everyone just kept on working like nothing was going on.

Th: And . . .
Verbal prompting

Cl: And then I asked Jay, the guy next to me, if this is some kind of drill or if we should just get the hell out of there.

Th: *And Jay said . . .*

This prompt is aimed at gaining specific details about the dialogue that may have taken place.

Cl: *Well, he said he didn't know, and by now I'm starting to get scared.*

Th: *Then what?*

The prompt communicates that the therapist understands the turn in the story and is ready to hear the next event.

Cl: *Okay, so the alarms are still going off. Everyone's just sitting around, working like nothing's happening. Now I'm looking for my supervisor. I looked everywhere—nothing. So I figured I don't care who laughs at me, I'm outta here!*

The primary advantage of prompting is its brevity: By interjecting short verbalizations, you are able to demonstrate attentiveness while unobtrusively prompting the storytelling. The conciseness of such prompts means that the "spotlight" never leaves the client for more than a moment, thus helping to facilitate the factual and emotional flow and continuity of the client's storytelling.

Open-Ended Requests

A variation on furthering involves submitting open-ended requests wherein a question is phrased in such a way as to suggest that you reasonably expect there to be more information available, rather than less or none. Consider this dialogue wherein the therapist's close-ended response, though supportive, implicitly caps-off the client's disclosure:

Cl: *Before we went to the movie, me and my buddies cut through a six-pack just to get the mood right.*

Th: *So a few beers; and that's all?*

Close-ended request

Cl: *Yep.*

The therapist's nonjudgmental response may be helpful in facilitating rapport; however, while the client is on the subject of beer, an important opportunity to gather a (more) comprehensive substance use history appears to have been passed over. The therapist's question, *". . . and that's all?"* carries a presumptive answer, that there should be no other substances involved.

Consider the therapist's alternate use of the open-ended request:

Cl: *Before we went to the movie, me and my buddies cut through a six-pack just to get the mood right.*

Th: [Friendly voice tone, moderate smile, unsurprised affect] *And what else?*

   Open-ended request

Cl: *Oh, these days, just beer. Sometimes some wine when I'm at a party, but that's all. Actually, about a year ago, I did some coke, but that was just like a once or twice thing. I mean, it's like it was just too much. My heart started beating like a million times faster and I got all sweaty and it was just too high-gear for me, so that's kinda not my thing. . . . Let's see, I guess I drink a little bit on the weekends, but I'm not like an alcoholic or anything. I mean, it's just a few beers with friends. . . . It's not like I sit around drinking alone.*

Here we see how openly asking, *"And what else?"* in a nonaccusatory fashion can open the door to a wealth of valuable supplemental information that may not have come to light otherwise. For example, suppose a client discloses that he or she has recently shoplifted. A useful open-ended request might be, *"When was the first time you can remember taking something without paying for it?"* Certainly, the client is free to say that this was the first time; conversely, this may be an opportunity to identify a history of such behavior. As a rule of thumb, make an effort to build questions that open the door to rendering richer, more detailed information and feelings.

Questioning

Throughout the course of the therapy, attentively listening to your clients will render much of what you will need to know. As in nonclinical settings, when you want to gather information that you do not have yet or request clarification or further details on an issue that has already been raised, questions open the door to further understanding.

Effective questioning is comprised of two parts: the question and the answer. First, when formulating a question, keep in mind that your goal is to *try to understand*. Maintaining a consistent sense of concerned curiosity about the client's life conditions will enable you to intuitively conceptualize appropriate questions that will facilitate further understanding. Second, *listen to the answer*. When taking in the client's response to your question, make an effort to set aside your preconceptions about the answer: the answer that you would *like* to hear, the way *you* would have answered the question, or what you *thought* the client was going to say. Listen to what the client is actually telling you. Listen beyond the words; absorb the multidimensional cues that travel along with the conveyance of the words. Cues such as the tone of voice, tempo of the speech, eye contact, and body language can be as important as the words. As you listen, take the time to integrate the information that is being rendered into your cumulative comprehension of the client's life circumstances. Therapeutic alliance and interventions are most effective when you understand your clients, collaborate with them to identify and pursue goals that are appropriate for them, and continually work toward customizing and implementing treatment plans that are concurrent with the client's life system. As you listen to your clients, value their words and emotional expressions: Think of the client as an expert on his or her life circumstances. The client is the only person who can provide you with first-hand knowledge (and feelings) of the multidimensional characteristics of his or her condition (McClam & Woodside, 1994).

Ask One Question at a Time

In the benevolent quest to efficiently gather and organize information about a client in a cohesive manner, it is natural to group related concepts and questions together. Occasionally a compound question may come to mind. A compound question, sometimes referred to as a "double-barreled" or "stacked" question, consists of more than one inquiry packaged into what sounds like a single question:

Cl: I come from a large family.

Th: How many siblings do you have, and do you get along with them?

Closer examination of the therapist's inquiry clearly shows us that two distinct questions requiring two very different types of answers have been submitted in a single burst: The first question, *"How many siblings do you have?"* involves an objective numerical response: *"I'm an only child."* *"I have two sisters and one step-brother."* The second question, *". . . and do you get along with them?"* is a subjective question, which can include some fairly complex and emotional responses ranging from the client providing a global response such as, *"Oh, we all get along great. We always have"* to varied and detailed accounts of relationship histories among the siblings, the client's relationship with each sibling, childhood history, who gets along with whom, and so forth. If a compound question comes to mind, this is not inherently bad. To the contrary, it suggests that you are engaged in the client's story and logically grouping related concepts together. Per this example, the strategy is to break the compound question into its discrete pieces and ask the questions one at a time. First ask, *"How many siblings do you have?"* The client may go ahead and include details regarding their names and the nature of their relationships with each other. If you require further information, then you may choose to continue with the related follow-up question: *How do you get along with them?*

A slightly more obvious form of compound questioning may involve separate questions submitted in a single burst:

Cl: *I have three children of my own and a foster child.*

Th: *How old are they? How do they get along? Do you have help raising four children?*

Just as before, the same principles apply. All three are reasonable questions; however, each one is asking for a very different type of information. Pitching multiple questions simultaneously is inefficient for a number of reasons: The client must decide whether to respond to the questions in the order in which they were asked, or the client may take on the task of composing responses to the three questions and then resequence them in order to facilitate more efficient responses. Regardless of the order in which the client chooses to respond, by presenting multiple questions simultaneously, you force the client to utilize mental energy less efficiently. In this case, the client must maintain a mental list of the other two questions while responding to the first. This can create unnecessary additional stress on the client and ultimately compromise the amount of attention that the client can dedicate to responding to the question at hand. Another possibility is that the client may become confused and frustrated in that he or she may attempt to formulate a single answer to respond to the multiple questions. We would expect that such an answer would be difficult, if not impossible, to organize or it would lack the level of detail that would be gained had the questions been posed one at a time. Additionally, submitting a barrage of questions may be perceived more as an accusatory interrogation rather than therapy.

Again, there is nothing inherently wrong with multiple questions coming to mind simultaneously. The strategy is the same: (a) Parse the inquiry into separate, discrete questions. (b) Decide which question comes first. (c) Ask the questions one at a time. (d) Listen to the answers. As you listen to the answers, be prepared to alter your strategy or abandon some of your follow-up questions accordingly. Some of the questions that you were initially considering asking may be answered along the way. Also, as new issues are revealed, more contextually relevant questions may spontaneously occur to you. Remember, therapy is a dynamic, real-time process. It is good to have a plan in mind, but be flexible enough to adjust your thinking and questioning in order to tend to what is being presented in the moment.

Buffering

Therapy involves a consistent exchange of information and feelings between you and the client. Without intending to, it is possible to be too expeditious and subject clients to a barrage of questions. *Buffering* involves providing some meaningful commentary in between questions. This serves to demonstrate your attentiveness, and it also sets a more humane tone and pacing to a dialogue consisting of successive questions. Consider reading this unbuffered dialogue aloud:

Cl: *I'm feeling a little anxious at home. I mean, I know it's my home, but somehow, I have this feeling that just won't go away. . . . It's like I keep thinking, "This isn't really my house." It's like I'm constantly waiting for the real owners to come busting in any minute.*

Th: *How long have you lived there?*

Cl: *About 2 months.*

Th: *Where were you living before that?*

Cl: *Hawaii.*

Th: *How long were you in Hawaii?*

Cl: *Six and a half years.*

Th: *Did you live in a house or an apartment?*

None of these questions is bad, per se; however, to the client, this rapid-fire stream of questions can begin to feel more like an interrogation than a therapeutic dialogue. Such a stream of questions is likely to be particularly offensive to American Indians, who may find it disrespectful to be confronted with a lot of questions (Ho, 1992; Thompson et al., 1993; Walker & LaDue,

1986). To avoid resorting to this intrusive-sounding question and answer format, consider putting something meaningful between the questions to buffer the inquiry process. This can take the form of interjecting some remarks that reflect changes in your impressions, thinking, feelings, or your conception of the story or problem as the client responds to your questions. Notice that the following dialogue is exactly the same as the prior example, except that buffering has been added, which is indicated by bold text.

Cl: *I'm feeling a little anxious at home. I mean, I know it's my home, but somehow, I have this feeling that just won't go away. . . . It's like I keep thinking, "This isn't really my house." It's like I'm constantly waiting for the real owners to come busting in any minute.*

Th: **Mm-hmm, sometimes it can take a while to feel comfortable in a new place.** *How long have you lived there?*

Cl: *We moved in about two months ago.*

Th: **Two months ago—that's not that long a time.** *Where were you living before that?*

Cl: *Hawaii.*

Th: **Really? What a unique state.** *How long were you in Hawaii?*

Cl: *Six and a half years.*

Th: **That's a long time. This is very different compared to Hawaii; it doesn't surprise me that it might take some time to get used to the change.** *You mentioned that you're living in a house now.* **I'm curious, when you were in Hawaii,** *did you live in a house or an apartment?*

This alternative approach involves including some brief facilitative feedback. The buffered version of the dialogue demonstrates the therapist's receptiveness and brings a warmer, less officious feel to the interaction, thereby facilitating the disclosure process.

Re-asking a Question

Occasionally, while listening to an answer, it will become clear that the client either remains silent or does not address the question that was asked. Per the model presented in Chapter 2 (Tourangeau et al., 2000), clients' responses are guided by a variety of factors: (a) Comprehension: To what extent did the client understand the question? Consider the client's vocabulary when assembling your questions without dumbing down concepts. (b) Retrieval: The client will need to access his or her memory to sort and select the information necessary to assemble a cogent response. This can take some time and effort depending on such things as the complexity, chronological span, and emotional depth of the question. For instance, a question like, *"What is your middle name?"* requires minimal effort, whereas asking, *"How many days did you feel depressed over the past 2 years?"* is considerably more involved. (c) Judgment: The client needs to decide which parts of the recalled information will be included in the answer. As mentioned earlier, clients may choose to disclose, withhold, alter, or fabricate components of a response depending on the sensitivity of the information and the client's sense of rapport and safety in the therapeutic setting. (d) Response: Clients may dodge or hesitate to respond to questions that involve heavy, hurtful feelings.

Consider this passage wherein the client's response appears to be inappropriate with respect to the therapist's question:

Th: You seem a little subdued today; did something happen?

Cl: Lavender.

Th: I don't understand. What does lavender have to do with your mood?

The client's response, *"lavender,"* makes no sense. The therapist checks for misunderstanding.

Cl: Oh, today, on the way here, I smelled lavender. I think some lady was wearing it out there. My mom used to wear lavender all the time. I guess it just made me think of her.

Th: Yes. Sometimes a smell can trigger memories or feelings. How long has it been since you and your mom have spoken?

Cl: I'm just remembering, when I was a kid, on the weekends, my mom used to make waffles from scratch for breakfast. She'd use the syrup to spell out my initials "J.G." in the little waffle squares.

The client provided some interesting historical information but did not respond to the question asked.

Th: [Smiles] That's fun. I've never heard of that being done before. It sounds like there were some good times there. How long has it been since you and your mom have spoken?

The therapist courteously acknowledges the client's historical information and then gently re-asks the question.

Cl: A little over a year. I guess I'm missing her.

Occasionally, re-asking a question can be met with strong resistance. As the therapist, you have the privilege to identify your observations and voice your concerns and reasons for wanting to explore a particular topic more thoroughly, but ultimately it is essential to respect the client's boundaries. If a client is truly unwilling or unprepared to talk about something, then it would not be appropriate to insist on it at that time.

Close-Ended and Open-Ended Questions

Close-ended questions are designed to elicit a brief, specific type of response: *yes, no,* a number, and so forth. Some examples of close-ended questions are inquiries such as: *"Are you over 18?" "Are you married?" "How many children do you have?" "Have you ever practiced unsafe sex?"* The advantage of close-ended questions is that they are focused to concisely gather a specific piece of information. The primary disadvantage of close-ended questions is that the responses typically lack broader subjective or emotional details.

Open-ended questions offer more latitude in terms of the client's response so as to prompt storytelling: *"What brought you into therapy?" "How do you like to spend your spare time?" "What kind of music do you like?"* Open-ended questions delve beyond *yes* or *no* inquiries, providing the client more literary license to compose responses using his or her own words and feelings. In some cases, clients may communicate richly detailed information that you may never have thought about. Table 5.1 shows examples of close-ended questions and their open-ended counterparts.

Table 5.1   Close-Ended Versus Open-Ended Questions

Close-Ended Questions	Open-Ended Questions
Did you go out to dinner after the movie?	What did you do after the movie?
Do you take any prescription medications?	What drugs do you use?
Are you over 18?	How old are you?
Are you upset?	How are you feeling?
Do you have a dog?	What pets do you have?

Consider the first close-ended question in the preceding example: *"Did you go out to dinner after the movie?"* Suppose the client replies, *"No."* Were you to continue using close-ended questions, the interview might begin to sound something like this:

Th: Did you go out to dinner after the movie?

Cl: No.

Th: Did you go to the beach?

Cl: No.

Th: Did you go to the park?

Cl: No.

Clearly, this unproductive interview begins to sound and feel more like a tedious game of 20 questions. Consider how this dialogue might go had an open-ended version of the same question had been asked instead:

Th: What did you do after the movie?

Cl: We started with a drive down Main Street. Then we stopped at this shop that had all these great out-of-print books and old movie posters. I've always loved old books. Anyway, I guess I started to feel more relaxed when we held hands. . . .

The open-ended question spares both you and the client from having to engage in a lengthy guessing game and provides the client the opportunity to articulate essential details that could not be rendered by the exclusive use of close-ended questions.

Consider the second question: *"Do you take any prescription medications?"* This question implicitly limits the scope of the client's response boundaries. Essentially the message could be taken as *"Tell me (yes or no) if you take prescription medications only,"* whereas asking the open-ended version of this question, *"What drugs do you use?"* allows the client to discuss prescription medication while also including a broader range of substances in the response (over-the-counter drugs, illegal substances, herbs, nutritional supplements, etc.).

Both close- and open-ended questions have their place in the therapeutic process. Close-ended questions are useful when a specific, concrete answer is required: *"Are you thinking of killing yourself?"* *"Did somebody hit you?"* *"Are you pregnant?"* More often, open-ended questions are preferred in therapy as they tend to facilitate deeper factual and emotional exploration and understanding. If you find yourself using a lot of close-ended questions, you may wish to take a moment to (mentally) rephrase such inquiries as open-ended questions, as demonstrated in Table 5.1, and consider which version of the question is most appropriate. Keep in mind that despite your diligence in using open-ended questions, you may still receive brief (one-word) responses. In such cases, it may be appropriate to make a more forthright request for further elaboration.

Avoid Asking Accusatory Questions

In the interest of maintaining a positive working rapport, questions should be phrased in a nonjudgmental manner. Questions that are phrased in an accusatory or judgmental manner are likely to be met with resistance and possibly deception. Consider this exchange:

Th: *What do you like to do for fun?*

Cl: *Well, last Friday I got a call early in the morning from my buddies. They were heading out for a surf day. I just picked up the phone, called in sick, and we had one hell of a day!*

Th: *Do you think it's fair to your employer and coworkers for you to call in sick when you're not really ill?*

The therapist's question carries a guilt-laden message, which can damage rapport and impede further disclosure on this and potentially other issues. Does this mean that you need to censor your curiosity, that you should stay away from discussing difficult issues such as consequences related to the client's behaviors? No. In fact, as the therapist, you are obliged to explore such topics with your clients. If you really want to know the impact that the sick call had at work, the preferred strategy is to form your inquiry in a more neutral or even positive fashion:

Th: *A Friday adventure makes the work week shorter and the weekend longer. Sounds like you had a blast. So, what was it like when you went back to work on Monday?*

This second version of the therapist's follow-up question aims to gather the same information, but in a more open, positive, and nonjudgmental manner, thereby facilitating rapport. The client essentially receives the message that it's okay to talk about breaking the rules. The client is not going to get hammered in here for being honest. As discussed earlier, this helps to confirm to the client that in therapy, the client has the privilege to raise and discuss any point that he or she needs to—even those that may cast the client in a less than flattering light—without having to fear an adverse reaction. It is very often such issues that most need to be processed; nonpunitive questions provide another opportunity to convey the notion that therapy is a safe environment for identifying and working through such issues.

Avoid Asking "Why?" Questions

"*Why?*" is not inherently a bad way to begin a question; however, asking someone why carries some rigid implications: Asking someone to tell you why is akin to demanding an explanation or adequate justification for something. This is likely to set off a defensive reaction (Benjamin, 1987). Further, asking why implies that the client *knows* the correct answer to the question. If the client does not know the answer to the "why" question, then he or she will likely become frustrated that you have demanded an answer that is beyond the scope of his or her knowledge or understanding. Another possibility is that the client *does* know the answer but is unprepared or unwilling to submit his or her reasoning—subject to your approval—again, potentially setting off a defensive reaction. Still another common reaction to "why" questions is the tendency of people to build their responses using facts or excuses. This can lead to a departure from the productive discussion of feelings, as in the following example:

Th: I see from your record that you tested positive for cocaine.

Cl: Mm-hmm.

Th: Why do you use cocaine?

Cl: I dunno. I guess I shouldn't.

Finding an interviewing pathway that avoids *why* questions is not always simple, but the information gathered is often more useful. Consider this alternate, more open dialogue:

Th: I see from your record that you tested positive for cocaine.

Cl: Mm-hmm.

Th: That's a pretty common drug. I'm curious . . . when did you first try cocaine?

Cl: Oh, about 5 years ago.

Th: What was going on 5 years ago?

Clearly this dialogue is not only more comfortable, but we can see that this guided line of inquiry is likely to render more therapeutically valuable information, which could include details, such as the client's baseline social functioning, course of the substance use, possible recovery efforts, emotional vulnerabilities, or usage triggers. Although it may seem like the long way around asking a simple "why" question, the value of this detour is evident.

Avoid Asking Multiple-Choice Questions

Our lives are laced with multiple choice questions. Anyone who has entered a voting booth, taken an exam, responded to a survey, or ordered a pizza has been subjected to multiple-choice questions. Multiple choice questions have the convenience of providing a short list of prepared answers from which to select; however, in the subjective realm of therapy, it may not be possible to assemble an all-encompassing list of choices, as in this brief dialogue:

Cl: *I've been having such a hard time with my brother lately.*

Th: *Do you like him, love him, hate him?*

Cl: *I don't know. . . . I guess I love him.*

Although the therapist provided what might be considered the three most likely responses, the structure of the answer set may lead the client to believe that the correct answer must be one of the choices on the list. Consider the following alternative wherein the therapist asks an open-ended question instead:

Cl: *I've been having such a hard time with my brother lately.*

Th: *How do you feel about your brother?*

Cl: *It's hard to say. I guess I don't have any one feeling. Sometimes he doesn't answer my calls or e-mails for months at a time, and other times he calls me and mails me odd and wonderful stuff. It's always been kind of a mixed bag with him . . . kind of hot and cold. . . . I guess my feelings just depend on what's going on at the time. I guess I just wish things were a little more stable between me and him.*

We can see that the client's actual answer to the multiple-choice version of the question might have been somewhere between "none of the above" and "some of the above." Although multiple choice questions are not inherently forbidden, consider the advantages of using open-ended questions instead.

Compared with multiple choice questions, open-ended questions are easier to assemble and offer more latitude in terms of the richness of the client's response.

Avoid Asking Biased Questions

Despite efforts to conduct yourself as an objective professional, it can be challenging to restrain your personal opinions, wishes, or positive intentions when composing questions. Although having an opinion about what would be best for the client is not intrinsically bad, embedding such messages within the context of a question can solicit less than genuine responses, as in this case:

Cl: *I was really dreading this birthday. It was supposed to be like a milestone for me, and when I look at what's in my life, it's just not what I wanted. It's been over a month, and every day, it just keeps getting worse and worse. I just don't know how much more of this I can take.*

Th: *But you're not thinking of killing yourself, are you?*

Cl: Um . . . [Pause] *no.*

In this dialogue, despite the apparent benevolence of the therapist, the therapist's question, as it is presented, is implicitly loaded with a correct answer: The client is expected to deny suicidal thoughts. The client, in a vulnerable state, may feel as if he or she is being pushed into providing the therapist's preferred answer for fear of the consequence of responding incorrectly. In this case, even the well-intended biased question may lead the client to artificially deny any suicidal ideation, potentially placing the client at grave risk.

Consider this unbiased inquiry:

Cl: *I was really dreading this birthday. It was supposed to be like a milestone for me, and when I look at what's in my life, it's just not what I wanted. It's been over a month and every day, it just keeps getting worse and worse. I just don't know how much more of this I can take.*

Th: *Are you thinking about killing yourself?*

Cl: *Well, I can't say that I haven't ever* thought *about it . . . but I mean, I'm sure it's something that everyone* thinks *about at one time or another. I think I'd be too scared to actually do something like that, but to be honest, these past few weeks have been so dark, it just seemed like it's maybe not so out of reach.*

This time, the therapist asks the question in a direct and unbiased fashion. Although this may be an uncomfortable subject, it is relevant and necessary. Asking the question in this unbiased fashion communicates multiple facilitative messages: It lets the client know that someone is appropriately concerned about his or her safety; it provides permission for the client to speak honestly about his or her feelings, thoughts, and intentions; and it offers the opportunity to more accurately assess the client's risk to him- or herself so that appropriate protective measures can be taken.

In the therapeutic realm, the client is not the only one who is challenged to deal openly with difficult topics. You must also approach each session with honesty and courage. In the first example, the therapist's bias tips the client's response in a direction that eases the therapist's mind but compromises the client's safety, whereas the therapist in the second dialogue demonstrates the courage to ask the essential question in a manner that is genuinely open to the client's truth—whatever it may be.

Directing

Unlike casual conversations, the therapeutic relationship is, by definition, a productive relationship. Part of your responsibility as a therapist is to keep the discussion focused on issues that are relevant to the therapeutic goals. The following skills can be used to keep sessions on track.

Returning

Returning involves going back to a point that the client mentioned prior. Sometimes, an issue that sounds clinically significant or interesting might be mentioned in passing. You may immediately request the client to elaborate on that point. Other times, you may recall an issue that was raised earlier in the session or discussed in a prior session. As information accumulates, it can be valuable to selectively revisit previously mentioned issues.

Cl: *I'm really not excited about my lovely stepmom's birthday. It's next week.*

Th: *I remember you mentioning that family gatherings don't usually go well . . . like what happened on Thanksgiving.*

The therapist returns to impressions gathered from prior sessions.

Cl: *Thanksgiving . . . right. [Sigh] Thanksgiving, New Years, birthdays, Wednesdays. . . . With my family, anytime's the right time for a fight.*

Th: Tell me a little more about your "lovely" stepmother. You mentioned that she's loud and how hard that is for you.

The therapist returns to a point that the client raised in this session, requesting clarification as to the nature of the stepmother.

Cl: Oh, she's a gem. She can yell loud enough to break crystal. . . . There's just no pleasing her.

In this case, returning serves to bring out potentially useful details regarding the strain between the client and the stepmother and difficult overall family dynamics. Providing such links may help to identify recurrent trends or behavioral patterns that could become the focus of therapy.

Returning not only demonstrates your attentiveness in the current session but, by identifying and including relevant information gathered from prior sessions, shows that you are actively accumulating a working comprehensive image of the client's overall life circumstance.

Resuming

Resuming provides an effective means for facilitating the continuity of the therapy from session to session. At the beginning of a session, you may request that the client resume from where he or she left off at the last session: *"Last time you mentioned that you were going to see your doctor about your insomnia."* Alternatively, the suggested "resume point" may involve continuing to process a salient topic raised in the midst of the prior session: *"In our last session, you talked about wanting to move, that you were tired of where you were living and you were looking to change things."* Avoid vague resume prompts like, *"Last time we met you were really mad."* When cueing a client to resume, tell the client specifically where you would like him or her to pick up the storytelling.

Th: Last time we were talking about how you and your brother have had trouble getting along and that it gets worse when one of you drinks.

The therapist provides a specific brief summary framed in an open-ended (question) fashion.

Cl: Yeah. [Silence]

Th: I'm wondering how you're doing with the two goals that we talked about last time: your wanting to patch things up with your brother and also wanting to get your drinking under control.

The therapist pursues the resuming effort via a more focused open-ended cue, engaging the client to report on the goals set in the prior session.

Cl: *I've thought about it a lot, and right now I'm really not ready to call him, but I have gone back to the AA meetings. I've been to three so far.*

The therapy resumes in a meaningful manner.

In addition to being used to provide for a meaningful entry into the present session, resuming can also be used in midsession. As an illustration, suppose the client's topic departs toward non-goal-related social conversation. Such discussions are not inherently bad, but such dialogues can just as easily take place outside the therapeutic environment with friends or family. In such instances, you may recommend making better use of your limited time together and then suggest resuming discussion of more critical goal-related issues that typically span sessions.

Resuming can also be a valuable skill for handling the "doorknob effect" wherein the client raises a substantial issue near the end of the session as he or she is reaching for the doorknob to leave, deliberately leaving insufficient time to address potentially uncomfortable issues (Lukas, 1993).

Th: *That's all the time we have for today.*

The therapist is appropriately closing the session on time.

Cl: *Oh, I guess I forgot to tell you. . . . I've been accepted into the police academy.*

This is a significant life event.

Th: *Congratulations. I didn't know you'd applied. I'd like to hear more about this in our next session.*

The therapist recognizes and effectively copes with this doorknob effect via (promised) resuming.

This is the first part of a two-part resume wherein this session closes with, *"I'd like to hear more about this in our next session."* It would be appropriate to flag this issue in the client's case notes as a reminder of where to pick up the therapy in the next session. The therapist would initiate the second part of the resuming at the opening of the next session: *"Last time, just as we were wrapping up, you mentioned that you'd been accepted into the police academy."* In terms of professionalism, it is considered inappropriate to extend sessions except in cases of genuine emergency conditions, such as the client expressing an intent to physically harm him- or herself or others. If the client habitually raises significant issues during the last moments of the session, then discussion of this propensity, starting at the beginning of a session, may be warranted.

Redirecting

When the therapeutic dialogue departs substantially from the focal topic, you may *redirect* the client to get the session back on track. In order to redirect, you must first be aware of the departure from the goal-directed nature of therapeutic dialogue. This can be fairly easy when the client changes topics abruptly; other times, it may be more elusive: The dialogue may gradually drift off topic. Such switching can be motivated by the client's emotional discomfort with the topic at hand. You can initiate redirection by acknowledging that the conversation has shifted, tentatively speculate as to the feelings that may have motivated the shift, and gently but deliberately redirect the client back to the prior topic. For sake of brevity, this client makes a relatively abrupt switch:

Cl: *This has just been one of the worst weeks ever. I hate funerals.*

Th: *Your cousin . . . the one who was receiving hospice care?*

Cl: [Nods] *He was such an easy guy to know, ya know? I wish you could have known him.*

Th: *From what you told me about him, it sounds like he was a good guy.*

> The therapist encourages the client to keep focused on the funeral and the client's feelings associated with it.

Cl: *See these shoes? . . . I got them for a special occasion. I've kind of been saving them.*

Th: [Nods]

> The therapist presumes the client will continue talking about the funeral.

Cl: *I bought these shoes online. A friend gave me the Web site, but I never took it seriously. I mean, who would buy shoes online? It's like, how can you try them on? And every monitor is different, so how do you know if the color's really right or not. I don't know . . . somehow it all worked out okay. It's like people are buying stuff online now more than ever. I bet the real winners are the delivery services!*

Clearly the client has shifted to a less stressful topic.

Th: *Who'd have figured they'd turn out to be your "funeral shoes"?*

The therapist attempts to redirect the client back to the topic of the funeral.

Cl: *You'll never guess what I paid for these shoes. I mean, who'd have thought that a Web site would have a "bargain basement"? Look at these shoes . . . name brand shoes. Guess how much!*

The client persists in the off-topic conversation.

Th: *Jess, the shoes are very nice; I'm sure you got a good deal on them. I'm wondering, though, if by talking about your shoes, you're trying to stay away from talking about how hard it is to lose your cousin Jake.*

The therapist makes a firmer but compassionate effort to redirect the client back to discussing the funeral.

Cl: *[Cries] I know. I know. I mean, for over a year, I knew he was going to die, so I thought I was like 99% ready for it. Look at me! . . . I guess it doesn't work that way.*

The redirection was effective.

When considering redirecting, try to avoid the temptation to redirect on the first sign of the client's departure from the topic at hand; he or she may need a brief break from a tough topic and may return on his or her own. Also, consider that the therapeutic realm is an environment of exploration and an opportunity for self-discovery. It is natural that as the client verbalizes facts and feelings, associations are built. One thought reasonably leads to another. Although focus is certainly of concern, consider providing fairly liberal latitude for the therapeutic discussion to advance. Providing such space for expansion may render valuable details that help to paint the clinical picture in a more comprehensive manner, which may reveal essential therapeutic findings such as correlations, behavioral patterns, coping adaptations, unidentified strengths, or usable resources. If you are uncertain if redirecting is appropriate, it may be useful to summarize the seemingly tangential story-telling and ask how that fits into the bigger picture.

Specificity

Therapy typically involves gathering a comprehensive understanding of the client's life and then selectively focusing on key issues that appear to be the source of the problems. When a problem or circumstance is expressed in vague terms, it can be difficult to get a meaningful grip on it. In the same way that an archer needs to know the precise location of the target, you, as the therapist, must be equally purposive in terms of gathering specific information in order to be effective. When the client's language seems to be comprised of vague, unclear, or overgeneralized information, it is time to solicit more meaningful details.

Cl: *I just don't know what to do. Everything's screwed up.*

     It is clear that the client is dissatisfied and at a loss for how to proceed. Two concepts require clarification: (1) "Everything" suggests that there may be more than one confounding issue, so you need to gather a list of what *everything* consists of. (2) "Screwed up" suggests that these issues are bothersome; further information is needed regarding the nature and magnitude of *each* problem (some problems feel "heavier" than others).

Th: *When you say, "Everything's screwed up," what's on the "everything" list?*
     The therapist respectfully requests that the client specify what "everything" consists of.

Cl: [Sigh] *Just everything!* [Pause] *First of all, my doctor told me that I need to lose weight, so I've been on this diet for a month now and I've followed it perfectly, so after one month of this, I've lost a grand total of three pounds, plus, for about the last week, my blood pressure has been back up in the 170s, and that's with taking all my medications. And then I have this insane instructor who hit us with a reading list that's not only physically impossible, but the material is completely boring, and to top it all off, Dave's back, and he "wants to talk"! No wonder my blood pressure's up!*

Per the therapist's expectations, the client has moved from an unaddressable, generalized expression of frustration (*"Everything's screwed up."*) to specific individual problems: #1 weight loss problem, #2 hypertension, #3 academic stress, #4 Dave's back.

The therapist has effectively moved the client from an unworkable, vague reference to specific, addressable problems. From here, further details about each discrete problem can be gathered making it possible to assess the weights and treatment priorities. Might resolving problem #1 reduce or resolve problem #2? Could problem #3 and #4 have caused problem #2? Elucidating such details may reveal valuable linkages, thereby suggesting meaningful intervention strategies for this system of problems.

This technique can also be utilized when only one problem is expressed. Upon exploring a problem that initially seems singular in nature, it may become clear that there is more than one confounding component. Solutions may more readily emerge when problems are broken down into their constituent parts.

Focusing

Focusing differs from redirecting; whereas redirecting guides the client from less to more clinically significant discussion, *focusing* serves to hone down the number of different topics raised in therapy, essentially limiting and prioritizing the number of different issues to be processed at any given time. Clients tend to report more improvement with respect to issues that are the subject of clinical focus than those that are not (Blizinsky & Reid, 1980). A good rule of thumb is *the effectiveness of the intervention is inversely proportional to the number of topics raised.* In other words, the more problems that are included, the shallower the discussion becomes with each topic. Without focus, the therapy can degenerate into haphazardly switching from topic to topic, producing multiple, potentially unrelated half-baked ideas that are unlikely to coalesce in any meaningful manner.

You can realistically expect a client to voice several problems concurrently. As mentioned earlier, when engaging in in-depth discussion, it is normal for one idea to naturally prompt the recollection of related ideas, feelings, or memories. When this happens, consider summarizing each one, perhaps sequencing them in some organized fashion (grouping related topics, sorting based on how closely correlated each topic is to the central therapeutic issue, etc.). Then ask the client to select the first thing that he or she would like to work on. Alternatively, you may choose to take a more active role in the selection process, pointing out the issues that seem most significant or those that appear to be most closely related to the central problem in the therapy. Although we acknowledge that our clients' lives can indeed be complex and problems can be intertwined, it is not feasible to focus critically on more than one issue at a time. Hence, priorities must be assigned.

Cl: *My father-in-law arrives tomorrow night. Not only does he smoke up the house and make rude demands left and right, but he loses things. Everything! Remote controls, silverware, his keys, my keys. . . . Everything he touches vanishes or winds up broken, and he never takes any responsibility for it. If that's not bad enough, my boss left on vacation last week and won't be back for 9 more work days, which just about triples the tower in my in-basket. And on top of all that, my car conked out again. This time they have to replace two cylinders and I'm stuck with this clunker loaner monstrosity that doesn't even have a radio for at least another week. It's going to cost me a bundle to get that slop-machine back on the road again.*

Item 1: Father-in-law.
Item 2: Extraordinary workload.
Item 3: Car trouble.

Th: *Well, we've got three things here: the father-in-law, the workload, and the car. Which one do you want to talk about first?*

The therapist reflects the list and prompts the client to select an issue to work on.

Cl: *Oh, [Sigh] how about the car. . . .*

Th: *The car. Interesting choice. I was figuring you might want to talk about your father-in-law since we've been discussing the stresses between your families. I'm also remembering that you said you'd already made up your mind about the car; didn't you and Mark agree that when the repair budget crosses the $2,000 line, it's time for a new car? . . . Or has that changed?*

The therapist summarizes the determination that the client made about the car in a prior session, which supports (re)focusing on an alternate entry point.

Cl: *Yeah, this repair should run about $1,700, so I guess that puts the car about $300 from the dump.*

The client appears to accept the rationale for the refocusing.

Th: *I certainly get how what's going on at work and the trouble with the car are impossible to ignore. . . . The extra stress is definitely real, but I've seen you get through work surges and car trouble before. Maybe a better use of our time might be to discuss what's going on with your family.*

To facilitate meaningful engagement, the therapist acknowledges the emotional weight of the two issues being deferred at this time (the car and work) and proposes focusing on the family issue.

Cl: *Oh, my family's fine. . . . I love them all, really. It's just my father-in-law, Richard. He's just so . . . Richard!*

The client embarks on discussion regarding the relevant family stressor. At some point, the therapist may point out that the recent stresses related to work and the car could reasonably exacerbate the conflicts at home.

Regardless of your thoughtful recommendation as to which topic should be the primary focus of the session, it is ultimately the client's prerogative to pursue the topic of his or her choice, even if it appears to be a less significant problem. Alternatively, as in this example, you may wish to challenge the client to consider the limited time available for therapeutic contact and encourage the client to opt for more substantial topics. Per this dialogue, it would be appropriate to ask, *"Pretend for a moment that you're not involved in any therapy, that we never met. Now, which of these problems do you think a person would put themselves in therapy to address: father-in-law trouble, in-basket trouble, or car trouble?"* In this context, car trouble clearly stands as the least plausible topic for the therapeutic setting.

Another strategy for prompting the client to address more substantial issues is to ask the client: *"If you could just snap your fingers and suddenly one of these problems would automatically fix itself forever, which one would you choose?"* Prioritizing problems from most to least significant can be a powerful strategy for maximizing the effectiveness of each session and the therapy as a whole.

Proposing Alternative Perspectives

Each individual is endowed with his or her unique point of view. As such, the therapeutic process affords the opportunity to provide an additional perspective with respect to the client's view of his or her issues. As you listen and process the client's story, you may come to see correlations, patterns, or alternate interpretations that may have eluded the client. Provisionally providing your take on the client's situation can be useful in advancing the therapeutic process.

Reframing

When a client presents a story that casts the client in a neutral or negative light, it may be possible to realistically represent the same information with a more positive twist, an alternate, more facilitative perspective. Reframing can be a useful skill when working with clients who present with a narrow or self-critical point of view. This may be accomplished by repackaging the same information or incident with a more objective or more positive view.

Cl: *I hate what I've come down to. I mean, look at me . . . a college drop-out. Until 2 weeks ago, I was homeless, living on the streets. I'm just a stupid loser.*

The client has revealed two major losses in his life.

Th: *I know you've been through a lot, but really, in the light of what I've already come to know about you, it's hard for me to think of you as a loser.*

Reframing prematurely may sound as though the therapist is ignoring or minimizing the client's problems, so the therapist begins by acknowledging what the client has coped with thus far.

Cl: *How do you mean?*

Th: *I get that you're not exactly feeling like a genius considering where some of your decisions have taken you lately, but think about this: Could a stupid person have ever been admitted to a first-rate university? Would a stupid person be savvy enough to know how to survive on the streets? You survived on the streets for 10 months; I'm betting most people wouldn't be resourceful enough to last 10 days. You also had the intelligence to find an exit off the streets, and you've been granted readmission to the university. A stupid person could not do any of those things.*

The therapist again acknowledges the client's perspective and then presents a list of life accomplishments that are inherently incompatible with stupidity.

Cl: *Huh! I never thought of it that way. You sort of do need to know what you're doing to get by on the streets.*

When reframing, take care not to deny the client's reality. Do not minimize the client's (emotional) experience. For instance, suppose the client says, "*I just got laid off.*" With all good intentions, one might be tempted to impulsively respond, "*Oh, you're bright; you'll find another job.*" Though on the surface, this may sound positive, it fails to respectfully attend to the emotional weight of the client's message. A more facilitative reply may involve reflecting a relevant recap of the client's history to lay the foundation for meaningful reframing: *"You've been talking about how things have been unstable at work for some time now. The reality of being laid off is never easy. I'd imagine you've got some stress right about now. You know, considering how unsatisfying you found the work, I'm wondering if this might be your big chance to consider an alternate career path that might get you out of the cubicle. You always seem to light up when you talk about flying; maybe this is your opportunity to make it something more than a hobby."* This approach acknowledges the client's feelings while introducing a supplemental meaning to having been laid off as an opportunity to embark on a potential career change.

Actively maintaining an understanding of your clients, coupled with a genuine positive regard, helps reframing come naturally.

Interpreting

Interpreting involves correlating gathered information and submitting an overall impression to the client in a tentative manner. Often this involves citing patterns in the client's behaviors, feelings, or thoughts. Interpretations also provide a means for proposing potential cause-and-effect coping cycles.

Whether the client directly or implicitly asks you for an interpretation, it is important to phrase your answer tentatively; bear in mind that interpretations are inherently subjective. It would be presumptuous to assign definitive meanings to events, leaving little or no room for the consideration of alternate ideas. Try to stay away from phrases that imply that you are holding *the* correct answer (*"This means . . ." "Clearly, this is about . . ."*); instead, consider more speculative, less authoritative phrases (*"I'm thinking this may have something to do with . . ." "I'm starting to see something of a trend here . . ."*).

Although it would not be warranted to withhold a clinical impression indefinitely, persistently providing the client with your interpretations could unintentionally rob the client of valuable opportunities to engage in meaningful introspective thinking and deprive the client of the chance to gain a sense of independence. Collaborate with clients to solicit their *own* interpretations. Try to be patient with *your* interpretations. You can always go second.

Cl: *I had this really weird dream: I'm not sure where I was. Anyway, I look at my wrist, and my watch is melting. Then I run into this homeless guy, and I want to give him some money and when I go to reach for my wallet, there's no pocket there. Then I turn around, and the whole city has just turned into desert—nothing but tan sand for as far*

*as the eye can see. And it's quiet. It's all so quiet. What's that all
about?*

Th: *What do you think it means?*

The therapist encourages the client to interpret his or her own dream.

Cl: *I don't know.*

Th: *What do we have? A disintegrating watch, a homeless guy, a lost wallet, a city that vanishes, silence. Do you see anything that might link
these things together?*

The therapist's summary models a way of thinking about such abstract
problems and solicits the client's interpretation.

Cl: *Huh! . . . Lots of sad stuff . . . missing stuff. . . .*

Th: [Nods] *I'm wondering if this might be a reflection of some of your
recent losses.*

The therapist provides some guidance, still leaving room for the client
to engage in the (therapeutic) interpretation process.

Cl: *Maybe Sara and the kids going on vacation without me. . . .*

The recap (*"What do we have?"*) plus the follow up open-ended question
(*"I'm wondering if . . ."*) invites the client to actively partake in the interpretative process. This style of communication helps engage the client by
conveying, *"I'm just speculating here. . . . Speculations don't have to be
perfect. . . . Right now, we're just playing with ideas. . . . Now you try one."*
You might even consider saying some of this out loud to help nurture the
client's participation.

Avoid the temptation to promptly assign definitive interpretations. Such
a propensity may unintentionally perpetuate an inappropriate controlling-
dependent relationship wherein the client begins to perceive you as the all-
knowing advice guru and him- or herself as the uncertain fool. Each step of
the therapy needs to actively encourage the client's empowerment, incrementally advancing toward self-sufficiency.

Generalizing

Generalizations can serve to identify both facilitative and dysfunctional
patterns in the client's life. Such patterns can involve recurring feelings,
(in)actions, events, thoughts, as well as notable patterns in those involved in

the client's system. Generalizations can be enlightening to clients in that the events of their lifetimes occur naturally over the course of years, whereas therapy happens within a more concentrated time frame (months, or perhaps weeks), selectively highlighting significant events. In therapy, events that were initially chronologically distant may (deliberately) be presented side by side with more recent events, revealing potentially overlooked progressions or repetitive trends. Such exploration may suggest the source of a maladaptive pattern and ultimately meaningful solutions.

Clients may conceptualize their lives as having discretely separated venues. As such, a client may think of problems at work separately from problems at home or in the client's private life. Thoughtful generalization may reveal some common coping patterns or repeating themes that play out in more than one domain.

Thoughtful generalizations may suggest meaningful treatment plans, which may involve identifying recurring problems, pointing out sequences of events and consequences that the client may not be fully aware of, establishing baseline behaviors, and implementing goal-related therapeutic interventions. In addition to identifying recurring *symptomatic* dysfunctional routines, historical exploration may point toward the *origin* of such maladaptive routines, which may become a useful focus for the therapy.

As a rule of thumb, it is advisable to allow yourself the time necessary to gather information regarding the client's life before submitting premature generalizations. As historical and present information accumulates, you or the client may naturally form impressions and begin to identify emerging patterns.

Generalizations need not always be negative. Although it can be tempting to focus exclusively on the client's dysfunctional patterns, it is essential to attend to, and actively identify, the client's strengths (*"You seem to have a reputation for finishing first." "It sounds like your family puts you in the driver's seat when they run into a crisis."* etc.). Drawing positive generalizations can facilitate coping by actively reminding clients of their proven ability to effectively face challenges. Remember, therapy involves not only focusing on the *problematic issues* but also aiding in the *identification of strengths*. These strengths ultimately constitute the client's solving skills that will fuel the accomplishment of the client's therapeutic goals. Consider the following guidelines when building therapeutic generalizations:

Be specific: Generalizations that cite specific incidents and details are more effective than those involving vague references. Simply stating, *"You can't get anything done on time. What's that about?"* lacks empirical support and, depending on the delivery, may be perceived as accusatory. Consider this more detailed presentation: *"This issue of not getting your taxes in on time makes me think of a few other things that we've discussed: your girlfriend's complaints about you being late for dates, your not getting to work on time, your missing your flights. I wonder what might be going on here."* Citing *specific* elements can be therapeutically facilitative in that this enables the client to focus on *actual* aspects of his or her own behaviors as opposed to focusing on how negative you are being.

It is also advisable to avoid the use of extreme or absolute language (always, never, etc.). Such expressions are seldom accurate and as such, are easily refutable. Consider more accurate alternatives (often, more times than not, tend to, etc.).

Encourage exploration and elaboration: As you cite specific examples in proposing your generalization, be open to corrections, elaboration, and addendums. Actively solicit the client to identify patterns or trends in his or her storytelling. As information is progressively rendered, valuable details may be recalled, facilitating the synthesis of more meaningful generalizations.

Avoid accusations: When identifying what seems like negative or dysfunctional trends in the client's behavioral history, try to avoid the temptation to phrase generalizations in an accusatory manner. Consider a case wherein the client is discussing a history of incomplete projects. Instead of saying, *"It sounds like you're a quitter,"* which is likely to be met with defensive resistance, take the time to compose a more objective adaptation: *"It seems like there's a pattern of stopping before the projects are 100% finished."* This second version carries less of an accusatory tenor; hence, we would expect the client would be more open to such a statement and the discussion that would follow. Remember that the goal of assembling generalizations is not to punish the client but merely to propose what appears to be a recurring pattern that may be worthy of addressing.

Discuss history: Exploring the history of emerging themes may reveal the source of dysfunctional behaviors. Such exploration may shed light on a precondition or antecedent event (X) that appears to be closely followed by an adverse reaction (Y): *"It seems like whenever X happens, you almost automatically do Y. When was the first time that X happened?"* Such correlations may become the focus of clinical attention: *"Can X be reduced?" "Can you learn to predict or control X?" "Could you learn to interpret X in some different way?" "When X happens, other than Y, what else might you do?"*

Relate findings to therapeutic goals: Engage the client to explore how the identified patterns may be contributing to the frequency or severity of the clinical problems at hand. Treatment plans can be modified to utilize positive coping patterns while taking strategic steps to address negative patterns.

Th: *How are things going between you and Ron?*

Cl: *I still haven't called him. He keeps leaving me messages, but I just can't call him back.*

Th: *. . . after he criticized your new haircut?*

Cl: [Nods]

Th: *You know, this reminds me of the time a few weeks ago when your instructor wrote you a note telling you not to use footnotes in your papers.*

Provisionally presenting a seemingly similar event from a different context.

Cl: *That's not the same thing.*

The client realistically refutes this provisional generalization; providing further details may elucidate the therapist's thinking.

Th: *You're right, it's a very different thing, but I remember you telling me that you received an e-mail from that instructor offering to discuss redrafting the paper and you held off on replying. That keeping silent part just seems similar to me. I'm wondering if there might be other times when you've run into a conflict with someone and played the silent card. Anything like that come to mind?*

The therapist proposes the similarity between these incidents and inquires further.

Cl: *Hmm . . . well, whenever me and my dad would get into it, he was so hard, it was like being grilled on the witness stand. It was like, the more I'd say, the worse he'd get, so I just started saying nothing, figuring, don't give him any more ammunition. It's not like I could ever win, so what's the point of stretching this out. I'll just shut up and that way we can get to the end of this quicker.*

The client's input provides valuable clues as to the origin of this silent response to hurt.

Th: *It sounds like that might have been the only way to deal with your father at the time. I'm wondering if you might be carrying some of that "cut to silence when things get rough" strategy forward with other people.*

The therapist proposes a generalization based on the recent events and also the client's supplemental contribution.

Cl: *Oh, yeah, . . . but this time it's with people who probably* wouldn't *slam me.*

The client follows and acknowledges the point of the generalization.

In addition to being a means to prompt clients to explore problems at hand more thoroughly, astute generalizations may also provide insight as to the antecedents of such problems. Identifying the recurring nature of problems does not have to be packaged as repeated failures but rather a therapeutic opportunity wherein addressing the source of the problem may pave the way to resolving multiple current problems or future manifestations of the problem.

Identifying and Resolving Discrepancies

The quality of the therapy largely depends on the exchange of genuine information and feelings. Tactfully citing inconsistencies can guide the client toward more thorough exploration of his or her condition and also enhance your comprehension of the client's situation.

Challenging

One of your primary goals, as a therapist, is to achieve an understanding of the client's life circumstances in an objective and supportive manner. In the midst of discussing emotionally laden material, clients may unintentionally express misinformation, misconceptions, overgeneralizations, inconsistencies, or partial truths. In such cases, it is appropriate to identify and challenge the client's assertions.

Challenges are most effective when they are specific and concise. Specificity promotes the robust reality of the challenge; conciseness helps present the challenge as focused and constructive. The more verbose the challenge, the more it is likely to be ignored as a tedious or accusatory lecture. Use challenges strategically; be aware that stacking challenges back to back may put the client on the defensive.

Cl: *Work's still kind of on the hectic side, but I think I'm finding ways to get by. I just get a little buzz when I get home and that pretty much takes things down.*

Th: *A little buzz? Like with what?*

Gathering further details.

Cl: *Oh, just some pot, you know, just to relax. It's no big change in my life. I mean I've smoked it for years. It's not like I'm turning into an addict or something. Why? Do you think I'm an addict or something?*

The client's reply is moderately defensive.

Th: *Well, at this point, it's hard to know if you're addicted. The only reason I'm asking about this is because when we first started working together, I remember you telling me that you smoked pot but only on the weekends. Now you're telling me that you're up to daily. Based on your own account, this is a change.*

The therapist appropriately resists labeling the client as an addict but tactfully points out that it would be wrong to passively let the client's assertion (that the client's drug use has *not* changed) stand.

Cl: *Okay. True. I guess sometimes I do smoke more than I used to.*

The client accepts the reality of the challenge.

Challenges need not always be negative in nature. The following dialogue utilizes a form of reframing to propose a positive challenge to the client.

Cl: *I'm such an idiot. I was running like 50 copies of something. Anyway, about half way through, the machine started making this loud grinding noise that just kept getting louder and louder, and then it started kicking out all these black mangled pages really fast and it started to smell weird . . . like something electrical was burning. So like an idiot, I couldn't find the off switch so I just kicked the plug out.*

Th: *First off, I know you. You're quite intelligent. You're not an idiot. Second, copy machines don't fail because somebody's smart or dumb. They just fail. . . . That's just what they do. Finally, it sounds like that machine was headed for a meltdown. In an emergency like that, I wonder if other people might have the presence of mind to cut the power at the source.*

The therapist systematically challenges the client's self-deprecating theme in a positive fashion.

Cl: *You're right. I guess that might have prevented a fire or a short circuit or something. That stupid thing is always breaking down. . . . The repair contractor is out about once a month doing something to bring it back to life.*

The client accepts the therapist's challenge that copy machine failure is not a sign of idiocy.

Both of these diverse examples demonstrate how it is possible to challenge the client's assertions without damaging rapport. One of the most powerful therapeutic skills is the ability to provide an alternate, more objective perspective on the client's condition. Without denying the client's sense of the situation, you have the privilege to tactfully submit your perspective, even if it contradicts the client's presentation.

Confronting

Confrontations can be thought of as a more robust challenge to a client's assertions. Appropriate confrontations use some of the same techniques as submitting therapeutic generalizations and challenges; however, the confrontations differ in that the ultimate goal is to identify and process discrepancies that may resolve with clarification.

In order to be facilitative, confrontations need to be focused and pertinent to the therapy. Consider the following guidelines for building and delivering effective confrontations:

Be specific: Raise specific facts, quotes (as best as can be recalled), time lines, and incidents that appear to be in conflict or implausible. In order to maintain focus, try to point out (only) one specific discrepancy at a time. One way to accomplish this is to cite the incongruity in the form of a "You said . . . but . . ." statement ("You said *you were a citizen,* but *now you're telling me that you're worried about being deported.*") (Hackney & Cormier, 2000). If you become aware of multiple discrepancies, consider addressing the most significant one first. Raising several conflicts simultaneously is likely to impart some negative feelings such as embarrassment, intimidation, or anger, which may put the client on the defensive.

Encourage exploration or elaboration: In the midst of submitting your recap of contentious elements, provide the client with the opportunity to submit further specifics, clarification, and corrections. As further information is rendered, be prepared to accept that you may have formed one or more misconceptions. Even the most attentive listener can lose or distort a piece of information along the way.

Avoid accusations: The goal of the confrontation is not to punish the client for lying. Your goal is merely to point out what appear to be inconsistencies in the story as you understand it and to respectfully seek clarification.

Present confrontations tentatively: Remember, your goal is to *try to understand*, not trap the client. Maintaining the perspective of genuinely trying to better comprehend the client's circumstances will help to elucidate the truth in a nonthreatening manner. The entry into a confrontation will likely set the tone for the remainder of the session. Keep in mind that not all inconsistencies are intentional efforts to conceal the truth or mislead. It is possible that you may not be recalling all of the facts with perfect accuracy. Alternatively, the client may have inadvertently failed to mention some essential piece of information. Keep in mind that as therapy advances and as rapport is built, the client may feel more trusting of the therapeutic process and progressively reveal more genuine information, which may conflict with prior guarded distortions or omissions. An open and nonjudgmental attitude on your behalf can greatly facilitate the resolution of conflicting or incomplete information and also provide the opportunity for the client to correct for less than true disclosures made during the course of therapy.

As with generalizations and challenges, submit confrontations firmly but tentatively. The focus of a confrontation may take a variety of forms, depending on the nature of the apparent discrepancies:

Factual conflicts: *"I remember you telling me that you were an only child, and now you're talking about your sisters."*

Time line conflicts: *"I thought you were living on the east coast 5 years ago, but now it sounds like you were on the west coast."*

Action conflicts: *"Two weeks ago you were telling me how undependable your ex has always been, and now I'm hearing that he's moving back in with you."*

Emotional conflicts: *"I notice that you smile whenever you talk about your aunt's death."*

Thought conflicts: *"Up until now, you've been telling me how much you treasure your home, and now you're thinking of selling it."*

Solicit the client's discussion: Per these examples, confrontations can be constructed to facilitate the therapeutic process. In the context of therapy, the purpose of confronting a client is not to point an accusatory finger. A confrontation provides an opportunity for the client to correct misstatements, discuss what may have inhibited him or her from initially being more honest, correct your potential misunderstanding, or clarify his or her story by providing further details.

Cl: *I'm not sure I'm ready to see my parents this weekend.*

Th: *Your* parents? *Didn't you tell me that your father passed away when you were a kid?*

The client's use of the plural term "parents" presents as inconsistent with a prior story; the therapist addresses this perceived discrepancy.

Cl: *Oh, yeah, he did, but I was only two when my dad died, so I really hardly remember him. My mom married Rob when I was four, so I pretty much just think of Rob as my father.*

The client uses this opportunity to address the discrepancy and provide further details regarding family structure and history.

Th: *Okay, I wasn't clear on that. That makes sense.*

The therapist appropriately takes responsibility for this misunderstanding in a nonpunitive fashion, as opposed to accusing the client of being unclear.

In some cases, clients find themselves in a place where they need to correct a lie they may have told earlier in therapy:

Cl: *I have to work a week of nights. I hate that. It really throws my sleep off.*

Th: *Really? I didn't know painters worked at night.*

The therapist points out the implausibility of the client's statement.

Cl: *Yeah, well, I'm not really a painter. I don't know why I told you that. I really drive a cab.*

The client corrects a prior lie.

Th: *Oh, okay. I'm glad you're telling me now.*

The therapist seamlessly accepts the corrected information. As opposed to taking a punitive stance (*Aha! So you lied to me!*), the therapist casually expresses gratitude for the clarification, implicitly communicating multiple facilitative messages: *"I'm not mad at you for lying. I commend your courage to admit the truth. I'm wondering if you're coming to feel more comfortable here. By the way, if you have other things that you'd like to go back and correct, it's okay to do that. We don't punish here."* The therapist may want to take a moment to actually verbalize some of these messages to the client.

Maintaining a positive, nonjudgmental perspective sets the tone in such a way that the client has the privilege to more readily correct or include further information without fear of retribution. Confrontations are ultimately about improving the quality of the information exchanged by clearing up ambiguities and advancing closer to the truth. The more genuine information that is disclosed in sessions, the more effective the interventions can be.

Educating

Teaching, per se, is seldom the primary goal in most forms of therapy; however, it is equally inappropriate for you to unconditionally hold your tongue when it comes to providing the client with therapeutically relevant information. Although theoretical orientations, clinical settings, and client characteristics can vary substantially, there is usually some latitude with respect to the sharing of quality information that you consider pertinent to the client's needs.

Informing

On occasion, a client may present with a direct question, incomplete information, or misconception regarding a therapeutically relevant issue. Alternatively, you may see the need to introduce a relevant piece of information into the therapeutic realm. In such cases, you have the opportunity to provide applicable information. In your role as a therapist, clients are likely to recognize you as an authority figure; some clients may presume that you hold a virtual font of encyclopedic information. Informing needs to be handled prudently. Withholding relevant information may be considered negligence, whereas providing too much information may unintentionally foster a dependent relationship (Benjamin, 1987).

Generally speaking, therapists tend to be bright people who are motivated to help, but everyone has limitations with respect to his or her range of knowledge. Nobody can be expected to know everything. As questions emerge in therapy, it is important to be genuinely aware of the scope and depth of your knowledge. When providing information, consider including a statement indicating your level of expertise with respect to the issue at hand. Honestly stating your competence coupled with the information that you are giving allows the client to assign the appropriate credibility weight to it, as in the following examples:

Low expertise:

Cl: *My sister needs a kidney transplant and we're fraternal twins. I want to help her. Do you think I could be a donor?*

Th: *That's very commendable of you, but unfortunately, transplant compatibility criteria are a little beyond my scope. I think you're going to need to speak with your sister's physician for that answer.*

Instead of guessing at such a complex issue, the therapist redirects the client to pose the question to an appropriate expert.

Moderate expertise:

Cl: *I hate telemarketers! The next time one calls, I'm going to just yell every foul word I can think of into the phone. I couldn't really get in trouble for making an obscene phone call, since they're the one who called me, right?*

Th: *I'm guessing you wouldn't be the first person to do that, and frankly, I've never heard of anyone getting in trouble over anything like that. My only concern here is that I know that these services work out of different states, each with its own telecommunication laws, so I'd guess there may not be a single answer to your question. Not being an attorney, I honestly don't know if you could get in trouble.*

The therapist begins by telling the client that what he or she is proposing may indeed be correct (*"I've never heard of anyone getting in trouble over anything like that . . ."*) but ultimately admits to not having a definitive answer. The therapist points out the multiple dimensions of the question (*"I know that these services work out of different states, each with its own telecommunication laws . . ."*), which suggests the need for the client to do further research.

High expertise:

Cl: *About the only thing I really use regularly is pot, but it's no big deal. I read somewhere that it's not addictive, so since I can quit whenever, I'm not going to worry about it.*

Th: *Well, I've taken courses in addictionology and neurochemistry, and some of what you're saying is true: You're right in that so far the research suggests that marijuana does not have physically addictive properties, but there are studies indicating that some people can develop a psychological dependence, which can be more powerful than a physical addiction.*

The therapist's citation of courses adds credibility to the statement contradicting the client's assertion. Notice that the therapist is tactful and respectful, even when delivering contradictory information with high confidence. In the interest of maintaining rapport, instead of the therapist outright saying that the client is completely wrong in his or her naive assertion, the therapist begins by identifying the elements of the client's statement that are correct (*". . . some of what you're saying is true. You're right in that so far . . ."*). If rapport were to collapse in the midst of the therapist's response, then the client may feel resentful and reject the remainder of the therapist's message. The therapist then goes on to provide the appropriate supplemental information *(". . . but there are studies indicating that . . .").*

In the interest of being helpful, be prepared to set your ego aside. It can be challenging to admit to clients, and to yourself, that you are not the all-knowing, all-seeing therapeutic oracle. Keep in mind: You need not be a know-it-all in order to provide quality therapy; nobody, no matter how experienced, holds all the answers. That is what research and ancillary experts are for.

Consider informally monitoring the frequency with which you find your-self giving information. Whereas withholding therapeutically relevant information from clients is a disservice, becoming a persistent compendium of answers to a client may unintentionally foster dependence. Instead of providing a multitude of answers, you may want to utilize a client's persistent questioning as an opportunity to direct the client to appropriate information resources (local agencies, expert professionals, relevant literature, credible Web sites, etc.), thereby promoting independence and empowerment.

Advising

Advising in the therapeutic realm varies substantially from social or casual advice giving. Socially speaking, friends offer or request advice as a regular part of their communication: *"If I were you, I'd do this." "Where should I go on vacation?" "I did XYZ. You should try it!"* Advice can come in a variety of magnitudes ranging from virtual demands: *"You absolutely have to come and see this movie with me,"* to gentle recommendations: *"Have you thought about cutting your hair?"* In the therapeutic context, there are competing factors to consider when contemplating giving advice: As with informing, too much advising may foster a sense of dependency and potentially compromise the client's sense of self-determination. Conversely, withholding meaningful advice may lead to a worsening of the client's untended condition; additionally, persistently not giving advice may reasonably cause the client to question your expertise (Kadushin, 1990).

In the therapeutic setting, you will need to achieve a thoughtful balance when considering advising. Advice should be administered in a focused, purposive manner that is synchronous with the client's life system, including values, beliefs, living situations, resources, and goals. The following guidelines provide a collaborative template for assembling and delivering meaningful therapeutic advice that respects the client's self-determination and empowerment at each step:

1. *Identify the client's problem:* A client may present with multiple problems. It can be risky to assume that the client wishes to address all of the problems in the therapeutic setting. It is possible that peripheral issues may be mentioned to facilitate thorough storytelling, but the client may intend to manage selected issues *outside* of therapy. Further, it is presumptuous to assume that it is solely your responsibility to identify the problem that the client most wants to work on. It is possible that the client may prioritize the problems differently. For instance, suppose a client presents as homeless; initially, one might presume that the client considers the homelessness as the primary problem. Conversely, the client may not see his or her homelessness as a critical issue and instead may be seeking help for an entirely different concern (needing access to medication, transportation, seasonal clothing, etc.). Hence, the first step in therapeutic advising is to have the client identify which specific problem(s), if any, the client is seeking to resolve. As the therapist, you need not be passive in this process. If the client is unable to articulate the problem(s), then you may wish to provide helpful prompts to solicit specificity or problem-solving priority: *"If you could have one problem just go away forever, what would it be?" "You've mentioned three problems: X, Y, Z. Put these in order. Which would you like to see resolved first?"*

2. *Identify the client's goal:* Once the problem has been identified, gather details as to what the client conceives as the resolution to the problem. Avoid the temptation to assume that you can intuitively derive the goal without consulting the client. For instance, suppose that one of the problems a client identifies is smoking. It may be tempting to impulsively presume that the client's goal is to quit smoking. In actuality, the client may identify any number of reasonable goals related to smoking: Perhaps the client's goal is to cut down from three packs a day to two packs a day. Maybe the client wants to stop smoking in the car. Bear in mind: 100% solutions may not be the client's goal, nor may such solutions be feasible. Another distinct possibility is that the client has identified smoking as a problem, but the client is not willing to do anything about it at this time; hence, there is no goal with respect to this problem. The fact that the client identifies a problem does not necessarily mean that the client's mission is to address the problem. This is the client's privilege.

Prompt the client to select which problems the client would like to work on; for each problem, aim to identify a reasonable goal. If there is hesitation, you may provide appropriate prompts to help cue the client's thought process: *"You mentioned that you'd like to work on X. If X were resolved, what might it look like?"*

3. *Solicit solutions:* Engage the client in identifying possible solutions. Consider starting by exploring the history of this problem. If this is a persisting or recurring problem, inquire regarding when this problem started and what was going on when this problem began. Did some incident or circumstance propagate or worsen the problem? What has or has not worked in the past? Does the client think that solution, or a modified version of it, might work this time? If this is a novel problem, then prompt the client in a collaborative fashion to assemble potential solutions: *"What do you think might work here?" "What are you willing to do?" "What's your goal?"* An additional source for potential solutions may involve engaging the client in a brainstorming session to generate an array of alternatives. From there, feasible ideas can be selected and combined to build applicable solutions.

4. *Advise (provide provisional options or strategies):* In addition to solutions that are generated collaboratively, your fresh, more objective view of the problem—combined with a reasonable understanding of the client, the client's system, available resources, behavioral theories, and clinical experience—may provide additional valuable perspectives with regard to problem solving. Thoughtful recommendations may be offered in a *provisional* manner, subject to the client's approval: *"Have you ever thought about . . . ?" "Have you considered . . . ?" "What about . . . ?" "What do you think might happen if . . . ?"* Phrasing advice in the form of active inquiries, subject to the client's approval, helps to actively engage the client in the solving process, thus fostering the client's sense of self-determination, even in the light of advice being given by a perceived authority figure.

Cl: *This week, my old roommate just showed up at my door, totally unannounced, and pretty much took up residency on my couch.*

Th: *So you're looking for a way to get the old roommate out of your place as tactfully and as promptly as possible?*

The therapist presumes that the roommate is an unwelcome guest.

Cl: *Not at all. We're best buddies; we always have been. I couldn't be happier!*

The client rejects the therapist's assumption.

Th: *Oh, okay. Then is there a problem?*

The problem is not as obvious as the therapist thought; hence, the therapist turns to the client to articulate the problem, if any.

Cl: Yes. *The problem is that I want us to have some good time together,*
but by the time I get home from work, I'm totally exhausted, and the
weekends are all jammed up with errands and stuff.

1. Identify the client's problem.

Th: *It sounds like you're wanting to spend more "quality time" together.*

Cl: *Right! I mean, I'm a day person, not a night person. I get really tired*
at night.

Th: *So you're looking for some extra daytime hours.*

2. Identify the client's goal.

The therapist pitches his or her conception of the problem.

Cl: *Right. But there's only 24 hours in a day, and half of those are night*
time, and most of the rest is work.

Th: *Yeah. Have you ever run into anything like this before, when you've*
found yourself suddenly needing some extra daytime hours to do
something?

3. Solicit solutions.

Cl: *Hmm. Well, about a year ago, when I moved, my boss let me use some*
sick time and vacation time to take a few days off to get things
together. I think I've got about 17 or 18 hours banked up at work, but
that'd only give me enough for two days off.

Th: *Have you thought about taking some unpaid time off? Do you think*
that might work?

4. Advise (provide provisional options or strategies).

Cl: *Yeah, I've been thinking about that. I know my boss would be okay*
with it, but I'll have to take a look at my budget and see if that'd work.

This dialogue demonstrates the potential misconceptions that can occur
if the problem and goal are not specifically articulated by the client.
Ultimately, both you and the client should work collaboratively to assemble
suitable solutions. Depending on the nature of the problem and the avail-
ability of resources, multiple alternate solutions may be assembled. Consider
utilizing the momentum of the problem-solving process as an opportunity to

formulate additional alternatives that may be implemented along with the initial plan or used as a backup strategy.

Notice that in social settings, advising may only involve Step 1, identifying the person's problem, and then promptly leap to Step 4, advising. Paradoxically, the *last* step in the presented therapeutic advising process involves actually giving advice. Consider the rationale of the first three steps of this model. They all involve gathering information. To summarize: In order for advice to be suitable, it must be tailored to meet the specific dimensions of the client's characteristics and the nature of the client's problem, and must target a specific goal. Advice that is uninformed or hastily delivered is likely to be perceived as a poor fit, misguided, and ultimately unusable.

The professional helper, though well intended, needs to use advice and information giving sparingly. Providing too much advice can unintentionally foster a counterproductive sense of dependency on the client's behalf (Kleinke, 1994).

Role-Play Exercise 5.1

Resume the Résumé

Chris has been out of work for several months and has lost momentum in seeking another job. In addition to eating poorly and isolating, Chris's sleeping and waking hours have become erratic. Much of the day involves endless snacking, watching television, and playing on the computer.

Client

- When the therapist asks you about work-seeking efforts, express that you know you should be doing something to look for work but find yourself depressed and easily distracted. Provide extensive details of alternate activities that you have become obsessed with (television shows, Web sites, computer games, etc.).

- Discuss how when you sense hurt (rejection letters, poor performance on interviews, etc.), it causes you to doubt your abilities and withdraw.

- Mention your feelings (anger, envy, jealousy, etc.) toward your employed friends or family who glibly tell you to just stop lying around and get a job.

Therapist

- **Open-ended requests** (p. 109)
  Ask Chris to articulate therapeutic goals (deal with the disabling depression, cope with harsh friends, etc.).

- **Re-asking a question** (p. 114)
  Ask what, if anything, Chris is doing to find work. If Chris embarks on extraneous dialogue, tactfully acknowledge the information that is given and then re-ask your question.
  "It seems like you've been spending a lot of time doing XYZ. I'm still curious about . . ."

- **Reframing** (p. 130)
  If appropriate, propose an alternate way of viewing this period of unemployment.
  "In our last session, you mentioned that you'd received a substantial inheritance. If money's not an issue, maybe you could consider this time off work as the vacation you said you've been needing."

Role-Play Exercise 5.2

Never on a Monday

Lee willingly agreed to spend the weekend helping a friend complete a project (painting, moving, etc.). Despite diligent efforts, the job was not completed by Sunday. Lee decided to take Monday off work to help finish. After the job was finished, Lee felt taken for granted and has started to resent this friend.

Client

- Discuss your history of making meaningful sacrifices for your friends and family that go unthanked and unnoticed.

- Talk about your supervisor's negative reaction to you calling in sick again or lost wages.

- Assert that as a good friend, you expect nothing in return for your services.

Therapist

- **Resuming** (p. 123)
  Regardless of where Lee begins, at the beginning of this session, ask Lee to resume with the story that was started near the end of the last session.
  "Last time, you mentioned that you were going to help a friend with a weekend project. How did that go?"

- **Specificity** (p. 127)
  Ask Lee to provide additional actual examples of times when voluntary helping resulted in resentment.

- **Challenging** (p. 137)
  If Lee claims that he or she expects nothing in return for helping, suggest that it does sound as if Lee has expressed resentment and does expect some appropriate form of reciprocation (a verbal thank-you, a nice dinner, some additional attention, etc.).

Day of the Condo

Robin has been living comfortably in an affordable apartment for the past several years. The owner just notified the tenants that the building is scheduled for demolition to make way for luxury condominiums. Robin has 30 days to move out.

Client

- Express your sense of betrayal by the owner with whom you have always been friendly.

- Over the past several years, you have been involved in a relationship that has had some ups and downs. Your significant other sees this as an ideal opportunity for you to move in. Although this sounds compelling, express your concerns.

- Spontaneously depart from your discussion of moving. Switch to discussing something completely unrelated (a peculiar person you saw outside the building, your satisfaction or dissatisfaction with a television show, your sudden craving for a food, a song that you cannot get out of your head, etc.).

Therapist

- **Close-ended questions** (p. 116)
  Ask about the length of the relationship, the location of the apartment building, how long Robin was living there, if it was a good building, etc.

- **Open-ended questions** (p. 116)
  Ask about the nature of the relationship.
  "Give me some examples of these ups and downs."

- **Returning** (p. 122)
  If Robin switches to an unrelated topic, acknowledge the departure and attempt to return to the subject of the imminent move.

Role-Play Exercise 5.4

Aunt Trap

Rene's aunt occasionally becomes drunk and calls repeatedly at inopportune hours, angrily shouting unfounded accusations and obscenities. Rene finds these calls very distressing and has addressed this problem with her on multiple (sober) occasions. She always apologizes and agrees to more civil communication. Unfortunately, the troublesome calls have persisted.

Client

- Explain that the timing of the most recent call spoiled your enjoyment of an otherwise happy event (your birthday, promotion, vacation, etc.).

- Discuss the history of these dysfunctional calls in terms of facts (how long this problem has been going on, increasing frequency or severity of the calls, etc.) and also the emotional factors (the caustic effects on your relationship with her, how the stress of these calls spills over into other parts of your emotional life, how awkward it is repeatedly trying to reestablish meaningful contact, etc.).

- Ask the therapist if you should try to fix this problem again or just cut your contact with her completely.

Therapist

- **Furthering** (p. 106)
  Ask specific questions regarding the client's relationship with the troublesome aunt:
  "What's typically said in these calls?"
  "What, if anything, do you like about her?"
  "Are you interested in preserving this relationship?"

- **Informing** (p. 142)
  Explain that someone who is intoxicated is not in a reasonable state of mind, that such conversations are inevitably unproductive.

- **Advising** (p. 144)

  1. Identify the client's specific goal.
     "What do you want to happen?"

  2. Solicit solutions.
     "What has or hasn't worked before?"
     "Any new ideas?"

  3. Offer advice provisionally.
     "What if you tell her, 'This is unacceptable. I'm not going to talk to you when you're like this,' then hang up and take the phone off the hook for a few hours?"

Role-Play Exercise 5.5

Pat's Pile o' Problems

Pat presents as overwhelmed, barely knowing where to start. Multiple problems have emerged recently (car trouble, possible layoffs at work, vacation cancelled, best friend is not communicative, sleeping poorly, relational difficulties, an unresolved misunderstanding with a family member, etc.). Generally, any one of these problems would be manageable, but together it feels like too much.

Client

- Initially, skip from topic to topic, giving scant details. You may randomly return to topics already mentioned, repeating information or providing additional information and feelings. You may convey one or several emotions (anger, confusion, frustration, etc.).

- Begin to discuss a selected topic and then halt once or several times. If the therapist prompts you to continue, then offer some further discussion wherein you continue your storytelling or provide details as to why you paused (how you are feeling, what you are thinking, things you might be remembering, your wishes, etc.).

- If the therapist asks you to provide details on a selected topic, then do so. At some point, abruptly shift to a different problem.

Therapist

- **Focusing** (p. 128)
  Recap and acknowledge the relevancy of each problem that the client mentioned and ask the client to select one issue to begin. If the client has trouble selecting a starting point, ask him or her to eliminate items that can wait. You may want to make a written list of the problems.

- **Redirecting** (p. 125)

    If the client departs from discussing a relevant issue, then ask the client to return to that point.

    "Just a moment. A minute ago, you were telling me about X. Now you're telling me about Y. X sounded like it was important. Before we go on any further with Y, could you tell me a little more about X?"

- **Prompting** (p. 108)

    If the client pauses in his or her storytelling or if you want more information on a particular issue, then use a few words to cue the client to continue discussing a selected topic.

Video Interview Self-Critique Exercise

Overview

In addition to learning the skills presented in this text on an individual basis, there is an ineffable art to integrating and implementing these skills in a meaningful manner. Reviewing a video recording of your performance can provide valuable insights as to your use of selected skills, physical presence, and the overall quality of your interaction with clients. Observing yourself will afford you further opportunity to build your therapeutic proficiency by identifying your strengths, as well as areas for continued improvement. You may consider repeating this exercise over time, enabling you to track your growth and areas for further refinement.

Setup

Role-Play Partner

Due to the legal and ethical issues concerning client confidentiality, it is recommended that you do not use an actual client or client's story line for this exercise. You may wish to enlist the help of a willing friend to play the part of the client. Students may choose to pair up—one portraying the client, the other as the therapist—and then exchange roles.

Staging

Place two chairs facing each other in relatively close proximity to each other. The chairs should be positioned so that when the two participants are seated comfortably, they can reach out and just touch fingertip to fingertip. The chairs should be angled slightly to face toward the camera as shown in Figure 5.1.

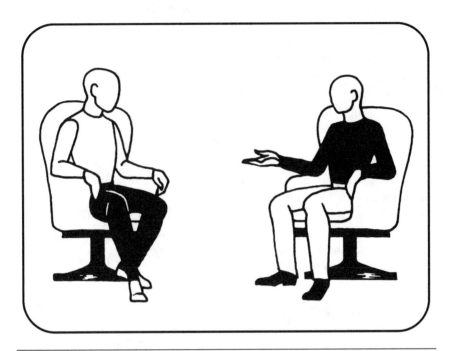

Figure 5.1   Camera's View of the Role-Play

SOURCE: Dean Cameron.

Mount the camera on a tripod or place it on a flat, stable surface. Position the camera's view to capture a "two-shot," making certain that the full body, from head to toe, of each participant is in the frame. This will enable you to observe your overall presence as you interact with the client.

Implementation

Role-Play

You have probably discovered through your experience with the role-plays in this text that you need only specify a few performance parameters in order to embark on an effective role-play. Scenes that are heavily scripted or rehearsed tend to come off as more rigid and lack the spontaneity that one would normally encounter in a natural dialogue setting. Consider selecting a role-play exercise from this book or invite the person playing the client to surprise you with an issue of his or her choosing. The story line of the role-play may be fictitious, based on actual events, or some blend thereof.

Aim for a duration of about 15 minutes. A simple timer can be useful. Alternatively, you may want to use a clock positioned off camera within your line of sight. Just before beginning the role-play, set the clock to 5:45. Hence, when the clock reaches 6:00, you know that 15 minutes have elapsed without having to be distracted with time calculations.

Debriefing

At the end of the role-play, stop the recording. Before reviewing the video, take some time to debrief. Consider using the same debriefing protocol specified in the section "Guidelines for Implementing Role-Play Exercises" (p. xiii). Compared with the role-plays offered thus far, this is a longer performance involving potentially multiple skills and issues; hence, consider allowing some extra time for the debriefing.

Self-Evaluation Guidelines

Begin by reviewing the recording solo. Later, if you wish, you may choose to ask a colleague to review all or parts of the role-play with you to solicit feedback from another point of view.

It is recommended that you assemble a brief report detailing your observations of the sessions. The following guidelines may provide a useful template to systematically assess your performance. This written portion of the exercise will facilitate your critical review and also serve as an inventory of your evolving skills, detailing proficiencies and areas for further development.

Section I: Characteristics of the Client

- Describe the client's attributes (name, gender, approximate age, cultural background, initial demeanor, presenting problem, etc.).

Section II: Goals of the Interview

- What was your initial goal of the interview?
- Did this concur with the client's goal?
- As the interview progressed, did other goals emerge?

Section III: Skills Used
(Complete this section detailing your use of three to five different skills)

- Reason for selecting the skill
- Example of the use of the skill
- Client's response
- Effectiveness of the skill
- Missed opportunities
- How might the interview have been different?

Section IV: Overall Impression of the Interview

- Goal achievement
- Quality of therapist-client relationship
- Flow of the interview (tempo, pauses)
- Use of body language or anomalous movements
- Interviewing skill strengths
- Interviewing skills which have shown improvement
- Areas for continued improvement
- Plan for improving interviewing skills
- Thoughts and feelings regarding evolving interviewing proficiency

Overview of
Appendixes A, B, and C

Skill Integration

Thus far, for purposes of clarity, the clinical communication skills have been demonstrated in the form of brief dialogues, primarily focusing on only one skill at a time. In order to see these skills integrated in a more natural context, Appendixes A, B, and C contain transcriptions of three 50-minute sessions consisting of Weeks 1, 5, and 10, exemplifying the beginning, middle, and end of a short-term therapy model.

Short-Term Therapy

Short-term therapy, typically consisting of 1 to 20 sessions, with an average of about 6 sessions, emerged in the early 1960s as a therapeutic alternative to the more lengthy mainstream psychoanalytic methods of the time (Bloom, 1997). Short-term therapy should not be confused with crisis intervention therapy. The primary goal of crisis therapy is to restore the client to his or her precrisis state, whereas longer-term therapy promotes the development and implementation of new skills that enable the client to address his or her problem(s) and advance beyond the baseline state (Wells, 1994).

Short-term therapy can be characterized by four components: (1) *planning*—identifying specific problems and their corresponding goals, (2) *collaboration*—fostering a therapeutic alliance, (3) *timing*—prompt and focused therapeutic efforts to be executed during and between sessions, (4) *empowerment*—proactively engaging the client to embark on solving or growth efforts (Eckert, 1993).

In terms of efficacy, research has revealed that significant progress can be made in as few as the first three sessions. Improvement tends to be the greatest in the early sessions of therapy (Barkham, 1989). It has also been shown that longer-term therapy does carry greater improvement, but with diminishing returns over time (Howard, Kopta, Krause, & Orlinsky, 1986), and that therapeutic gains tend to endure regardless of the duration of the therapy (Lambert & Ogles, 2004; Nicholas & Berman, 1983).

Termination

Termination, though ultimately common to all forms of human contact, is endemically embedded in the practice of short-term therapy. Some forms of short-term therapy can specify a predetermined number of sessions to accomplish the task at hand, essentially putting a positive motivational spin on the therapy, the implication being that the therapist, a knowledgeable figure, shares with the client the expectation that a positive outcome is achievable within the designated time frame (Garfield, 1989).

Though a predictable phase of the therapeutic process, termination is not without emotional threads. As the therapeutic relationship is built, both the client and the therapist typically develop a sense of the other person. This may consist of feelings such as admiration, pride, or enjoyment of the other person; hence, finalization of the therapeutic relationship can represent a mutual loss for both the client and the therapist (Leigh, 1998). The process of therapeutic termination itself can be considered a valuable growth opportunity, enabling the client to master skills for coping effectively with the many endings that one inevitably faces throughout the course of life (Maholick & Turner, 1979). To avoid termination coming as a devastating surprise, the transcriptions in these appendixes demonstrate that termination is not reserved solely for the concluding minutes of the final session. To the contrary, notice that termination is addressed beginning in the very first session and progressively occupies more of the session time as the end of the therapeutic term approaches. Such discussions provide the opportunity for incrementally citing progress accomplished to date, feelings associated with the progress, the work that is to be done, the amount of time left to do it, and the pending termination of the therapeutic relationship.

Appendix A

Session With Dusty—Week 1: Initial Session

Th: *Hello. I'm Dr. Knapp.*

Introduction (in waiting area)

Cl: *Oh, hi. I'm Dusty.*

Th: *You're right on time. I'm glad you could make it. Please come in.* [They enter the office. The therapist closes the door, sits down, and gestures to the seats available. This allows the client to select a seating position that suits his or her distance comfort.]

Rapport, Nonverbal cue

Cl: *Okay.*

Th: *Do you prefer to be called "Dusty," or some other name?*

Rapport

Cl: *"Dusty's" fine. Everyone calls me "Dusty."*

Th: *Okay, Dusty. Did you have any trouble finding the office?*

Rapport

Cl: *No, no, the directions were very clear.*

Th: *Okay, good. I see from your paperwork that this is your first time in therapy.*

Start where the client is

Cl: *Yeah, first time ever.*

Th: First time ever. Did you have any questions before we get started?

Reflection, Open-ended question

Cl: Ummm, yeah. So, the limit is, what, 10 sessions?

Th: Your benefits specify a maximum of 10 sessions. We can evaluate as we approach 10, and if necessary, it looks like we can apply for an extension of up to 2 more sessions.

Informing

Cl: Sounds pretty short.

Th: Short-term therapy is a fairly common model these days. We'll go for 10 sessions and see how things go. Lots of people can accomplish some meaningful stuff in 10 sessions.

Informing

Cl: Okay, that's good to know. [Pause] Also, something else. One of the forms on the clipboard that I signed . . . it said something about limitations on confidentiality. I'm not sure I got all that. Just how much of what we say here is really confidential?

Th: Yes, let's go over that. [Therapist reviews the client's copy of the document] This paragraph states that the issues discussed in therapy will remain confidential, that nothing you say here will be disclosed except as mandated by law.

Informing

Cl: Okay, that's this part [Client points to the document] about if I was a risk to myself or others, or if I was abusing a kid or someone elderly . . . then legally, you'd have to report me.

Th: Correct.

Informing

Cl: But like if I told you something like that I was . . . having an affair or cheated on my taxes then you couldn't tell that?

Th: That's right.

Informing

Cl: *So if, say, my boss called up and wanted to know how things were going here, you'd say . . .*

Th: *I'd say: "I can neither confirm nor deny any knowledge of Dusty."*
Informing

Cl: *Really?*

Th: *Really.*
Reflecting, Brief verbal

Cl: *And if he wanted to know more?*

Th: *If he wanted to know more, I would tell him that legally, I cannot have any further conversation with him without written consent signed by the individual in question. And then I would end the call.*
Reflecting, Informing

Cl: *Wow. Okay. Well, seeing as I'm not a child molester and I haven't beaten anyone up, and I'm not suicidal, [Laughs] I guess I'm on good ground here.*

Th: [Smiles] *Sounds like it.* [Pause] *Did you have any other questions at this time?*
Open-ended question

Cl: *No. I'm okay with that. I guess it makes sense. It's just that I've never been in therapy before, so this is all new to me, so I just . . . I guess I just wanted to know how all this works . . . make sure that all of this is . . . okay.*

Th: [Nods] *Mm-hmm. It's important for you to know how this works, especially where confidentiality begins and ends. There's some more details here* [Points to form]. *This copy of the informed consent form is yours to keep. If any other questions come to mind later, you can always ask.*
Brief verbal, Reflecting, Informing

Cl: *Okay. That's good to know.*

Th: [Smiles and nods] *Okay.* [Pause] *Where would you like to begin?*
Start where the client is

Cl: *Well, um,* [Pause] *I've just been really stressed out lately. I haven't been sleeping too well.*

Th: *Uh-huh.*
Brief verbal

Cl: *Umm . . . [Pause] I don't really know where to begin.*

Th: *When did you start feeling stressful?*
Specificity

Cl: [Laughs] *hmmm, uh.* [Laughs]

Th: *I see in your paperwork that you mentioned a problem sleeping. When did you first notice the change in your sleep?*
Re-asking a question

Cl: *It's been within the last few months, um, ever since I went back to school.*

Th: *You went back to school?*
Reflection

Cl: *Uh, right. I got my associate's degree about 12 years ago and my career opportunities seem to be limited without a bachelor's degree, so I decided to go back.*

Th: *What prompted your decision to go back?*
Furthering

Cl: *Unemployment.* [Laughs]

Th: *That could do it.*
Brief verbal

Cl: *Yeah.*

Th: *What kind of work were you doing?*
Specificity

Cl: *Um, mostly unskilled office stuff.*

Th: *Uh-huh.*
Brief verbal

Cl: *Not anything that had much opportunity for advancement in terms of position or even salary.*

Th: *I'm curious: Was there lack of work, or were you unsatisfied with it?*
Close-ended question

Cl: *Both.*

Th: *Both. Okay. And so you made the decision to go back to school.*
Reflection, Summarizing

Cl: *Right.*

Th: *Uh-huh. How has that been?*
Open-ended question

Cl: *Well, uh, it's a little scary. I mean I'm older now, old enough to be the parent of some of these younger students.*

Th: *It sounds like being among a younger population makes you feel a little out of place?*
Empathy

Cl: *I feel out of place, yes. I mean, there are some students my age, and some even older than me, and that . . . that helps, but it's still very odd.*

Th: *And that makes sense, because in terms of age, you are something of a minority there.*
Validation

Cl: *Yes, definitely.*

Th: *Did you go straight into the university?*
Close-ended question

Cl: *No, I actually took a few courses at the community college level first, just to get my feet wet and see if this would be something that I could do. So, but I did very well in those classes. Um, I got A's, so I figure it was just time to make the leap.*

Th: *Mm-hmm.*
Brief verbal

Cl: *So I applied, I was accepted, now I'm in it and it's a little [Laughs] . . . I'm nervous, I guess. My first midterms are coming up, and it's been some restless nights.*

Th: *School's a big job.*

Validation

Cl: *Yes.* [Laughs] *Very much so.*

Th: *Do you feel that you're able to keep up with the assignments?*

Close-ended question

Cl: *Um, yes.* [Pause] *I just have trouble just getting myself to start the big projects.*

Th: *Could you give me an example of a big project?*

Specificity

Cl: *Yes. For instance in one of my research classes I'm taking, there's a 15-page paper due at the end, and in a couple weeks, we have a 5-page paper due. Um, at least the 15-page paper isn't due all at once, but the 5-page paper . . . it feels perhaps like it's a bigger project than it really is, but my mind seems to be inflating the size of some of these things, so it's* [Pause] *I guess that's why I'm nervous . . . about all this.*

Th: *When you talk about it, you sound nervous.*

Empathy

Cl: *Yeah.* [Laughs] *Because it's new. I'm . . . don't know if I'm just hung up on the age thing . . . maybe I . . . maybe that's something I . . .*

Th: *It sounds like there's more than one thing going on in terms of school: The regular stress of keeping up with the demands of each course—attending the courses, homework, readings, papers, presentations, plus being a minority in terms of the age.*

Summarizing

Cl: *Yeah.*

Th: *Any one of those can be stressful, and here they are combined.*

Validation, Normalizing

Cl: *That sounds about right.*

Th: *I'm just curious: If you could have either of those solved, which would you rather have go away, the age difference or the workload?*

Close-ended question

Cl: [Silence]

Th: *. . . to be among peers your own age, or a reduction in the course work?*
Re-asking a question

Cl: *Well, the lazy side speaking, I guess I would go for the work load.* [Laughs]
*Uh, then again, if I decreased my workload, and take fewer classes, then it just
prolongs this whole experience. I mean, I'm looking at 2 . . . 2$^1/_2$ years to get
my bachelor's degree, but if I take fewer classes at a time, then I'm looking at
maybe 3 or 4 years and I don't know that I really want to . . .*

Th: *How many units are you taking right now?*
Close-ended question

Cl: *Twelve.*

Th: *Twelve.*
Reflection

Cl: *Just enough to be full-time.*

Th: *Twelve* is *a full-time student.*
Validation

Cl: *It's busy.*

Th: *That* is *a full load.*
Validation

Cl: *I also qualify for the student loan, and the financial aid, so . . . which
helps. . . . It takes a little bit of the stress off that I have the extra money coming in to keep me available to do this.*

Th: *Sure. Sure. School is a very consuming project; the money's helpful in that the
more hours you don't have to work, the more hours you can use for school.*
Summarizing

Cl: *Right.* [Silence]

Th: *What else is going on in your life?*
Open-ended question

Cl: *Well, in order to do this . . . in order to do this, I had to give up my independence—my apartment, . . . and I moved in with my parents.*
Underlying problem

Th: *You moved in with your parents?*
Reflection

Cl: *Right.*

Th: *I noticed on your information sheet, in the family information section, that you list your mother is living local, and your father lives in another state.*
Confronting

Cl: *Oh, right. Yes, my father does live in another state. [Laughs] I'm living with my mother and* stepfather. *My father and me, well, we don't have much to do with each other, . . . but that's a whole other story. I just refer to my stepfather as my father. It's just easier and less distant. I mean, he's a good guy. . . . I mean, he really is part of the family.*

Th: *Okay. That makes sense. I get it. What's it like living with your parents?*
Open-ended question

Cl: *[Laughs] Well, they're in their late 50s and, ya know, early 60s now, and I'm in my 30s, so it feels like we're maybe all too old for this arrangement, but they're supportive. . . .*

Th: *Uh-huh.*
Brief verbal

Cl: *I'm not sent to my room like a child would be, but I do find myself going in there and closing the door a lot. . . .*

Th: *Uh- huh.*
Brief verbal

Cl: *[Laughs] . . . just, just to not be around them . . . um, perhaps to hang out with them in the front room would be too much of a reminder that [Laughs] I'm a 30-something person living like a teenager or a 20-something.*

Th: *When you talk about your parents, it looks like you've withdrawn a bit. Your arms are folded, your shoulders are hunched together. You seem to draw in a bit.*
Observational cues

Cl: *Yeah, well, it's . . . it's not that easy to talk about things. . . . Well, it's just not that easy to talk to them. Um, my mother, in particular . . . is not easy. My dad . . . stepdad, really . . . he's pretty easy going . . . um, although we've never been so close to where I'm divulging . . . ya know . . . uh . . . deep dark secrets to him, or anything, but my mother has a very hard time dealing with specific details about my life. She tends to get agitated or judgmental or upset very easily, and I find myself filtering what I tell her anyway.*

Th: *So you find you have a more open communication with your stepdad than your mother?*
      Reflection

Cl: [Pause] [Proceeds slowly] *Yes and no, although I do limit what I tell him as well.*

Th: [Nods]
      Nonverbal attending

Cl: *Just perhaps in a less neurotic way, I guess.*

Th: *When you talk about the difference between what you would converse with your mother about, compared to what you would converse with your stepfather about, give me an example of a topic or an issue that would be a "stepfather" thing that wouldn't be a "mom" thing.*
      Specificity

Cl: *Uh . . . my mother's smoking. She smokes like a chimney. She always has, and she always will. She at least doesn't smoke in the house, and that's a relief, uh, but it bothers me that she smokes at all. She constantly smells like cigarettes. It's tough to be around her.*

Th: *So it's hard to tolerate the presence of a smoker?*
      Interpreting

Cl: *Right.*

Th: *But getting back to what I asked you before: You mentioned that there are certain things that you withhold from discussing with your mother, more so than what you withhold from your stepfather. Can you think of a specific example . . . maybe something that happened recently, that you conferred with your stepfather about but not your mom?*
      Re-asking a question

Cl: [Pause] *Um, simple everyday activities . . . I won't give her as much details as I'd give him.*

Th: *Mm-hmm.*
Brief verbal

Cl: *Like if I'm going out to meet some friends for dinner or whatever, I usually am more forthcoming with him about that than I am with her.*

Th: *What is it about his way that makes it easier for you to be more forthcoming with him than with your mother?*
Specificity

Cl: *Because when my friends do come around, which is hardly ever . . . since I moved in with them, I can count three times. Seriously, in a little over a year . . .* [Laughs] *three times, um, when people come over to the place, and they both tend to hover around the person like they're very curious about this person in Dusty's life. . . . Ya know, like they're finally getting to see someone that I interact with outside their home. They're both very curious, but my mom is exceptionally super nice and super sweet. . . . She's trying very hard to win this person over, but my stepdad, he's more easy going. He's not trying to be their best friend. My mother's trying to be supermom, or something, like one of those implausible TV sitcom moms, and she goes a little overboard and I can't stand watching it. . . . It makes me ill, because I know that's not really her.*

Th: *Who is the real "her"?*
Specificity

Cl: *The real her? It's not super nice and sweet. I mean, I wouldn't say she's a shrew, but the real . . . the real her curses, and isn't all nice and refined and "let's have tea"* [Laughs] *and what-not. . . . She's no TV mom. . . .* [Laughs]

Th: *Nobody is. . . . That's all fake anyway.*
Validation

Cl: *Right.*

Th: *It sounds like this "artificial mom" performance makes you feel uncomfortable.*
Empathy (speculative)

Cl: *Definitely. Most definitely.*

bere's a certain stress at home . . . an adult living at home. It sounds like
: are some forgone privileges. You mentioned that you have a room of
own. . . .
Summarizing

Cl: *I do have a room of my own with a door I can shut.*

Th: *I'm guessing you keep the door shut often?*
Close-ended question

Cl: *When I'm in there, yeah. And even when I'm not, actually.*

Th: *So privacy is important to you.*
Summarizing

Cl: *Very much so.*

Th: *Now before you went back to school, you were living independently?*
Redirecting

Cl: *Yeah, I had lived alone for 5 years.*

Th: *And what was it like living alone compared to living with your parents?*
Open-ended question

Cl: *I could come and go as I pleased, any time of the day. I didn't have to check
in with anyone. I didn't have to answer to anyone. [Pause] I didn't have to
worry about disturbing anyone . . . coming in late at night.*

Th: *So there was a sense of independence there. . . .*
Summarizing

Cl: *Definitely. Definitely.*

Th: *. . . and not having to explain yourself . . .*
Prompting

Cl: *. . . not having to explain myself [Pause] . . . not having to worry about am
I going to be questioned about why I got home so late.*

Th: *The freedom.*
Summarizing

Cl: *Thank you! Yes.*

Th: *Yeah. So that's a source of stress.*

Interpreting

Cl: *It's not something I think about every day but now that you mention it, it's . . . it's . . . it's just something's really always there.*

Th: *Mm-hmm.*

Brief verbal

Cl: *I suppose that since the time I moved in with them I've gotten used to it in a way . . .*

Th: *Mm-hmm.*

Brief verbal

Cl: *. . . but it's still not fun.* [Laughs]

Th: *As an adult, there's things that we want to do, and nobody can explain all of the small things that they do that might be seen as peculiar by someone else. It may be hard knowing that you're being monitored on a day-to-day basis . . .*

Normalizing

Cl: *Right.*

Th: *. . . where before, it sounds like you were freer to be more spontaneous.*

Summarizing

Cl: *Yeah, it definitely felt more spontaneous when I was living in the apartment by myself.* [Pause] *The other thing . . .* [Laughs] *the other thing is I have cats, and I brought them all with me and my mother, and my stepfather, but mostly my mother, have adopted them as their own . . . unofficially. My mother has beaten me, on a consistent basis, to feeding them.*

Th: *How do you mean?*

Clarification

Cl: *She takes it upon herself to feed them, give them fresh water, and . . .* [Pause]

Th: *What do you think the motivation is?*

Open-ended question, Specificity

Cl: *Well, she knows . . . she thinks . . . well, I'm not married, and I'm an only child, and I've decided I'm never going to have kids, so perhaps she thinks this is the only version of grandchildren she'll ever get to experience. But sometimes it feels as if my territory has been invaded.*

Th: *They used to come to you for care, feeding, affection, attention. . . .*
Summarizing

Cl: *They still do because they've been with me so long, but it almost feels like she's trying to infiltrate my position.* [Laughs]

Th: *It sounds like you miss the role of caretaking for your cats.*
Interpreting

Cl: *Ya, I don't feel like I want to share that.*

Th: *Being their parent, as it were.*
Interpreting

Cl: *Right, right.*

Th: *And it feels like that space has been invaded; part of your role has been absorbed by your mother.*
Interpreting

Cl: *Right.*

Th: *Without your . . .*
Prompting

Cl: *. . . consent*

Th: *. . . and that's a loss to you.*
Empathy

Cl: [Laughs] *Yeah.*

Th: *I get it. Have you talked to her about this?*
Close-ended question

Cl: *Not in depth. She tried buying the cat litter, and she got the wrong kind . . . two times in a row, and was . . . I tried not to sound as angry as I was, because*

. . . because even as the words were coming out of my mouth: 'Why did you buy this? You know that I buy this.' I knew that this was perhaps a little neurotic. . . . I guess I was feeling very self-conscious that I was angry about this . . . um . . .

Th: *. . . and that gets back to something you mentioned earlier: That you're not as forthcoming with your mother as your stepfather, and even with your stepfather, it sounds like you subtract off a lot of information.*

Returning

Cl: *Right. A lot of editing.*

Th: *A lot of editing.* [Pause] *If you were at an editing console . . .*

Reflecting, Focusing

Cl: [Laughs] *Okay . . .*

Th: *. . . and cutting the film of your life that your mother would view in the screening room . . .*

Cl: [Laughs]

Th: *. . . what percentage of film do you think would be left on the cutting-room floor?*

Close-ended question

Cl: *Hmm . . .* [Pause] *Probably about 95%.*

Th: *That's a lot of editing.*

Interpreting

Cl: [Laughs] *Yes it is!*

Th: *And how much film would be on the floor for the version that your stepfather sees?*

Close-ended question

Cl: *Mmm . . . anywhere between 90 and 95% . . . somewhere in there . . . about 90%.*

Th: *So he gets the "edited for television" version too?*

Interpreting

Cl: [Laughs] *Yes.*

Th: *That's a lot to subtract out.*
Interpreting

Cl: [Sadly] *Yeah.*

Th: *That's a lot of secrets to keep.*
Interpreting

Cl: *Yeah, it does feel like I'm keeping a lot of secrets. It's just that I want my privacy.*

Th: *And you're entitled to all the secrets that you want to keep. I'm thinking that working to guard all that information is one of the causes of the stress that you've been experiencing.*
Validating, Interpreting

Cl: *How do you mean?*

Th: *Well, for every secret, that's information that you have to keep tabs on. That's information that can't get out. For every item locked away, there's an associated anxiety: "What if this secret were to get out?"*
Interpreting

Cl: *I see. Yes. Definitely.*

Th: *That's a far leap from living independently.*
Summarizing

Cl: *Right, I didn't have to think about editing myself for anybody. . . . The cats didn't care.*

Th: *Exactly. You didn't have to justify or hide anything or worry about what might happen if something were revealed; you could just be. Tell me about some of the things that you had the privilege to do when you were living alone that you can't do, or it's difficult to do living with your parents.*
Interpreting, Specificity

Cl: *Have overnight guests!* [Laughs]

Th: *You don't think they would approve of that?*
Furthering

Cl: *I would feel extremely awkward, so I haven't even tried.*

Th: *Was having an overnight guest something you did very often?*
Close-ended question

Cl: No, *because most of the time I valued my own privacy to the extent of . . . I didn't really want that many people staying over especially if, ya know,* [Begins pounding fist on chair] *you meet somebody new and you're gonna fool around . . .* [Pause] *and somebody new . . . I wouldn't want someone staying around until daybreak anyway, I don't think.*

Th: Mm-hmm.
Brief verbal

Cl: *But, I just . . . I guess I'm just mostly a loaner. . . .*

Th: Mm-hmm.
Brief verbal

Cl: *. . . in that regard.* [Stops pounding fist on chair] *I mean, I do like to socialize, but . . .*

Th: *Socialize? How?*
Specificity

Cl: *Well, I belong to a bowling league.*

Th: *A bowling league?*
Reflection

Cl: *Yeah.*

Th: *How long have you been bowling?*
Close-ended question

Cl: *Oh, a few years. A friend got me involved. It's fun. You've got your friends on the team. Then there's all the people on the other teams. I like this league because it's friendly for the most part. Everyone cheers when you get a strike, no matter what team you're on, so I like that. It's fun. Feels good. Anyway, it sort of sprouted me into this whole other social thing.*

Th: *So that gets you out of the house . . .*
Prompting

Cl: *It gets me out of the house. It's fun to do on weekends . . .*

Th: *Do you still bowl?*
      Close-ended question

Cl: *I still bowl.*

Th: *What's your average?*
      Close-ended question

Cl: *170 . . . around 150 on a bad night.* [Laughs]

Th: *Not bad. So that's something that you can still do even under the watchful eye of family life.*
      Validation, Reframing

Cl: *Right. But there's still a lot of stuff at home that I don't feel comfortable with, like I'm not comfortable inviting those friends over just to hang out like I was before. I used to host regular parties at my place, you know, every couple months, you know. I'd just have friends come over and play board games. It was very simple stuff, and it was a lot of fun, but I wouldn't feel comfortable doing that now. I mean, my parents go to bed at 7:00, even on the weekends.*

Th: *So it sounds like your freedoms have been trimmed down in exchange for returning to school.*
      Generalizing

Cl: [Pause] *Right.*

Th: *This is quite a dedication to a higher mission: that you're willing to give up the independence of living alone, . . . all the privileges and freedoms that go with it to advance to a future with a more satisfying potential. I think that speaks a lot to your character.*
      Validation

Cl: [Silence]

Th: *Immediate gratification is always an option, but you're choosing to forgo that in favor of something bigger, something more important down the line in the future . . . something more substantial.*
      Validation

Cl: *Well, in a way, I kinda had no choice.*

Th: *Well, you always have a choice.*
Confronting

Cl: *Well, the idea of going back to school had been there for years . . . ever since I bowed out. But there was no real incentive to do so, ya know. I was living on my own. I had a nice comfortable day-to-day existence. The only way to get my feet moving again was to lose that sense of comfort . . .*

Th: *Mm-hmm.*
Brief verbal

Cl: *. . . so, perhaps, I . . . I have that as an incentive.*

Th: *I guess what I'm saying is that it seems to me that your mission is commendable, in that when people are unsatisfied, very often, they'll sit and just continue to be unsatisfied—they may complain, but maybe take no action. There are a variety of ways to alleviate a feeling of dissatisfaction or unhappiness. Some people shoot drugs; some people spend compulsively; there's any number of unhealthy, self-destructive things that people can reach for when their lives are not as satisfying as they'd like. None of these activities really address the problem at hand, the dissatisfaction. Now, what I'm hearing here, is that you're willing to suspend some of the immediate gratification and invest in a more rewarding, fulfilling future.*
Reframing, Validation

Cl: [Silence]

Th: *Just to review: You've willingly forfeited some of your freedom, some of your independence, some of your privacy, and taken on a mission that is genuinely challenging, consuming, doesn't pay very well . . .*
Summarizing

Cl: [Laughs] *. . . it's a little scary too.*

Th: *. . . it's a little scary too, and somewhat socially uncomfortable being around peers who aren't quite your age. And even with all that, you are still showing the motivation and dedication to proceed. That's pretty commendable.*
Reflection, Empathy, Validation

Cl: *It's hard to take compliments* [Laughs] *but thank you.*

Th: *You're not used to compliments?*
Close-ended question

Cl: Not really. Not that I never get them, . . . it's just that it never seems to feel like a perfect fit.

Th: Where do your compliments typically come from?
Furthering

Cl: [Pause] I don't know. [Pause] I don't know.

Th: Where do they not come from?
Furthering

Cl: [Pause] I feel like I should have an answer for that, but I don't.

Th: It's okay. Maybe that's going to take a little thought. Maybe it's going to take a little feeling.
Empathy

Cl: [Laughs] I think so.

Th: It's okay; we can get back to that later. How are you feeling right now?
Open-ended question

Cl: Umm . . . [Pause, sighs] a little more relaxed. [Pause] Uh . . .

Th: There's no wrong answer here.
Prompting

Cl: [Laughs] I know, I'm trying really hard to search. [Pause] Well, I feel more relaxed. I guess I feel a little better about myself than when I first walked in here.

Th: What feels lighter?
Specificity

Cl: Well, I wasn't quite sure how this was going to go [Pause] or what I should say [Laughs] or how I should say it.

Th: You're doing fine.
Validation

Cl: Okay [Laughs] thanks!

Th: I'm curious: If you could have one wish right now, what would you take?
Open-ended question

Cl: Oh, you mean aside from the winning lottery numbers?

Th: Okay. [Therapist theatrically snaps fingers] You now have the winning lottery numbers. Now what?
Specificity

Cl: [Laughs] Wow, thanks! Now get back in your bottle! [Both laugh]

Th: Well?
Prompting

Cl: Okay. Tuition.

Th: Financial help would be useful.
Reflection

Cl: Financial help would be useful. It would be wonderful if I could live on my own again while I do this, but I also doubt whether or not I would be as fueled to get through this program quickly and get my degree.

Th: So it sounds like living in some social discomfort with your parents acts like something of an academic motivator . . . to get through school expeditiously, shortening your time with them. It's interesting that you chose the financial help which would enable you to live independently to continue the educational mission. Notice how you didn't wish for a degree.
Summarizing, Challenging

Cl: Oh.

Th: As if a genie-granted degree wouldn't provide you with the educational experience and personal and professional growth that you seem to be craving.
Interpreting

Cl: Right. The lottery money wouldn't change my mission. It would just make it a little easier to be a student. [Pause] I'm wanting to do this because most of the jobs I've held over the past 10 to 15 years have been [Pause] well, boring and unchallenging. At least they weren't challenging in an intellectual way or an emotional way.

Th: You wanted to be able to use more of who you are?
Interpreting

Cl: Exactly. [Pause] Yeah! Exactly.

Th: *And that wasn't happening in those positions?*
Generalizing

Cl: *No. I had one job that came close a few years ago.*

Th: *Mm-hmm. What was that job?*
Specificity

Cl: [Pause] *I worked in a funeral home.*

Th: *You worked in a funeral home?*
Reflection

Cl: *Yes. It was . . .* [Laughs] *. . . I worked in a funeral home.*

Th: *What did you do in the funeral home?*
Specificity

Cl: [Laughs] *Well, it was just an office assistant type . . . secretarial job, but . . .* [Silence]

Th: *Did you deal with the public?*
Close-ended question

Cl: *A little bit. I worked with the public and the office staff . . . both. I dealt with the public, and I dealt with the funeral directors, and those people.*

Th: *What made this position more satisfying than the others?*
Specificity

Cl: *I was doing something that actually mattered.*

Th: *Mm-hmm.*
Brief verbal

Cl: *That we were dealing on a day-to-day basis with a subject that people are in deep denial about anyway.* [Pause] *There was nothing . . .* [Pause] *it was the most* [Pause] *honest work that I ever did.*

Th: *Honest?*
Prompting

Cl: [Pause] *The . . . well, the death care industry is . . .* [Pause] *it's like this was the first job in which I was part of a team, or even individually making a real difference in someone else's life. I'd never felt that before.*

Th: *Your other jobs haven't provided you with that?*
Generalizing

Cl: *No. I mean, I worked for an insurance company, and the sole purpose there is for them to make money, at least that's how I perceived it then.*

Th: *So was that more of a paper-pushing job?*
Clarification

Cl: *Just moving papers around.*

Th: *Got it.*
Brief verbal

Cl: *In other jobs, it was just customer service, listening to people's petty complaints.*

Th: *I'm curious: In returning to school, do you have a particular goal in mind? A particular career pathway you've been thinking about?*
Specificity

Cl: *Well, I thought I wanted to go into teaching . . .*

Th: [Nods]
Nonverbal attending

Cl: *. . . that was an aspiration of mine when I was younger, but . . .* [Pause]

Th: *Teaching at what level?*
Specificity

Cl: *High school, middle school. Well, maybe more high school. I'm not really that comfortable around young . . . young, hyper children.*

Th: *And it sounds like your decision has evolved?*
Open-ended question

Cl: *Uh, yeah, that's a good way to put it.* [Sigh] *Like I said, teaching was an aspiration of mine when I was younger. Anyway, I have a few friends who are teaching and I've spent a lot of time talking to them, and what I'm seeing is that right now, and recently, the climate for teachers seems to have been gradually getting worse and worse, in terms of pay, benefits, bureaucracy, working conditions, et cetera, et cetera, and I don't know that I have the stomach to deal with all that.*

Th: *Mm-hmm.*

Brief verbal

Cl: *So even though I do want to get my degree in history, since I love history, I love the study of the way things change over time, . . . I've always liked that . . . I'm just not sure I can use that degree toward something other than teaching. I don't want to pigeonhole myself.*

Th: *How do you mean?*

Specificity

Cl: *I don't want to pigeonhole myself with a degree in something as specific as that, just as I don't like that I've already pigeonholed myself by not having a degree.*

Th: *Right. To speak to that point, you understand that holding a bachelor's degree is not the same as a technical school. Someone who goes to technical school to repair refrigeration units is pigeonholed to repair refrigerators and air conditioners and that's pretty much it. The basis of the university degree is, as you know, the general education, plus the emphasis in a particular subject. Many people recognize the university degree as signifying that this is a person who has the capacity to take on a large project and come out the other end. If nothing else, it's a demonstration of competency and dedication. Lots of people will believe in that as a preferable, employable person: you've proven yourself.*

Validation, Informing

Cl: *That makes sense.*

Th: *It sounds like you've already come to terms with the notion that it's important to you to earn a history degree, whether history is going to be the focal point of your career or not.*

Summarizing

Cl: *Right! Because I already learned, firsthand, that not having the degree closes a lot of doors for me.*

Th: Mm-hmm. *What kind of doors would you like to see pop open?*
Specificity

Cl: *Hmm.* [Sigh] [Pause]

Th: *Rub a lamp!*
Prompting

Cl: [Laughs] *Well . . .* [Long pause]

Th: *It's okay if you don't know that right now. That might be something you'll want to spend some time thinking about.*
Normalizing

Cl: *Yeah.* [Pause] *I don't really know. I thought . . . at different points in my life, I have thought of going into human resources. I seriously even tried a couple of times to get human resource assistant jobs, hoping that would lead into something else, but to even get beyond the assistant position, you would have to have a bachelor's degree in something,* [Fist pounding chair] *most preferably, human resource management . . .*

Th: Mm-hmm.
Brief verbal

Cl: *. . . or business management. I didn't have that, so I didn't spend too much time in my life fussing over that one goal. That would be another goal that I would be willing to revisit, and I actually have given it some thought. I just don't know if a history degree will get me there, if that's ultimately where I decide I'm better off being.* [Stops pounding fist] *Because I know that in human resources, you wouldn't be doing the same thing as teaching, but you would kind of be helping people find their way in . . . you know . . . some fashion. You're helping match people with jobs. You know, I worked retail management for a while, and even though that was grueling, low-paying, and thankless, uh, hiring new people and training them and seeing them take on this new job and grow into their new position was gratifying. You know, helping them . . .*

Th: *Right. One of the recurring themes I keep hearing is your passion to work with and help people.*
Summarizing

Cl: *Yeah, I suppose I . . . yeah, okay. I . . . I guess the funeral home was where I really started to feel that for myself.*

Th: *People at their most vulnerable point.*
Interpreting

Cl: [Softly] *Definitely.*

Th: *People who have a lot of needs that have to be met in a timely and efficient manner. People who needed special handling . . . and you were there . . .*
Interpreting

Cl: *. . . even in the limited capacity that I was . . .*

Th: *. . . even in the limited capacity that you were, you report that as being the most gratifying employment experience you ever had. This suggests a propensity for wanting to help. What I'm thinking is you kind of stalled on the "What do you want to be when you grow up?" question, and that's okay because we don't need an answer before midnight tonight.*
Reflection, Summarizing, Validation

Cl: [Laughs]

Th: *I'm starting to wonder if it might be a good idea to confer with the university career guidance counselor to do some talking, and maybe some diagnostic testing, and see what kinds of recommendations they can provide. You already know you like to work with people; it sounds like you don't want to be a "cubicle and calculator" employee.*
Advising

Cl: *Each job that I've had that was like that was increasingly difficult to deal with* [Pounds fist on chair] *and I ended up staying at those jobs shorter and shorter.* [Stops pounding fist on chair]

Th: *It sounds like a pattern's emerging. It sounds like you're coming to identify what your talents are, and with anyone, that's the beginning. A simple template: Find out what you naturally have a flair for and get some education and training so you can grow in that direction—your direction—and you'll just get great at it. So, it sounds to me like you're on your way. You've identified where you shine, and the question now is, "Who is going to have the privilege of you?"*
Generalizing

Cl: [Pause] *Right now it's just my four walls and a closed door.*

Th: *For now. But there is a future down the line. Where you won't be living with your parents. Where you will be at the end of this phase of your academic education. Where you will have the privilege to work with people in a more meaningful way. Is this something that sounds plausible to you?*

Validation, Normalizing, Close-ended question

Cl: *It sounds definitely like something I want. I suppose I'm not 100% convinced of its plausibility. Maybe because I haven't seen it yet?*

Th: *Well, it's not there yet. Do you think that's something you want to work toward?*

Close-ended question

Cl: *Most definitely.*

Th: *I'm not here to read your future; I'm just trying to connect the dots that you're presenting.*

Clarification

Cl: *Hmm.*

Th: *Does this sound reasonable?*

Close-ended question

Cl: *Yeah.*

Th: *Something else that strikes me: I'm feeling some low self-esteem, or some lack of self-confidence. Is that something that you see?*

Empathy

Cl: [Sigh] [Pause] *Yeah.* [Pause] *Uh.* [Pause] [Sigh] *Haven't had much luck in the dating department, and being the age that I am, and feeling that I'm just behind in life . . . you mentioned the "not knowing what you want to be when you grow up." I feel like I've already grown up and still not figured out the answer to that question. I feel like I'm running behind.*

Th: *Running behind?*

Prompting

Cl: *Yeah.*

Th: *What are your peers doing?*
Open-ended question

Cl: *Uh.* [Pause] *Well, some are married, some have kids. A lot of them have kids or have been in relationships or they're at least financially independent, and you know, even if they're single, they're living on their own, or maybe they have a roommate and at least they're living the life of an adult. . . .*

Th: *Their careers are in progress?*
Summarizing

Cl: *Their careers are in progress . . . some don't care . . .*

Th: *School is behind them?*
Summarizing (speculatively)

Cl: *School is behind them, um,* [Pause] *yeah, some have their masters, their PhDs, what-not . . .*

Th: *Sounds like that's some of what you're working toward. It also sounds like there's some comparisons going on.*
Summarizing

Cl: *Yeah, but I feel like . . . I mean, I know that I'm making them in my own head. I don't know if anyone else is. I suppose I'm on guard a lot, just waiting for that other shoe to drop.*

Th: *What shoe?*
Specificity

Cl: [Pounds chair] *Well, I guess the advantage to being the age that I am is that I know that they aren't judging me as harshly as I'm judging myself, or if they are, to hell with them. But, there is still a little of that person on my shoulder going . . . shaking the finger, and sometimes it takes the shape and form of my mother.* [Laughs] [Stops pounding]

Th: *And if you had to give a voice to the person on your shoulder shaking their finger, what would that sound track sound like?*
Specificity

Cl: *My mother's voice.*

Th: Saying . . .
Prompting, Specificity

Cl: [Sighs] *Why aren't you there yet?!*

Th: *It sounds like that's what you're saying to yourself. And what's the answer to that question?*
Interpreting, Open-ended question

Cl: [Silence]

Th: *The question: "Why aren't you there yet?"*
Re-asking a question

Cl: [Pause] *Because I'm still trying to figure out where "there" is.*

Th: *Sure. Maybe part of that answer is "I'm on my way." Because the mission is in progress; you haven't stalled.*
Reframing

Cl: [Pause] *Well, I've stalled in the past, perhaps I'm stalling now.* [Pounds fist] *I guess I'm carrying around the guilt, from when I was in neutral.*

Th: *How do you wish things had gone?*
Open-ended question

Cl: [Laughs] [Sighs] *I don't know. I don't know. I mean, there have been so many twists and turns. . . . One of the things I hate about job interviews is that question, "Where do you see yourself in 5 years?" Who the hell knows where they're going to be in 5 years?! What's wrong with people asking that dumb-ass question?!* [Starts pounding fist] *But at a job interview, you can't say, "What the hell's wrong with you for asking that dumb-ass question?" You have to smile, and keep your hands folded, and be all proper and polite, not show your true geeky self, and come up with an answer. I've never had an answer because I . . . at any given point in my life, I look back 5 years and think, "Would I have predicted this?" and the answer is almost always "No!"* [Stops pounding fist].

Th: *Right.*
Brief verbal, Validation

Cl: *So I don't know where I'm going to be in 5 years. Does that even answer your question?*

Th: *The real reality is that we don't know where we're going to be in 5 minutes.*
       Normalizing

Cl: *That's true.*

Th: *It's okay to not know where you're going to be in 5 years. More than anything, the impression that I'm getting is that you have knowingly sacrificed a lot in order to push this mission forward . . . to have the potential for opportunities that you wouldn't have otherwise in 5 years. What you'll have in 5 years is opportunities and privileges that you don't have now. Right now, you're in the preparation mode, so that you can put yourself out there. So you can have those satisfying occupational experiences that you've had glimpses of, and the privilege to see who you are on the inside, and where you shine as a person, and where your talents lie. And with a little more of a fine focus, as these years march on, I imagine you'll come to have a closer approximation of where you belong, and what's worthwhile, and where you'll want to put yourself. What do you think?*
       Normalizing, Generalizing, Open-ended question

Cl: [Sighs] *I hope you're right.*

Th: *Think of it this way: Maybe it's like assembling a puzzle, with only having a brief look at the cover. As more pieces start to come together, the picture begins to emerge, and over time, there are fewer stray pieces to sort through, so it gets faster and clearer as you march along. I'm figuring that as you proceed, you're going to come to know more about yourself, what kind of opportunities are out there, and eventually, the two will converge into a meaningful match. For now, it sounds like you're doing what it takes to make your life line up and make more sense.*
       Reframing

Cl: [Pause] *Yeah, yeah. It rings true. It sounds as if I'm supposed to pat myself on the back at this point.* [Laughs] *I guess I have a hard time doing that.*

Th: *Mm-hmm. For now. We only have a few minutes left. Let me just recap some of the things that we've talked about: You came in initially complaining that you're feeling stressed and that it's starting to interfere with some of your sleeping. You moved in with your parents, which in many ways compromises your sense of independence, freedom, spontaneity, and privacy. School—both*

the academics and the peer age difference—is a source of some other stresses. There's some uncertainty about the future, where once you had an image of teaching but not any more, and that'll probably involve doing something else. That not knowing is a source of anxiety. It sounds like dating hasn't been as satisfying as you'd like it to be. And a sense of feeling somewhat behind in life . . . not quite in step with your peers in terms of your life accomplishments. I think we can work on some of these things through the course of therapy, and over the next week, I'd like you to think about which one of these you'd like to place first. During the next week, I'll encourage you to consider selecting one, or maybe two that you'd most like to see resolved—maybe the most substantial goals—and we'll begin there next time.
Summarizing

Cl: *Okay.*

Th: *Do you have any questions before we wrap up for today, or anything you'd like to add?*
Open-ended question

Cl: *Well, the thing with the dating . . . maybe it's just because I never knew what I wanted out of life, so how should I know what I want out of another person?*

Th: *Sounds reasonable. We can talk about that next time.*
Managing the "doorknob effect"—set a resume point for next session

Cl: *Okay.*

Th: *Thanks for coming.*
Rapport

Cl: *Thanks.*

— END OF SESSION —

Appendix B

Session With Dusty—Week 5: Midtherapy

Th: *So, how're you doing today?*
Open-ended question

Cl: *Pretty good.*

Th: *Yeah?*
Prompting

Cl: *Yeah, the sleep is . . . I'm having an easier time sleeping.*

Th: *You're sleeping better?*
Reflection

Cl: *Yeah, well, the imagery stuff that you suggested to me before, it seemed a little odd at first. . . . I guess because I'm just not used to doing that.*

Th: *Okay, so you were waking up about one to three times a night?*
Summarizing

Cl: *Yeah about that.*

Th: *And then you would be up for anywhere from about an hour to 90 minutes, is that right?*
Summarizing

Cl: *A couple of hours sometimes, yeah.*

Th: *A couple of hours.*
Reflection

Cl: *Yeah.*

Th: *And tell me what's going on with your sleep these days?*
Specificity

Cl: *Well, I mean, I still wake up occasionally, but what I've started doing like, like the one suggestion you gave me about, just picture yourself at the beach. Um, and like I would get all worked up over a test, and be woken up and find myself just, you know, stressing about that. And what I started doing was, well what you said, just stay in bed and close my eyes and picture myself on a beach . . .*

Th: *Mm-hmm . . .*
Brief verbal

Cl: *. . . and then there's this box that's washing up on the beach and I just kind of mentally put the word "test" on it . . .*

Th: [Nods]
Nonverbal attending

Cl: *. . . and the waves just come up and grab it and slowly wash it off to sea. Sometimes it tries to come back, but I just keep the waves . . . I just sort of mentally keep the waves coming in a little harder. And oddly enough it does . . . it did work. I guess I didn't think it would, just because I'm not used to doing that but . . .*

Th: *Well, the trick is it helps keep you relaxed in bed and helps keep you from getting worked up.*
Interpreting

Cl: *Right, right, but before I would get all worked up and want to get out of bed, so I would just get out of bed and just get my adrenalin up. Here I have something different to concentrate on. So I'm kind of distracted from getting out of bed, oddly enough.*

Th: *So the box drifts off out of sight, and about how long would you say it takes you to drift back to sleep?*
Reflection

Cl: *Not long. Ten minutes, I guess.*

Th: Okay.

Brief verbal

Cl: I don't know as I fall . . . as I'm drifting off to sleep, I'm no longer keeping track of time. [Laughs]

Th: So that's quite an improvement over getting up two or three times in the night and losing at least 3 to 4 hours of sleep in a night.

Interpreting

Cl: Right, yeah, I would get about half of the night's sleep.

Th: Okay. And what's the quality of your days now that you're able to sleep more continuously at nighttime?

Furthering

Cl: Better. I'm a lot more alert. I'm a lot more functional and productive. I'm retaining things from class.

Th: Mm-hmm . . .

Brief verbal

Cl: I guess my confidence has gone up a little bit too, doing a lot better on the tests.

Th: Sleep is a pretty strong predictor of the quality of what your next day is going to be like. During sleep the mind's able to reorganize and sort things out. It gives the mind a chance to rest so you can be alert and clear for the next day. And it sounds like your performance is improving and your self-satisfaction is improving along with that.

Informing, Summarizing

Cl: Definitely.

Th: Mm-hmm. What else is going on?

Open-ended question

Cl: Well, I took that vocational guidance test that we talked about.

Th: Yeah. How did that go?

Furthering

Cl: Well, it was all online, so I mean I didn't have to . . . it's not like I had to get dressed to go do it, which I guess was good because there were 70 or 80 questions and, and . . .

Th: *What were the questions like?*
Clarification

Cl: [Laughs] *Well, just about like, what do you like? I mean, asking if I'm good with numbers, if I like speaking in front of crowds, whether or not I like working directly with people. And then it has this grid where you're supposed to mark off if you strongly disagree or you're neutral on it or you strongly agree or anywhere between . . .*

Th: *Like a scale?*
Clarification

Cl: *Yeah, like a scale.*

Th: *Uh-huh. And how long did it take for you to get through the test?*
Close-ended question

Cl: *About an hour I guess. . . . I didn't rush. I wanted to be thorough. I mean, I was at home doing it online, you know online, so . . .*

Th: *And how did you feel answering these questions?*
Open-ended question

Cl: *Well uh, I guess I'm surprised at how simple the questions were. I mean, I suppose . . . I don't know what I expected, to be honest.*

Th: *And what kind of thing did it tell you after you finished answering all these questions?*
Open-ended question

Cl: [Laughs] *Well, there really weren't any results at the end. All it did was give me a phone number to call, so that I could* [Laughs] *set up an appointment to go talk about it with some professional. . . .*

Th: *On campus?*
Clarification

Cl: *Yes, yeah, on campus.*

Th: *Okay. So it sounds like there might be some subjective evaluation and advisement that goes along with this test.*
Clarification

Cl: *I would hope so . . .*

Th: *Uh-huh.*
      Brief verbal

Cl: *. . . otherwise why make the appointment?*

Th: *Well, there are advantages and disadvantages there: The disadvantage is you don't get an immediate report. The advantage is you get to sit down in front of a live person who's presumably an expert with this stuff, and you can have an interactive experience, get advice, ask more questions . . .*
      Reframing

Cl: *Right, well I guess I'll be doing that. I'm on a waiting list for an appointment right now.*

Th: *When is your appointment set for?*
      Close-ended question

Cl: *Like 3 weeks from now.*

Th: *Okay.*
      Brief verbal

Cl: *So I have the appointment. It's just that I'm on the waiting list to get in.*

Th: *Well, it sounds like you're taking a very active hand in trying to answer a question that you articulated near the beginning of therapy, knowing that you're building something better by going back to school, that it may not turn out to be a history teacher, but it's clear that you're actively looking for what that next right answer and what some of your choices might possibly be.*
      Summarizing

Cl: *Exactly. Well it's also easier [Laughs] to tackle this question when you have . . . I guess, when you are given a direction to go. I mean I don't know that I would have actually gone for this test, but it looks like this was a good route to take. . . . We'll see . . . we'll see.*

Th: *Were there any particular questions that grabbed you or surprised you in any way?*
      Specificity

Cl: [Laughs] *Actually, yeah, umm, the question about whether or not . . . how you feel about public speaking, you know, speaking in front of crowds.*

Th: *How do you feel about speaking in public?*
Furthering

Cl: *Kind of mixed. I mean I get a charge out of it sometimes. I guess it depends on the subject matter, you know . . . if it's just a speech about, you know, math, of course, I am not going to care. But umm, I took a film history class, and I had to give a speech on a movie. Umm, and that was definitely, you know, something that I was interested in so I enjoyed doing that.*

Th: *Were you able to select the film?*
Close-ended question

Cl: *Yes, we were allowed to select the film.*

Th: *Well, it follows that you wouldn't have selected a film that you had no interest in . . .*
Interpreting

Cl: *Right.*

Th: *. . . and it sounds like talking about a film that you're strongly interested in, there would be a lot of motivation and there would be a certain enthusiasm in talking about it, as opposed to something that you have no passion for, like math.*
Interpreting

Cl: *Right, yeah, when it's something that I care about and that I'm interested in, then the public speaking is a little easier. Otherwise, I tend to get nervous and flub my words and become just very self-conscious and almost bored.*

Th: *Again, I'm seeing that when you hit on something that you're interested in, there's a lot of enthusiasm and you see that your performance goes way up.*
Generalizing

Cl: *Definitely.*

Th: *It seems like that's been a trend throughout the therapy here.*
Generalizing

Cl: Yes.

Th: Do you see that?
Close-ended question

Cl: [Laughs] Yes, I do.

Th: Okay, and you'll be having an appointment in a few weeks?
Reflection

Cl: You're right—about 3 weeks.

Th: Okay. Could you keep me posted on what comes of that?
Close-ended question

Cl: I will.

Th: I'm curious: Having answered all those questions, what do you think you're going to hear at that meeting?
Open-ended question

Cl: Well, I don't really know. This is the first time I'm going to be meeting with some-body to discuss this type of thing, so I don't know what they're going to say.

Th: Did your answering pattern to the questions seem to suggest anything to you as you were taking it, or maybe in retrospect?
Close-ended question

Cl: Well, there wasn't any . . . there weren't any questions that my answer . . . there weren't any questions where my answers surprised me.

Th: [Nods]
Nonverbal attending

Cl: At this point, I guess I do know what interests me and what doesn't, you know . . . what I enjoy and what I don't.

Th: Fair enough. What else has been going on since our last meeting?
Open-ended question

Cl: Oh, well, I put an application in for student housing.

Th: *So you're going ahead with that?*
Close-ended question

Cl: *Uh, yeah. I debated on [Laughs] how I felt about that. Well, my concern was that I would end up in some dorm with a bunch of like, you know, partying . . . young partiers, and I really do value peace and quiet.*

Th: *How do you know that won't happen?*
Challenging

Cl: *Well, I already talked with one of the people there at the student housing office and I guess what they do is they . . . even though I'm an undergrad student, they'll probably put me in with the grad students. Apparently that's a more serious crowd . . . older.*

Th: *I would think.*
Brief verbal

Cl: *And I would hope. [Laughs]*

Th: *Well, grad students typically are little bit different from younger undergrads in that most graduate students have given up a lot to be there.*
Informing

Cl: *I can relate to that.*

Th: *Sure. Many of them have given up careers, they've given up pay, they've given up established social lives to go back to school, and typically they're a little bit more composed.*
Informing

Cl: *You mean focused?*

Th: *Focused, composed, typically a little more emotionally set and stable. Probably a different house protocol. So that sounds like a good match for you.*
Informing

Cl: *Well, I guess we'll see. . . . . Um, I'm fairly optimistic about it. I mean, I may or may not have a roommate. I don't know. But I did request no smoking because I am not . . . I just . . . I don't know . . . I just want to be with a nonsmoker.*

Th: *Getting back to that earlier point that you mentioned—that you'll be among graduate students who are typically older than undergraduate students—I'm thinking of this in two ways: Number one, you've expressed some dissatisfaction about being among younger peers and some discomfort there.*

Returning

Cl: *It's awkward.*

Th: *Right, so this'll put you with presumably people closer to your age. But second, I'm thinking that there maybe another disparity. And I'm wondering how you'll be coping with that, the disparity that you being an undergraduate living among predominately graduate students. And in a prior session, you mentioned almost competitively that some of your peers are further along than you. I'm wondering how that might sit with you.*

Returning, Challenging

Cl: *Well, I guess I don't know yet. Well, in terms of dealing with the other students who are a lot younger than me, I'm starting to not care as much.*

Th: *Hmm.*

Brief verbal

Cl: *I guess I'm so busy worried about the work. It just doesn't really seem to be an issue. I suppose . . . I suppose when someone is in high school they care a lot more about those kind of social things. But I definitely don't. I mean, as I've gotten older my . . . the age range of the people I call friends becomes wider anyway. You know, these are just, sort of, people in the classroom to me.*

Th: *And age sensitivity does dissolve over time. For instance, in elementary school there's a world of difference between the kindergartner and the first grader. That one year is a world of difference. That one year is essentially 20% of your life, whereas the difference between, say, a 30-year-old and a 31-year-old, that same one-year difference is virtually undetectable. So that difference does tend to vanish over time, as I'm sure you've noticed.*

Informing, Validating

Cl: *Definitely.*

Th: *Okay, so instead of focusing on the age difference, it sounds like the classes are keeping you busier . . . focusing your attention more on the academics.*

Summarizing

Cl: *Definitely! Yeah, I just don't have as much time to worry about what now seems like petty things.*

Th: *So it sounds like you adjusted to your peers in a more adaptive fashion?*
Summarizing

Cl: *I suppose I have.*

Th: *Sounds positive. How are the classes going?*
Brief verbal, Open-ended question, Redirecting

Cl: *Well, they're challenging.* [Laughs] *They* are *challenging. But, um, I'm finding that as each test comes and goes, and I see the A's and the B's on these papers and these tests, that's very . . . that just sort of keeps acting as encouragement.*

Th: *Success breeds success?*
Interpreting

Cl: *Uh, yes, very well put . . .* [Laughs] *okay.*

Th: *You'd mentioned that when you were at the junior college, you were seeing A's showing up and appropriately pleased with that. You also mentioned that you were still a little bit skeptical: Could you continue to produce A's at the university level?*
Returning

Cl: *Right. That I know is definitely . . . I knew it would be more challenging. . . . I just wasn't sure if I was really up to it.*

Th: *And now you're seeing some evidence?*
Furthering

Cl: *I am seeing the evidence. I guess I really am up to this. And I don't think that I would have committed to living on campus and dorm if I . . . no, I wouldn't have been ready to live on campus at a dorm when I started this out. I guess I had to prove to myself, yes I can do this* [Pause] *before, I guess, jumping in with both feet.*

Th: *You had to confirm that this could float before you loaded anything onto it?*
Summarizing

Cl: *Definitely.*

Th: *Makes sense. And now that it's floating and you're on your way, how does that speak to your self-esteem in a broader sense?*
Open-ended question

Cl: [Silence]

Th: *Or does that speak to your self-esteem?*
Re-asking a question

Cl: *I don't know. I think I'm too busy to really* [Laughs] *analyze it. I've been so* [Laughs] *busy trying to concentrate on getting myself to sleep.*

Th: *Maybe that'll be an after-finals-are-over question?*
Close-ended question

Cl: *Okay, that's fair.* [Laughs]

Th: *Let's hold that one.*
Reflection

Cl: [Laughs]

Th: *How about your midterms? You should be around midterm time by now?*
Redirecting

Cl: *Yeah, yeah, the midterms are wrapping up.*

Th: *They're wrapping up?*
Reflection

Cl: *Mm-hmm.*

Th: *Okay, and how many of the courses threw midterms at you?*
Close-ended question

Cl: *All of them, all five! All of them!* [Laughs] *All of them!*

Th: *Take-home? In-class?*
Close-ended question

Cl: *Most of them were in-class. There was one that was actually like a 20-page take-home paper.*

Th: *Which do you prefer?*
Close-ended question

Cl: *Well, the in-class tests are stressful because there's all that anticipation ahead of time. But once it's done, I can say, "It's over, it's behind you." You can take it off your plate, you can wipe it from your mind, and then you just wait for the grade to come back. With the paper, it's an ongoing process. You're constantly revisiting it. And I found myself fussing over the final draft and determining that that was not the final draft, and I did that a few times. But the paper's in and we'll see.*

Th: *But in doing all those returning edits, what it sounds like to me is that you're really making an effort here to be successful . . . to draw as much out of each learning opportunity as you can. It makes me wonder if maybe there's something more than just seeking a high grade . . . as if you may be looking to build a greater version of you?*
Interpreting

Cl: *Well, I'm definitely doing this to improve myself . . .*

Th: *Mm-hmm.*
Brief verbal

Cl: *. . . and most definitely doing it to improve* [Laughs] *my opportunities.*

Th: *What I'm thinking is a student who's determined to just barely get through this, knows when to stop writing a paper and they stop early. They estimate what it's going to take to get a C and then they call it quits . . .*
Interpreting

Cl: *Okay.*

Th: *. . . It's a very different kind of student that returns back to a paper that they thought was a fully done deal and finds ways to actively improve it. That's a very different kind of student.*
Interpreting

Cl: *I never really thought about that before.*

Th: *How does that strike you now?*
Open-ended question

Cl: [Pause] *I think I deserve to treat myself to ice cream!* [Laughs]

Th: *I think you do too. Don't forget the hot fudge!* [Both laugh] *So it sounds like this is more than just checking off boxes, finishing out classes, fulfilling menial criteria. . . . It seems to me that you're reaching for something deeper than that.*

Interpreting

Cl: *Definitely! Well, I just . . . I didn't feel like the associate's degree prepared me enough, professionally or otherwise.*

Th: *You mentioned, I believe it was in our first session, that there was work sometimes but . . .*

Returning

Cl: *. . . it was innocuous, it was boring, it was unchallenging.*

Th: *Right.*

Brief verbal

Cl: *It was arduous just to get up in the morning and go to it.*

Th: *It sounds like you truly believe you deserve more than that.*

Interpreting

Cl: *I hope I deserve more. I guess if I really wanted to analyze it, I could say that by doing this I'm trying to prove to myself that I do deserve it.*

Th: *Well, as you said yourself, by taking student housing, you've jumped in with both feet.*

Reflection

Cl: [Laughs]

Th: *You still seem hesitant to admit that . . . to believe that you're all the way in this, and that it's working . . . you're working.*

Challenging

Cl: *Maybe I'll believe it more when I see the final grades for the first term.*

Th: *Makes sense. But the grades are moving in the direction that makes good sense now?*

Close-ended question

Cl: So far, so good.

Th: Not to cast any foreshadowing on this, but typically final grades are a composition of all of the grades along the way; the grades all add up. Typically, through my own experience in many years of college, the final pretty much moves in the direction of the assignments and your progress as you move through that course.

Informing, Self-disclosure

Cl: Do you mean the final exam?

Th: The final exam, the final grade, is pretty much predictable by say, about half way through. You kind of know if you are or aren't catching this class, and I've yet to see a final grade come out that was radically unexpected. Sometimes you can't tell if it's going to be an A or B, but you're never confused if it's going to be an A or a D.

Informing

Cl: Okay, yeah, that makes sense.

Th: In moving out, it sounds like there's a lot that could happen there. You discussed multiple times stresses related to being at home, self-editing among your parents: your mom and your stepdad . . . isolating yourself to a room with the door closed most of your waking hours, the general stress of having to forfeit adult-size freedoms.

Summarizing

Cl: [Laughs]

Th: Tell me a little about your expectations, your wishes, your hopes in terms of student housing.

Furthering

Cl: Well, I just hope I end up with a roommate. If I do have a roommate, and it sounds like I probably will . . . um, I just hope that the person is clean and tolerable. I mean I've had other roommates in my lifetime, [Pause] but I mean when you put two people together in a shared living space, I guess anything can happen, especially if you don't know one another. So this'll be different.

Th: You requested a nonsmoker?

Clarification, Close-ended question

Cl: *Right, that's really the only thing I feel all that strongly about.*

Th: *What matching criteria were there, other than presumably gender, that they take into account in matching roommates?*
Close-ended question

Cl: *None, I think.*

Th: *Okay, so smoking and gender.*
Summarizing

Cl: *Right.*

Th: *Okay. And it sounds like you have some concerns about how you'll socialize with this roommate. If you could have it your way, would you want to live solo?*
Summarizing, Close-ended question

Cl: *Yes!* [Laughs]

Th: *And what would be involved in living solo?*
Open-ended question

Cl: *Well, it'll cost about 20% more, and the room is about half the size.*

Th: *You think that might be worth it?*
Close-ended question

Cl: *Maybe. I'm leaning towards "yes," but the chance to save money is very tempting right now . . . especially right now.*

Th: *It makes sense. Money's always a concern, no matter how much of it you have. What's your parents' impression of you going off to live at the dormitory when there's a "perfectly good" room in their house and they're willing to have you? What's their take on all this?*
Summarizing, Validation, Open-ended question

Cl: [Laughs] *Well, they're for it. They're for it. Um, I think. . . . They kind of surprised me.*

Th: *How so?*
Specificity

Cl: Well, [Laughs] *they seem to be clued-in a lot more to my discomfort there than maybe I thought they were.*

Th: *So you underestimated their awareness?*
Clarification

Cl: *Yeah I did. I think so.*

Th: *Think of it this way: Suppose you were living in a house, your house . . . and the person who was living there with you, during all their waking hours reverted to their room with the door closed and gave you trickles of information when conversing "freely" . . .*
Challenging

Cl: [Laughs]

Th: *. . . do you think you might catch on that this person feels a little uncomfortable there?*
Challenging

Cl: *Umm, [Laughs] at the risk of incriminating myself, yes, I think I'd know something is up.*

Th: *Okay, so it sounds like your parents have come to recognize that you've missed some of your freedoms and privileges?*
Generalizing

Cl: *Yeah, well, they've been adults longer than I have, so I guess they understand this routine better than I do.*

Th: *Sure, sure, it makes sense. And what was their reaction when you mentioned that you were considering moving into student housing?*
Open-ended question

Cl: *Well, they were afraid I was going to take the cats with me.*

Th: *Oh?*
Brief verbal

Cl: *So although I don't like the idea of being away from the cats, the cats'll stay with them while I'm doing this.*

Th: *Does student housing take pets?*
Close-ended question

Cl: *No, no, I don't think any dorms do.*

Th: *Okay.*
Brief verbal

Cl: *At least that's what I'm told.*

Th: *You mentioned that your mother had formed a relationship with your cats and had taken to actively providing care, and you expressed some resentment about your mom incidentally taking over your parenting responsibilities. How do think you'll feel once you move out and the caretaking will be in her hands?*
Returning, Open-ended question

Cl: *Well, I know that she loves them and she cares about them, so I don't have to worry about whether or not they're safe or fed. So that takes some stress off of my . . . that takes stress off of me . . .*

Th: *Mm-hmm.*
Brief verbal

Cl: *. . . and in 2 years, if I'm ready to move out of the dorm and into my own place and they can't part with the cats, I've already thought this through. . . . It's, [Pause] well, . . . if that's where the cats need to be, then that's where they need to be.*

Th: *But that's 2 years down the road?*
Clarification

Cl: *Right. I mean anything can happen in 2 years. In 2 years, they may decide "get these cats out of my face," but I don't think that's going to happen. I think they're going to bond with them and that's just going to be their home from now on.*

Th: *You'll always have visitation privileges, I imagine?*
Clarification

Cl: *Right. At least my parents'll have them and not some total strangers. So they'll still be family.*

Th: *So it's not a half-bad solution?*

Summarizing

Cl: *It's not ideal, but right, it's not half bad. I mean, it's not bad at all.*

Th: *How far is the dormitory from your parents' place?*

Close-ended question

Cl: *Oh, that'd be about five or six miles. It's not far at all. I could actually just . . .* [Laughs]

Th: *So it's accessible?*

Close-ended question

Cl: *I could stop by every day if I wanted to, but I don't think that I'll want to, at least not right away.*

Th: *Right, and have you thought about living at the dorm in between sessions, or during summer sessions?*

Close-ended question

Cl: *Well, I'm going to summer school. I mean, I've already decided. I knew that. . . I knew that would be the case even before this semester began. So I imagine I'll just continue to live on campus during the breaks.*

Th: *Okay, sounds like a plan, and tell me a little bit more about the student housing. Have you seen where you'll be living?*

Furthering

Cl: *Yeah, and it's small, but I'm not losing any space. I mean it's the same size . . . the rooms are about the same size as what I already have.*

Th: *Okay, and will you be doing your own cooking, or will that be taking care of?*

Close-ended question

Cl: *I think it's taken care of. Well, there's cafeteria service.*

Th: *Okay, so you don't have cooking in your room, right?*

Close-ended question

Cl: *My cooking's not that great anyway, so . . .*

Th: *Okay.*
Brief verbal

Cl: *So this'll be fine.*

Th: *One less thing to think about.*
Reframing

Cl: *Yeah, yeah, actually it helps take the stress off even more, because there was a certain amount of guilt in my stepdad and my mom preparing all the meals. They wouldn't even let me do the cooking because I guess they know how bad my cooking is but . . .*

Th: *And how were their meals?*
Furthering

Cl: *Hmm . . .*

Th: *Not to your taste?*
Re-asking a question

Cl: *Not . . . well no, not good.*

Th: *Okay, but there was some guilt that you might have been overburdening them?*
Interpreting

Cl: *Right, yeah, I guess you could say I was eating out of guilt, certainly not because I loved the taste.*

Th: *Did they ever do anything to make you feel guilty?*
Close-ended question

Cl: *[Pause] I don't think so, no. I suppose as more time and distance is created between me and that living situation, I'll look back on it and see now that they, they really didn't.*

Th: *Mm-hmm. But it seems to me that maybe having your parents prepare meals persistently was one of the factors that helped keep you feeling in the parent-child mode.*
Interpreting

Cl: Definitely.

Th: Mm-hmm. And with that removed, I'm guessing you might have a better shot at feeling independent, as you said . . . coming and going as you wish without having to explain anything to anyone.

Interpreting

Cl: Right.

Th: Think of all the secrets you won't have to keep.

Reframing

Cl: [Laughs] Well, I probably won't be telling them any more than I already have. But they won't be around to see me coming and going, and I won't be thinking about their seeing me coming and going.

Th: So it sounds like even when you weren't living with them, there was a certain level of secrecy and confidentiality?

Challenging

Cl: It didn't feel like secrecy when I wasn't living with them. But yeah, definitely with them the information is just not traditionally shared, [Laughs] either about my life to them or, you know, about, you know, their daily lives to me.

Th: You seem to have a much brighter energy today than you have in our last couple of meetings. I'm wondering if some of these things that are about to blossom—moving out independently, living at the dorm, regaining some of your freedom, the pending outcome of the vocational guidance testing, classes progressing well. . . . I'm wondering if some of these bright spots down the road are loosening things up, giving you a brighter, lighter feel. What do you think?

Observational cues, Open-ended question

Cl: I agree, totally. Yeah! It just feels like there's more optimism in the day. I have more energy to start the day, and of course the sleeping . . . correcting the sleeping problem is helping that.

Th: Mm-hmm. And I think it's important to recognize that these things that are down the road—the bright outlook for the future of school based on positive grades coming back, the moving out and becoming more independent, . . . regaining that, the vocational guidance testing and the potential outcome of that. These aren't things that came to you accidentally. These are a function of your active hand. Do you see that?

Generalizing, Close-ended question

Cl: [Laughs] [Pause] *Well, I'm not in a habit of patting myself on the back. So it feels a little strange. But yeah, I am noticing that I've got things moving in a more positive direction than I had before, certainly more than I'm used to.*

Th: *Do you acknowledge that these things are all things that you caused to happen?*

Close-ended question

Cl: *Are you going to let me get away with not acknowledging them?* [Laughs]

Th: [Facial expression: challenging glance]

Nonverbal Attending, Silence

Cl: *Okay. Yes, I did do all that.* [Laughs] *Well, like I said, when I see the final grades for the semester, perhaps I'll ease up on myself.*

Th: *Fair enough.* [Pause] *I want to spend some time talking about the progress we've made so far. And I want to talk about where we stand right now in the therapeutic process in terms of termination. You remember at our initial session, we talked about the 10 sessions that your health plan provides?*

Redirecting

Cl: *We're about halfway through now, aren't we?*

Th: *We are halfway through now, yes,* [Pause] *and I want to talk to you about how you're feeling about being halfway through, and your impressions of the work we've done together.*

Reflecting, Summarizing

Cl: *Okay.*

Th: *How does it feel that we'll have about five sessions left here?*

Furthering

Cl: *Wow, I haven't really thought about it. I guess that I was getting kind of used to being able to come here and unload and talk about this stuff.*

Th: *Mm-hmm. Well, you'll still be coming here to unload and talk about this stuff. We're not done yet, which is why I raise this today. I think the halfway mark is an appropriate place to evaluate how far you've come and to identify specific goals that you'd like to accomplish during our remaining weeks. What advancements do you see that you've made since initially beginning therapy?*

Reflecting, Summarizing, Open-ended question

Cl: *Well, I'm much more committed than I was before. I mean I was before, but it seems as though . . . it's . . . I don't know.* [Pause] *It just seems like there's a deeper level of commitment that I wasn't aware of before that I'm now beginning to experience firsthand.*

Th: *As if you're more robustly invested in school?*

Interpreting

Cl: *Yeah, it's easier to get homework assignments moving.* [Pause] *Before, I was kind of a procrastinator, maybe that comes from being . . . you know, spending long periods of time at jobs where I just didn't like the work or the people or the subject matter* [Pounds fist] *or any of it. Uh, but now I'm doing something with a direct purpose that is designed to benefit me and not to just help somebody else make money.*

Th: *And isn't that an interesting observation—that when you're engaged in something that's meaningless to you, your performance is appropriately mediocre, compared to when you're engaged in something that you deeply believe in? Then you really throw yourself at it in a powerful and meaningful way. I'm figuring that that's going to be characteristic of whatever career you wind up selecting. This would be far more purposive than anything that you were able to incidentally land on before, jobwise.*

Interpreting

Cl: *Yeah, that makes sense.*

Th: *I have high hopes for the findings of the vocational guidance testing.*

Redirecting

Cl: [Laughs] *Well, we'll see. I don't really know quite what to expect. I don't even know who I'm meeting with.*

Th: *I'm sure you will when you get there.*

Rapport

Cl: *Okay.*

Th: *But what this tells me is that you're not a wandering, mediocre, "don't know where I'm going," lost-in-the-dark person. It seems to me, from everything you're telling me, that when you have a meaningful goal on your plate, you eat it all up. And that kind of power can be pointed at anything that's meaningful to you.*

Interpreting

Cl: *Well, if I can perform as well in whatever it is I become as I have so far as a student, I suppose the world is mine, right?*

Th: *I think you have every chance to do well there, and school's a pretty hard mission.*

Validation

Cl: *Yeah I'm learning that. I don't think that I realized that at the junior college level. . . .*

Th: *Mm-hmm.*

Brief verbal

Cl: *. . . Definitely not at the high school level. Well, in high school, I didn't even care, I don't think.*

Th: *You know, typically in a work environment it ends after 8 hours, and you typically report to one, maybe two supervisors. School, if it's done as you're doing it, is a "24-7" job. It's more than a full-time job, and instead of working for one or two supervisors, you're working for four or five instructors. In a lot of ways, I'm guessing that professional work is going to be something less of a challenge to you than your course work at the university.*

Informing

Cl: *[Laughs] Well, I guess if I become accustomed to a heavy workload like this, maybe I'll have to find additional challenges outside of just my job, right? [Laughs]*

Th: *I'm sure they'll be there ready for you, and I'm guessing you'll make some meaningful selections in doing so. Maybe you'll include a voluntary position— who knows.*

Rapport

Cl: *[Silence]*

Th: *How do you feel about knowing that in 5 weeks, we'll be done here?*

Open-ended question

Cl: [Sighs] [Pause] *Well, I guess I hadn't really wanted to think about that much, but* [Pause] *I'm probably going to miss coming here. No one else is willing to listen to me like this and help me work things through.* [Laughs] *Yeah, I'm going to miss this.*

Th: *Do you think you'll miss me?*

Close-ended question

Cl: *Yeah, I think I probably will.*

Th: *I think I'll miss you too.*

Rapport

Cl: *Why?*

Th: *Why do you think?*

Open-ended question

Cl: *Do I have to answer every question?* [Laughs] *I don't know, I don't know.*

Th: *Why do you think someone might miss you?*

Re-asking a question

Cl: [Pause] *Because I owe them money?* [Laughs] *Oh, well, alright is this where I have to acknowledge something positive about myself?* [Pause] *Okay, I'll be serious. Well, I guess I'm a nice person.* [Laughs] *I feel kind of silly saying that.* [Laughs]

Th: *What else?*

Prompting

Cl: *Oh . . .*

Th: *You're a growing person. You're evolving and changing. That's interesting. That's exciting.*

Rapport

Cl: *This is interesting to you?*

Th: *Isn't it interesting to you?*
      Challenging

Cl: [Laughs] *You're always answering a question with a question!* [Laughs]

Th: *Do I?* [Both laugh]

Cl: *Yes!* [Both laugh]

Th: *Are you interested or bored here? You seem engaged.*
      Re-asking a question

Cl: *This is interesting to me! This is interesting to me. It's 50 minutes where I can just talk about myself and worry about myself and not feel guilty about it . . . that I'm slighting someone else.*

Th: *And this is an opportunity for exactly that. What kind of goals would you like to see us working on between now and your last session?*
      Open-ended question

Cl: [Pause] *Well, I guess, uh, there's the issue of dating. I'm not exactly sure if it's such a great idea right now. I mean, I'm so busy, and I'm finding that, yeah, I still go out bowling, and I still have my friends. Um, I'm beginning to see a little bit less and less of them, but it doesn't feel like it's a problem.*

Th: [Nods]
      Nonverbal attending

Cl: *I guess I'm not quite sure. I mean, I'd like to have somebody special in my life, but I don't know if this is the right time.*

Th: *. . . that the emotional distracter, either positive or negative, may pull your attention away from your academics?*
      Clarification

Cl: *Right! Yeah, I don't know how another person would fit into all this. I don't know if there's room. So I mean it's . . . I mean I think about this from time to time and when I do it's a little bit lonely, but um, I guess I'm just so busy and . . . I don't spend too much time thinking about it . . . when I think about it.*

Th: *And how do you feel when you do think about it?*
Open-ended question

Cl: *Lonely.*

Th: *Lonely?*
Reflection

Cl: *I'm not getting any younger.*

Th: *You're not getting any younger?*
Reflection

Cl: *No.*

Th: *Well, we're all there.*
Normalizing

Cl: [Laughs]

Th: *You think that getting older makes you less attractive? Less of an interesting catch?*
Close-ended question

Cl: *Well, I do notice that when people notice each other, I'm noticing that the younger ones tend to get noticed more often than the older ones.* [Laughs]

Th: *Cosmetically?*
Clarification

Cl: *Right.* [Pause] *I mean, I know deep down that looks don't count but, um . . .*

Th: *I think, to some point, looks do count. We're very visual beings. I think we look at people and we make determinations. We look at their skin color, and it could set off prejudice reactions. That's old news. . . .*
Challenging

Cl: *True.*

Th: ...We look at someone who grooms themselves appropriately, and we make certain determinations on who we think they are and what they're like based on what they dress like, and so forth.
Challenging

Cl: Well, right now I'm not spending too much time priming and primping and studying the mirror.

Th: But aside from that, I think people do form meaningful opinions based on something that goes beyond the depth of the skin—who's in there—and it sounds like that's what you're working on building these days . . . the inside.
Reframing

Cl: I hadn't really thought about it like that, but yeah, you're right. Yeah, I am sort of rebuilding from the inside out . . . from the ground up perhaps.

Th: It makes me wonder if what's going on is something along the lines of "closed for remodeling."
Interpreting

Cl: Well, better to be closed for remodeling than closed for demolition.

Th: Absolutely. If you could have a sign on your T-shirt, would it say, "Closed for remodeling," or might it say something else right now?
Close-ended question

Cl: I don't know. Maybe it would say, "Check back in 2 years."

Th: "Dusty . . . grand reopening . . . 2 years?"
Reflection

Cl: [Laughs] Yes, yes.

Th: Sounds like a plan. You're okay with that 2 years?
Close-ended question

Cl: Well, I'll have enough to keep me busy in these 2 years. Two years, yeah, I think it'll probably be just okay . . . or, but who knows? . . . I mean, maybe someone'll find me [Laughs] instead of me finding someone else.

Th: *Never know how it works . . .*
Summarizing

Cl: [Pause] *I just keep thinking about this vocational testing thing. I just . . . I don't know what to expect. Um, I guess I'm afraid maybe they'll tell me something about myself that I don't already know and won't like.*

Th: *Well, you know, of course, that whatever it is that they tell you or don't tell you, that it's only in the form of recommendations. They're not going to implant a job chip in your palm* [Client laughs] *and send you off doing a job that they've determined you need to do. It's only a recommendation. And if you go, and it makes no sense, or it's unsettling, you know there are other vocational tests to take. There are lots of other options; there are lots of other people to talk to, lots of other resources. I'm not telling you to not be anxious or concerned or excited about this. I know you will be. But keep in mind, this is not the only answer. You know that.*
Informing

Cl: *Yeah, I guess.*

Th: *Okay. You always have first choice no matter what anyone says. You're a free person.*
Informing

Cl: *Yeah, I guess I'm not used to having first choice.*

Th: *Maybe as you come to reclaim some of your sense of independence, you may start to feel that way more often.*
Interpreting

Cl: *Sounds good to me.*

Th: *How are you feeling right now?*
Open-ended question

Cl: *Kind of energized.*

Th: *You seem that way . . . bright affect, sparkle in the eye.*
Observational cues

Cl: Yeah, I feel good right now! Maybe it's the sleep. [Laughs] *Maybe the sleep is making that more easy.*

Th: *It's hard to have an energetic day when you haven't done enough sleeping.*
Validation

Cl: Yeah. *Before, it was like I was about to doze off towards the end of like some of the classes.*

Th: *Was that the lecture or bad sleep?*
Close-ended question

Cl: [Laughs] *Both!*

Th: *Makes sense. I think I've had that class.* [Both laugh]
Rapport

Cl: *I'm sure I'll have that class again!*

Th: *Okay, so we'll be working on your feelings regarding your regaining independence through the student housing. We'll be talking about your social issues. We'll be keeping tabs on your sleep. And we'll see where this vocational guidance testing moves.* [Pause] *Do you have any questions or thoughts before we close up for today?*
Summarizing, Open-ended question

Cl: *Umm,* [Pause] *not that I can think of. Well, I just, I kind of don't want this. . . . I don't want this therapy to end.*

Th: *Yeah. That's not uncommon, but we'll be working on that as we approach our last appointment. Each session, we're going to dedicate some time to talking about what the ending of therapy means to you and how you feel about that. And just because therapy ends, it doesn't mean that it's the end of your personal growth. You know, the goal of therapy, at least from the therapist's perspective, is to get you as close to the best functioning that you can achieve at this time and to launch you in such a way that you can independently carry on, and do this for yourself. Does that make sense?*
Informing

Cl: *Yeah, it's a little scary, but yeah. It makes sense.*

Th: Okay. You know, the rationale is essentially: if we address the largest issue or issues, then that'll clear the plate and leave some of the smaller residual issues for you to solve on your own, applying some of the techniques and skills that you've acquired during these sessions, and with your self-awareness and your motivation, I think you can do exactly that.

Informing

Cl: [Pause] *Okay.*

Th: Okay. I'll see you next time.

Rapport

—END OF SESSION—

Appendix C

Session With Dusty—Week 10: Termination

Cl: *I just have so much going on in my head right now.*

Th: *What's going on?*
Open-ended question

Cl: *Well, okay, I guess for starters, I know we've talked and talked about this...*

Th: *Yeah.*
Brief verbal

Cl: *... but that meeting with the vocational guidance counselor...*

Th: *Yes.*
Prompting

Cl: *... just talking about all the different career options and of the human resources and the industrial trend, I just, I just... [Pause] I still keep thinking about that, but you know, I... since last time, you know, I met, I had a conversation with my uncle, you know the one that's been on dialysis.*

Th: *The renal patient... for 9 years?*
Reflection

Cl: *Right, um, and he's been doing this for like 9 years, and lot of this I didn't really know until we were talking about this, because one of the career options that came up was the health educator, you know, like training dialysis patients, which I don't think I would've even thought of that before. But apparently a lot of patients don't know how to cope with the treatment and so that person's job, if I were to go into that field... I'd basically be training them on how to cope with dialysis, and I just still keep thinking about . . . I don't know yet exactly how I feel about it, and this . . . it feels like it's very early in the game. But it's not. [Pause] It's kind of cool to know that there are all these options that I'd never even considered before.*

Th: *You know what this reminds me of? In our first session, you mentioned that the most satisfying job you ever had was working at the funeral home . . .*

Returning

Cl: *Right.*

Th: *. . . providing guidance and support for people who were at a very vulnerable spot.*

Summarizing

Cl: *Exactly, and even though I wasn't functioning as a counselor, per se, just the minimal interaction that I had with the people at the job that I held felt significant enough.*

Th: *It sounds like you want to keep moving along that same direction.*

Interpreting

Cl: *I think that might be the way to go. Yeah. [Pause] Because one of the issues that I had with teaching was the disciplinary role that you have to play with kids, and I don't think that that's something that I want. But if I were to do something like this, I would most likely . . . well, I'd be working with people who have a direct interest in what's being discussed. It wouldn't be like forcing children to stay in a classroom.*

Th: *Right. Children in the classroom can feel like prisoners, whereas among adult learners, it's an entirely different thing. There's a different level of maturity; it's more about them wanting the information . . .*

Generalizing

Cl: *Right.*

Th: *. . . and it's very focused, and so the conduct problems would essentially be subtracted out of the picture. So based on what you're telling me, that might be a better fit for you.*

Advising

Cl: *I think so.*

Th: *I'm wondering if you've spoken further with the career guidance center regarding what'd be involved, educationally, in qualifying for a position like that. I'm guessing maybe some sort of an advanced degree may be required . . . something like a master's in public health or health education?*

Open-ended question

Cl: *Well, definitely it is. I don't have . . . I mean, I'll have my bachelor's in history and . . . that's not enough to get me, you know, a job counseling dialysis patients. I'd have to go through an MS program for that. But I think it might be worth it. I'm just not sure if I'll want to go on to work on my master's right after graduating with the 4-year degree.*

Th: *Lots of people take a break between degrees and actually find the working world quite a respite from the academic world . . . in that, most jobs run you 40 hours; there's no homework, no prep work. You just do the job. Maybe, at some point, you might find yourself satisfied enough doing that job. Or maybe, at some point, you'll want to upgrade your skills. But lots of people find it's important to take a break in between academic programs. It can take a while for the school batteries to recharge, [Client laughs] but this certainly sounds like an interesting plan. According to my calendar, this should be the end of the term. Tell me how the classes have wrapped up.*

Advising, Open-ended question

Cl: *Well, finals are done.*

Th: *Mm-hmm.*

Brief verbal

Cl: *I took . . . well, I'd just had my last final shortly after our last meeting. A couple of the grades have come back, and one's an A and the other one's a B+, and it looks like the other three are going to be in the same range. I know one's definitely going to be an A in the humanities class that I thought was so difficult. I know I've got an A or at least an A- in that.*

Th: *How do you feel about that?*

Open-ended question

Cl: *Great!*

Th: *That's good work. You know, final grades are seldom a surprise. They're pretty much a reflection of however well or poorly someone's been doing in the class up until that point in the same way that finals are basically an accumulation of what's been covered over the course.*

Validating, Informing

Cl: *Right. I would've been in serious trouble if I wouldn't have kept up throughout the term.*

Th: *Right. It sounds like you're learning how to be a student.*

Generalizing

Cl: *Right.*

Th: *And to my knowledge, there's no particular class in "how to be a student." It's presumed that you can just do it . . .*

Informing

Cl: *Right.*

Th: *. . . and as with any skill, typically people get better at it as they go along. You find out what does and doesn't work, what does and doesn't need to be there.*

Informing

Cl: *Right. Well, I suppose I learned this from all the various different jobs I had. I don't know that I've ever applied it to school before, but the principle's pretty much the same in that you find out what they want and then you just give that to them, and the instructors are, in that regard, no different from my former supervisors.*

Th: *Interesting. A two-step model: Find out what they want and give it to them.*

Summarizing

Cl: [Pause] *Find out what they want and give it to them.* [Pause] *Yeah, pretty much.*

Th: *What else is going on?*

Open-ended question

Cl: *Well,* [Laughs] *you know that I have a part-time job on campus. Um, and I mean, it's only about 20 hours a week, but I don't really know. . . .* [Pause] *I kind of feel as though it . . .* [Pause] *I mean, there's no homework involved.*

I just show up and I do the job, you know? I'm just an office assistant, but I kind of feel like when I walk away from it after a shift that that's time that I could've spent studying. And my financial situation right now isn't such that I'm in dire need for cash. So I don't know if I want to keep this for next term.

Th: *That'll be something to consider . . .*
Prompting

Cl: *Mmm.*

Th: *. . . but you're right. Each hour that you spend working's an hour that you could be using to do something else. And it seems to me like the biggest "something else" in your life now is the academics.*
Reflection

Cl: *Definitely.*

Th: *Well, you might want to consider reducing your work hours . . .*
Advising

Cl: *Mmm.*

Th: *. . . maybe down to zero?*
Close-ended question

Cl: *That's kind of what I'm thinking.*

Th: *It's your choice.*
Rapport (Empowerment, Self-determination)

Cl: *Yeah. Let's see. What else is going on? . . .* [Sighs] *Oh, speaking of financial, my mom and stepdad are going to help me out financially* [Laughs] *with living on campus. I'll move in next week. It just seems like a lot of big changes that are happening right now.*

Th: *Those are big changes.* [Client laughs] *Did you wind up with a roommate or will you be living solo?*
Close-ended question

Cl: *Well, I'll be solo, so it's just going to be me and the four walls.* [Laughs]

Th: *And your independence.*
Furthering

Cl: *And my privacy . . . yeah.*

Th: *How does it feel to have reclaimed something as significant as that?*
Open-ended question

Cl: *It feels good. It almost doesn't feel real yet. I suppose once I'm actually in there and all the boxes are unpacked, then it'll feel more real.*

Th: *And that'll be* your *four walls.*
Interpreting

Cl: *Exactly.*

Th: *And no one'll be on the other side of that door.*
Clarification

Cl: *No, just on the other side of the walls.* [Laughs] *But it looks like this is a quiet dorm. I already met a couple of people, and this one guy older than me.* [Laughs] *That surprised me. That surprised me. But I don't know. . . . It doesn't look like I'll be living in the middle of "party central," so that's going to be good.*

Th: *So are the undergraduates housed in the same building, or are they somewhere different?*
Close-ended question

Cl: *I think it's clear on the other end of the block. I'm not sure exactly where they are, but I've been by the dorm building where I'll be living at all different hours and all different days, and it's pretty tame.* [Laughs]

Th: *Quiet?*
Close-ended question

Cl: *Very.* [Laughs] [Pause] *And that's what I need.* [Pause] *So I'm happy.*

Th: *Okay. How's your sleeping these days?*
Redirecting

Cl: *Oh, a lot better. Yeah, I rarely have sleepless nights anymore. Um, I mean, it was tough during finals, you know? I was waking up a little too early and*

I guess sort of anticipating that I'd be there to take the final. Uh, a couple of nights I had these bizarre dreams where I'd missed the final. . . . I was walking in 2 minutes before a timer rings and being told that I failed and I'm being kicked out of school, . . . [Laughs] *but you know I . . .* [Sighs]

Th: *What student hasn't had that dream?*
Normalizing

Cl: [Laughs] *I suppose that that's normal.*

Th: *And with the weight that you put on the importance of school, of course that dream would be present. The reality seems like it's working out pretty well though.*
Normalizing

Cl: *Certainly.*

Th: *So a little bit of early awakening. And how many times a week are you making it through the night without waking?*
Summarizing, Close-ended question

Cl: *About five or six.*

Th: *Okay, that's quite a leap from what it used to be with multiple awakenings each night.*
Interpreting

Cl: *Right.*

Th: *Okay, so it's a little bit of short sleeping . . . waking early, but not so much the broken-up sleep any more?*
Clarification

Cl: *Right. I mean it's not perfect but it's a lot better than it was.*

Th: *Yeah. How do you feel in general?*
Redirecting

Cl: *Umm . . .* [Pause]

Th: *On a range from relaxed* [Therapist gestures with left hand] *to anxious* [Therapist gestures with right hand], *where would you say you are now?*
Re-asking a question

Cl: *A little more relaxed* [Client points toward the therapist's left hand] *. . . a little more excited about, you know, the next term and this new living situation, that I'm guessing it'll be easier for me to concentrate on school. I'll be among peers when I'm not in my room. . . .* [Laughs] *I'll be going to my room and shutting the door, but I won't be doing it to keep anyone out like I was, you know, like I've been doing at home. But, you know, when I walk out of the door, I'll be interacting with other people who are, you know, working towards the same or similar goal as me.*

Th: [Nods]

Nonverbal attending

Cl: *I think that'll act as encouragement. . . . I think . . . I don't know . . . I'm . . . that's kind of what I get from the other people who've already been living on campus.*

Th: *Mm-hmm, and when you walk out of that door, you'll be among peers as opposed to parents.*

Summarizing

Cl: *Right.*

Th: *And while there's nothing inherently wrong with parents, they're not your peers.* [Client laughs] *And you mentioned that neither your mom nor your stepdad attended college. Now you'll be among people who understand your mission, maybe, more closely.*

Interpreting

Cl: *Right. And it's not that they aren't supportive. I mean, they're willing to finance this nonsense so, you know, they're definitely supportive as far as understanding what I'm going through.*

Th: *Nonsense?*

Confronting

Cl: *Well . . .* [Pause] *I guess I feel a little bit guilty about taking the money. I wish that I didn't have to. It'd be great if I didn't have to take the . . . accept the help. I guess that's what I think's nonsense. Definitely the school's not nonsense . . .*

Th: *Mm-hmm.*

Brief verbal

Cl: . . . *but yeah, I* . . . [Pause] *I guess I do feel conflicted about accepting the financial help.*

Th: *Well, sometimes there're solutions and sometimes the solutions aren't 100% solutions.*
Informing

Cl: *Right. I mean, even my mom kind of said, "So are you sure you want to do this? Why don't you just stay here at home?" And I felt like . . . like I don't want to explain it all over again. Like maybe she gets it or maybe she doesn't want to get it . . . I don't know.*

Th: *Yeah, but it sounds like this is going ahead and that they wish you well.*
Summarizing

Cl: *Yeah, and I think they're glad the cats'll still be around.*

Th: *And you'll still be able to see them, won't you?*
Close-ended question

Cl: *I'll still be able to come and spend time with them.*

Th: *Okay.* [Pause] *How do you feel about this being our last session together?*
Redirecting

Cl: *Umm* . . . [Pause] [Sighs]

Th: *Have you given that any thought?*
Close-ended question

Cl: *Yeah,* [Sighs] *a lot.*

Th: *Tell me a little.*
Furthering

Cl: *Well, I just feel like there's more to do like this . . . like maybe 10 sessions wasn't enough. I feel like I'm not finished here.*

Th: *And that's a valid feeling, because you're not finished. You're never really finished. Every day of your life, there's something to do. Just to review, the goal of short-term therapy is to identify, as we did in our first session together, the multitude of problems that you'd like to address—the things that you'd like to* see resolved in your life. And early in the therapy, the goal was to sort them out, to assign them priorities and start working on the most significant problem first, the idea being that if the largest problem is managed, then that should alleviate enough stress, so that you'll be able to concentrate and focus on working on some of the remaining problems. I think that's happened. I think a lot of that's happened. And as this therapy comes to a close, you'll take the skills and experiences that you've learned and applied here in these sessions—and in between sessions—and continue to apply them to maintain what's been built here. You'll continue to use these solving processes throughout your life . . . and to build on that. True, that after today, we won't be meeting any more, but based on what you've accomplished in these past 10 weeks, and the successes that you've achieved in between sessions, I'm confident you have what it takes to manage without consulting me. You've made quite a lot of progress here. Do you see that?

Validation, Summarizing, Informing, Close-ended question

Cl: Yeah, I think I do.

Th: [Pause] *In your own words, tell me what you see as being different in your life as it is now, compared to our first session.*

Open-ended question

Cl: *Well I couldn't sleep. I didn't know how to. . . . I don't think I had even the notion to move out of my parent's house, you know? That living situation . . .*

Th: *How important your independence was to you?*

Reflection

Cl: *Yeah, yeah, I don't . . . because living on my own just wasn't affordable anymore. I had somewhat resigned myself to something that I didn't really want.*

Th: *You'd settled?*

Interpreting

Cl: *I'd settled. Yeah, and I felt lousy. I guess I needed this to help remind me that I didn't have to settle. And not just with the living situation, but in terms of, you know . . . I don't have to miss a whole night of sleep; I don't have to sit and let my career goals be a big question mark. I mean, there are answers out there. I guess I just didn't have the energy yet to go out and get them.*

Th: *See, and that's another interesting point that we should talk about here: that you didn't realize that you felt bad. One of the things that I've seen here is that you came in with a great awareness of what your circumstances were, but at something of a loss of assigning feelings to these things. The purpose of pain* or hurt—whether it's physical or emotional—is to suggest that something's gone wrong. *Physicians use the characteristic of pain to begin diagnosing what's gone wrong with the patient: They actively assess the origin and severity of pain to diagnose: Where does it hurt? How much does it hurt? When did it begin hurting? Is there anything you do that makes you feel better? In therapy, we do a lot of the same things. We take a look at the living conditions, the emotions, and thoughts: When did it start hurting? What was going on when that hurt was occurring? And from there, we can map out what's emotionally stressed you and come up with some solutions. I think you've come to a point where you've become a lot more emotionally aware of yourself, and when you're seeing stress, or hurt, you now have the capability of saying, "I'm feeling this. . . . I should be feeling better. . . . I don't have to live my whole life like this. What can be done here?" I think you've sharpened your sense of self-awareness and your ability to assemble plans to address the problems and the pains that've been plaguing you. That advancement's been a running theme throughout the course of your therapy. I'm seeing you becoming more emotionally self-sufficient.*

Informing, Summarizing

Cl: *Thanks.*

Th: *What do you think?*
Open-ended question

Cl: [Laughs] *Well, I feel like that's true. I don't know why I'm hesitant to say that, but for some reason, it's still a little bit of a challenge to pat myself on the back and accept that I've succeeded in something. But then I don't know, seeing the A and B+ on the final grades for those two classes . . . yeah, I guess maybe. . . .*

Th: *Proof is in the pudding?*
Interpreting

Cl: *Proof is on the grade sheet.* [Laughs]

Th: *It's interesting that it still takes an external cue from an instructor on the grade sheet for you to know if you're good or not.*
Confronting

Cl: *Well, now, I guess I've been doing that all my life. Not just instructors but, you know, my parents and, you know, when I was younger anyway.*

Th: But what about right now, if I were to ask you, "What kind of student are you?" Just your gut feeling . . . forget what's on the grade sheets, tell me what kind of student you are?
Open-ended question

Cl: Dedicated.

Th: Dedicated. [Pause] Competent?
Reflection, Challenging

Cl: Yeah.

Th: Okay. You are that. [Client laughs] Still hesitant. . . .
Validation

Cl: [Laughs] No, I feel confident. Confident and competent. You know, I guess I needed this term to prove to myself that I could do it. And I can do it. I am doing it.

Th: Maybe one of your posttherapy goals could be learning to identify your own positive points and pat yourself on the back without the external cues.
Advising

Cl: [Pause] That's not easy, . . . but I guess that would be the next logical step.

Th: I think you're right; it may not be easy, but I think it's a worthwhile step in your continued growth. If right now you could write a letter to yourself and send it backwards in time 10 weeks, what would you write?
Reflecting, Redirecting

Cl: Ooh, that's a tough one. [Pause] [Laughs]

Th: I'll get you started.
Prompting

Cl: Oh, okay.

Th: Dear Dusty: [Client laughs] [Pause] I want you to know . . .
Furthering

Cl: *. . . that it's going to be okay.* [Pause]

Th: *Next paragraph . . .*
Furthering

Cl: *Try not to worry;* [Pause] *you'll get there.* [Pause]

Th: *Sincerely yours.*
Prompting

Cl: *Me.* [Laughs]

Th: [Smiles, nods] *Sounds good. Maybe that's something worth writing down.*
Nonverbal attending, Advising

Cl: *Do I have to write it down right now?*

Th: *You don't have to do anything.* [Pause] *How are you feeling right now?*
Open-ended question

Cl: [Pause] *Umm, good, but kind of sad that this'll all come to an end.*

Th: *Yes.*
Validating

Cl: *Which is kind of strange because, you know, I came in here not knowing what to expect, and I've really relied on coming here every week to . . . I mean, this is part of my regular routine. I don't know what I'm going to do with this time anymore.* [Laughs] *I'll have to find something on television I suppose . . .*

Th: *Maybe.*
Brief verbal

Cl: *Or maybe I can just spend extra time studying, right?*

Th: *Maybe. But let's talk about that. This has been a regular part of your life for 2½ months.* [Pause] *We've talked about what these sessions have been like for you. Let's talk about what it's been like in between sessions.*
Summarizing, Redirecting

Cl: *Well, you know, I guess I sort of go through the week kind of taking notes mentally on what to talk about here. Um, I guess,* [Pause] *more and more, with each week, I tend to take more mental notes but sort of check the things off on my own as the week goes by. So by the time I come here, I don't necessarily need to talk about it anymore.*

Th: Good. *This is exactly what we've been talking about . . . that you're growing and you're taking the skills that we're applying in our weekly sessions and applying them on the fly, as things are happening. You're taking the skills learned from these sessions and implementing them without having to run them past me . . . without having to check and see if you got it right. You can do this. You* are *doing this.* [Client laughs] *And like anything else, as you practice, you'll get better and better at this.*

Summarizing, Informing

Cl: *Yeah, uh, like you said—I think it was a few weeks ago—I'm solving these things on my own, whereas before I would just kind of let them pile up, and I wouldn't even attend to them. It was just kind of throwing things on the other side of the wall and letting them collect. I guess sooner or later the walls are going to give, and it'll all come falling back at you.*

Th: *Right, and when they all come piling back at you, they kind of lose their boundaries, and then it just looks like one massive problem with no beginning and no ending.*

Reflection

Cl: *Right, or like a sponge that when you drop it under the water, it weighs a lot less than when you pull it back out.*

Th: [Confused look]

Nonverbal attending

Cl: *Did that make sense?*

Th: *I guess I don't understand.*

Clarification

Cl: *Well, you know how a sponge is very lightweight when it's dry. And then you put it in water and you dunk it and it soaks it all in. And when you pull the sponge up, it's got all the water in it and it weighs more.*

Th: *It absorbs a lot?*

Reflection

Cl: *Right, so that's kind of what that stuff does when I don't . . . when issues come up and I don't deal with them. What I would do—at least in the beginning here with this—is I would . . . these issues would come up throughout the week, and I would actually write them down on a piece of paper, and I would save them. So that on the day to come here and meet with you, you could help me solve them. But what seems to be happening now is that the list of things . . . the list's getting shorter, and I'm actually taking care of them before I come here.*

Th: *So you're coping with them as they happen, as opposed to banking them up and then seeing what we can do with them together?*
Summarizing

Cl: *Exactly!*

Th: *So you're becoming more independent.*
Generalizing

Cl: *Yeah.*

Th: *Which means, it's okay to terminate therapy.*
Generalizing

Cl: *Oh, I don't like the word "terminate."*

Th: *What's a better word?*
Open-ended question

Cl: *[Pause] [Laughs] I don't know if there is a better word.*

Th: *Sometimes when people don't like "good-bye" . . .*
Normalizing

Cl: *I hate good-bye.*

Th: *How about "sayonara"?*
Close-ended question

Cl: *That's just "good-bye" in another language, right?*

Th: *Well this is an ending. And it's okay to feel a sense of loss here.*
Empathy, Normalizing

Cl: *Yeah, I know it's just depressing.*

Th: *It is a loss. It is depressing. [Pause] It is an ending. In a way, it's also a beginning, . . . the next step in your independence.*
Empathy, Normalizing, Informing, Reframing

Cl: *Well, I won't get to come here and talk to you anymore. I'm going to miss you.*

Th: *Thank-you. I'll miss you too.*
Rapport

Cl: [Pause]

Th: *And what kind of beginning will this be?*
Open-ended question

Cl: [Pause] *I just learn to do things more on my own.*

Th: *I think you're already doing that. I think you'll continue to do things on your own. And I think over time, you're going to come to learn something about yourself that no amount of therapy with me is going to get you. I sense a running theme of some low self-esteem that still seems to be present. And I'm guessing that after the therapy's over, as you reflect on the accomplishments in your life, you'll see that your solving capabilities will no longer at all be attributable to me or us. This advancement will land solely on you. And I'd hope that you'd monitor your progress and accomplishments as we have in here and know that none of those things happened per chance or by accident or by clever third party. They'll be a factor of your vision and your doing. I think that's going to do a lot for your self-esteem in a way that I can't do. When you fly solo, that perfect three-point landing's only yours and no one else's.*
Summarizing, Interpreting, Generalizing

Cl: *So, then I'll be able to take credit for it.*

Th: *Yes.*
Brief verbal

Cl: *And if I screw up?*

Th: *Then that'll be yours too. But Dusty, if you were going to screw up, you'd have screwed up by now.*
Challenging

Cl: *I guess so.*

Th: *Yes, there's the fear of screwing up, because when you're flying solo, and you screw up, it's clear whose fault it is.*
Empathy, Informing

Cl: *Mine!*

Th: *Yes. Yours. But I don't see you as a screw-up. You don't sit idle between sessions, nor do you go into a nosedive in between sessions. In fact, some of the most remarkable work that you've accomplished over these 10 weeks has happened in between sessions. If you were going to screw up, we'd have seen that by now. What do you think?*
Reflection, Generalizing, Open-ended question

Cl: [Pause] *Wow. I guess you're right. You're right.*

Th: *Yes, how does that make you feel?*
Furthering

Cl: [Pause] *Kind of empowered.*

Th: *Yeah. You're stronger than you think. Just to review: You know all of these changes and improvements that've happened over the last 10 weeks? . . .*
Validation, Summarizing

Cl: *What about them?*

Th: *Who do you think's responsible for those?*
Close-ended question

Cl: *You?* [Laughs]

Th: [Silence, serious gaze]
Nonverbal attending

Cl: *Okay.*

Th: *Hey, you need to get this: Did I get you enrolled in college?* [Client laughs] *Did I get you a room at the dorm? Did I get you A's in your classes?*
Summarizing, Challenging

Cl: Well, it was your idea to go to the vocational counselor. But, I mean, I actually went . . .

Th: You did all the hard work.
Reframing

Cl: Yeah, that's true.

Th: I just sat here and talked to you about it. It's one thing to talk about climbing Everest. You climbed it. They never announce the name of the guy who talked about it. All these changes that you've seen in your life, they've all been of your hand. You've done all the live work. And no matter how much you want to dodge it or deny it or shift it somewhere else, your life is your responsibility, and you've done some good solid work in these past 10 weeks.
Reframing

Cl: Thank-you.

Th: You're welcome. [Pause] Look in the mirror and say that, [Client laughs] because you've done some amazing things for yourself here. What do you think?
Generalizing, Open-ended question

Cl: I think you're right.

Th: You're smiling.
Observational cue

Cl: [Laughs] Because that wasn't easy to say. But I believe it.

Th: But that's what this has all been about. This therapy's not been about doing easy things; this therapy's been about doing meaningful things and positive things . . . and building the next higher version of you. [Client laughs] What's on your mind now?
Generalizing, Open-ended question

Cl: Well, [Pause] well, I know this is the last session but, I mean, can I come by and like just say "hi" at some point? . . . Just call and say hello or . . . ?

Th: If you want to, you can call me and fill me in on what's going on; that'd be fine. If I'm not here you can put it on the voice mail.
Informing

Cl: *Would it be okay if I came by in person . . . if I stop by and just say "hello"?*

Th: *Typically we don't do that.*
        Informing

Cl: *Why not?*

Th: *Because we've had a professional relationship. And it would be inappropriate to attempt to bend this into a social relationship. In fact, ethically, it's really not supposed to happen that way.*
        Informing

Cl: *Should I take this personally?*

Th: *I could see how you might feel that way, but I'd hope not. This is the way any therapist would handle relations with the client. There's an ethical principle called "dual-relationship" that, in short, means that you don't have your friends as clients, and you don't have your clients as friends. You don't have your friends as clients because you're emotionally invested and you really don't have the objectivity that's necessary to embark on quality therapy, . . .*
        Empathy, Informing

Cl: *That makes sense.*

Th: *. . . and you don't have your clients, or ex-clients, as friends because there's an undeniable residual authority that would be ever present. And that really wouldn't be an appropriate basis for friendship or peer-to-peer kind of relationship. I want you to understand this isn't about you.*
        Informing

Cl: *Okay.*

Th: *These ethics are in place for a reason. . . . They're in place to protect clients.*
        Informing

Cl: *I guess it's not like it is on TV.*

Th: *TV is pretend.*
        Reflection

Cl: [Laughs] *True.* [Pause] *I feel like I'm losing a friend.*

Th: *Well, it's undeniable that we've had something of an emotional contact here. You've disclosed a lot of very vulnerable information. I mean, who's a friend? . . . Somebody that you confide in and tell them your deep dark stuff, and I've been privileged that you've disclosed as freely with me as you have. Some friends help you through some rough times too, so it follows that you'd feel as if you're losing a friend. It is a loss. It's definitely a loss. I'm going to miss you, too. It's been a pleasure and an adventure coming to know who you are, what you're about, learn about your mission, help you connect the dots, help you clear the road and get from here to there, and I think that being witness to what you've built over these past 10 weeks has been quite a privilege. I'm proud of you, and I can see you're proud of yourself, no matter how you have to hesitate before you say that.*

Empathy, Validation, Summarizing, Normalizing

Cl: *[Laughs] [Sighs] So can we talk about at least just . . . I don't know how much time we have left, but can we talk about one more thing before we wrap this up for good?*

Th: *Sure.*

Brief verbal

Cl: *Well, I told you about the person I met, . . . the one with the keys locked in the car on campus.*

Th: *The wire coat hanger rescue?*

Clarification

Cl: *The wire coat hanger rescue, . . . [Laughs] yeah.*

Th: *Yes.*

Brief verbal

Cl: *Well, you know we went out a couple of times . . .*

Th: *Mm-hmm.*

Brief verbal

Cl: *. . . you know, but the age difference is just kind of . . . I don't know . . . I can just . . . I could feel it because this is about 8 years. I just . . . well, I've never been attracted to anyone who's younger than me. I just haven't. It just feels kind of strange, and . . . I don't know. I'm kind of thinking that . . . and I,*

I mean, I tried . . . [Pause] *We went out a few times. I'm kind of feeling like maybe I should just hold off on the dating thing for a while . . . just worry about school. I have my friends, you know. They see a little bit less of me now, but, you know, most of them understand.*

Th: *And that's your privilege. You know, there'll always be people out there.*
Validation, Reframing

Cl: *That's true.*

Th: *You might want to keep an open mind.*
Advising

Cl: *Yeah, you never know who might go drifting by. Maybe . . . if it was the right person . . . I guess I'll just have to wait and see.*

Th: *Sure.* [Pause] *You keep looking at your watch.*
Observational cue

Cl: *I just . . . I just don't want to end, and there's still time here, and I just . . . I just feel like I want to run the clock out.*

Th: *Dusty, what did you come into therapy for?*
Redirecting

Cl: *For help, or answers.*

Th: *About what? What were your goals?*
Specificity

Cl: *Uh, well, I wanted to correct the sleeping problem. I wanted to learn how to deal with my living situation. I wanted to figure out my career goal questions.*

Th: *And how did that all work out?*
Furthering

Cl: *Beautifully! Well, I mean, you know, the story isn't over yet, I guess, but . . .*

Th: *It's not over; it's never over. You know, the end of therapy doesn't mean the end of problems or the end of your mission. You know, sometimes therapy's like stopping for directions: you find out where you are; you talk about where you want to go; you get a map and some directions; and you move on. I think that's what this form of therapy, in a lot of ways, has worked out to be. I mean, in the same way that you wouldn't keep that same direction-giver in the back seat of your car for the rest of your life, you don't necessarily need to be in therapy to finish the rest of your mission. And there're going to be flat tires along the way, and there're going to be closed roads. And you're skillful enough that you'll be able to navigate the detours on your own. You've demonstrated quite an adaptability and independence, both in here and out there in between sessions. And I know you can carry that forward. What do you think?*

Informing, Open-ended question

Cl: [Pause] *Are you sure you don't want to ride around in my back seat with me?*

Th: *I get car sick.* [Both laugh]
Brief verbal

Cl: *Fair enough.*

Th: *This is a loss, and it is an ending. And this time next week, I'll be missing you too. But you have other places to be, and other things to do.*
Empathy, Reframing

Cl: *You don't think I need help?*

Th: *Do you?*
Close-ended question

Cl: *Well, I think I've gotten help.*

Th: *I think you're ready to fly solo, but this isn't the first time you've flown solo.*
Reframing

Cl: *True.*

Th: *Up until 10 weeks ago, you lived your whole life without a therapist to see every week, and somehow it's worked. And I think having come to the sessions and done the intense work that you've done, I think you can continue this work. There's nothing to suggest that you can't or won't.* [Pause] *You're smiling. What's behind that smile?*
Summarizing, Observational cues, Open-ended question

Cl: *I just feel really good right now. I feel sad that this is ending, but, I mean, I understand why, you know, and . . . but I feel, on one hand, I'm sad this is ending, but on the other hand, I feel like I'm walking out of here with a lot more.* [Pause] [Sighs] *I feel like I'm walking out of here stronger than when I first walked in 10 weeks ago.*

Th: *I can see that, and I'm a little sad that this is ending too. It's been quite a privilege to work with you and to see what you're evolving into. I see great things ahead for you, and please send me a picture of you in your graduation gown.*
Empathy

Cl: *And the funny hat!* [Both laugh]

Th: *Hey, I'm a great fan of funny hats. I'd very much like to see that. That hat signifies a lot.*
Validation

Cl: *In 2 years, when I graduate, will you remember who I am?*

Th: *Dusty, do you think you'll forget* me *in 2 years?*
Challenging

Cl: *Definitely not.*

Th: *I'll always remember you.* [Client becomes tearful, therapist offers a tissue box].
Informing

Cl: *Thank-you.* [Laughs]

Th: *Thank-you. What's on your mind now?*
Open-ended question

Cl: *Well, okay, I mean, I guess I understand this whole thing.* . . . *We can't hang out as friends or anything, but can I send you something for your birthday or something? What's your favorite wine?*

Th: *I appreciate that. I know you want to do something nice, but that really wouldn't be appropriate. You don't owe me anything like that. Your accomplishments, plus what you're going to go out and accomplish and contribute to the world are, to me, better than anything you can put in a box.* [Checks time] [Pause] *Well,* . . . *we're there.*
Empathy, Informing

Cl: [Pause] *So this is it, huh?*

Th: *This is it.*
        Reflection

Cl: [Sighs] *Umm, I guess I don't know what to say at this point.*

Th: *It's okay. You don't have to say anything.*
        Normalizing

Cl: *I feel like "thank-you" isn't enough, and I can't send you gifts, so I almost feel like I have to just pass this forward somehow.*

Th: *Well, in a way, maybe you will. You know, a lot of what we learn and how to cope and how to be who we are comes from what we observe in others. We observe things we like, or admire, or seem worthwhile, and we clip off a piece of that and make it part of our repertoire. And as you go out there, maybe, at some point, someone'll see some sharp coping skills and some good compassion that's within you, and maybe, in some way, they'll take that and make that part of themselves, and benefit from bits of what we've done here, and who you are as a person. Parts of this may well carry forward.*
        Reframing

Cl: *Maybe so.*

Th: [Pause] *I'm glad we had a chance to work together.*
        Rapport

Cl: *Me too.*

Th: *Take care.*
        Rapport

Cl: *I will.*

—END OF SESSION—

Appendix D

Ethical Standards of Human Service Professionals
National Organization for Human Services
Council for Standards in Human Service Education
Adopted 1996

Preamble

Human services is a profession developing in response to and in anticipation of the direction of human needs and human problems in the late twentieth century. Characterized particularly by an appreciation of human beings in all of their diversity, human services offers assistance to its clients within the context of their community and environment. Human service professionals and those who educate them, regardless of whether they are students, faculty or practitioners, promote and encourage the unique values and characteristics of human services. In so doing human service professionals and educators uphold the integrity and ethics of the profession, partake in constructive criticism of the profession, promote client and community well-being, and enhance their own professional growth.

The ethical guidelines presented are a set of standards of conduct which the human service professionals and educators consider in ethical and professional decision making. It is hoped that these guidelines will be of assistance when human service professionals and educators are challenged by difficult ethical dilemmas. Although ethical codes are not legal documents, they may be used to assist in the adjudication of issues related to ethical human service behavior.

SOURCE: Reprinted with permission of the National Organization for Human Services and Council for Standards in Human Service Education, copyright 1996.

Section I—Standards for Human Service Professionals

Human service professionals function in many ways and carry out many roles. They enter into professional-client relationships with individuals, families, groups and communities who are all referred to as "clients" in these standards. Among their roles are caregiver, case manager, broker, teacher/ educator, behavior changer, consultant, outreach professional, mobilizer, advocate, community planner, community change organizer, evaluator and administrator. The following standards are written with these multifaceted roles in mind.

The Human Service Professional's Responsibility to Clients

STATEMENT 1   Human service professionals negotiate with clients the purpose, goals, and nature of the helping relationship prior to its onset as well as inform clients of the limitations of the proposed relationship.

STATEMENT 2   Human service professionals respect the integrity and welfare of the client at all times. Each client is treated with respect, acceptance and dignity.

STATEMENT 3   Human service professionals protect the client's right to privacy and confidentiality except when such confidentiality would cause harm to the client or others, when agency guidelines state otherwise, or under other stated conditions (e.g., local, state, or federal laws). Professionals inform clients of the limits of confidentiality prior to the onset of the helping relationship.

STATEMENT 4   If it is suspected that danger or harm may occur to the client or to others as a result of a client's behavior, the human service professional acts in an appropriate and professional manner to protect the safety of those individuals. This may involve seeking consultation, supervision, and/or breaking the confidentiality of the relationship.

STATEMENT 5   Human service professionals protect the integrity, safety, and security of client records. All written client information that is shared with other professionals, except in the course of professional supervision, must have the client's prior written consent.

STATEMENT 6   Human service professionals are aware that in their relationships with clients power and status are unequal. Therefore they recognize that dual or multiple relationships may increase the risk of harm to, or exploitation of, clients, and may impair their professional judgment. However, in some communities and situations it may not be feasible to avoid social or other nonprofessional contact with clients. Human service professionals support the trust implicit in the helping relationship by avoiding dual relationships that may impair professional judgment, increase the risk of harm to clients or lead to exploitation.

STATEMENT 7 Sexual relationships with current clients are not considered to be in the best interest of the client and are prohibited. Sexual relationships with previous clients are considered dual relationships and are addressed in STATEMENT 6 (above).

STATEMENT 8 The client's right to self-determination is protected by human service professionals. They recognize the client's right to receive or refuse services.

STATEMENT 9 Human service professionals recognize and build on client strengths.

The Human Service Professional's Responsibility to the Community and Society

STATEMENT 10 Human service professionals are aware of local, state, and federal laws. They advocate for change in regulations and statutes when such legislation conflicts with ethical guidelines and/or client rights. Where laws are harmful to individuals, groups or communities, human service professionals consider the conflict between the values of obeying the law and the values of serving people and may decide to initiate social action.

STATEMENT 11 Human service professionals keep informed about current social issues as they affect the client and the community. They share that information with clients, groups and community as part of their work.

STATEMENT 12 Human service professionals understand the complex interaction between individuals, their families, the communities in which they live, and society.

STATEMENT 13 Human service professionals act as advocates in addressing unmet client and community needs. Human service professionals provide a mechanism for identifying unmet client needs, calling attention to these needs, and assisting in planning and mobilizing to advocate for those needs at the local community level.

STATEMENT 14 Human service professionals represent their qualifications to the public accurately.

STATEMENT 15 Human service professionals describe the effectiveness of programs, treatments, and/or techniques accurately.

STATEMENT 16   Human service professionals advocate for the rights of all members of society, particularly those who are members of minorities and groups at which discriminatory practices have historically been directed.

STATEMENT 17   Human service professionals provide services without discrimination or preference based on age, ethnicity, culture, race, disability, gender, religion, sexual orientation or socioeconomic status.

STATEMENT 18   Human service professionals are knowledgeable about the cultures and communities within which they practice. They are aware of multiculturalism in society and its impact on the community as well as individuals within the community. They respect individuals and groups, their cultures and beliefs.

STATEMENT 19   Human service professionals are aware of their own cultural backgrounds, beliefs, and values, recognizing the potential for impact on their relationships with others.

STATEMENT 20   Human service professionals are aware of sociopolitical issues that differentially affect clients from diverse backgrounds.

STATEMENT 21   Human service professionals seek the training, experience, education and supervision necessary to ensure their effectiveness in working with culturally diverse client populations.

The Human Service Professional's Responsibility to Colleagues

STATEMENT 22   Human service professionals avoid duplicating another professional's helping relationship with a client They consult with other professionals who are assisting the client in a different type of relationship when it is in the best interest of the client to do so.

STATEMENT 23   When a human service professional has a conflict with a colleague, he or she first seeks out the colleague in an attempt to manage the problem. If necessary, the professional then seeks the assistance of supervisors, consultants or other professionals in efforts to manage the problem.

STATEMENT 24   Human service professionals respond appropriately to unethical behavior of colleagues. Usually this means initially talking directly with the colleague and, if no resolution is forthcoming, reporting the colleague's behavior to supervisory or administrative staff and/or to the Professional organization(s) to which the colleague belongs.

STATEMENT 25   All consultations between human service professionals are kept confidential unless to do so would result in harm to clients or communities.

The Human Service Professional's
Responsibility to the Profession

STATEMENT 26   Human service professionals know the limit and scope of their professional knowledge and offer services only within their knowledge and skill base.

STATEMENT 27   Human service professionals seek appropriate consultation and supervision to assist in decision-making when there are legal, ethical or other dilemmas.

STATEMENT 28   Human service professionals act with integrity, honesty, genuineness, and objectivity.

STATEMENT 29   Human service professionals promote cooperation among related disciplines (e.g., psychology, counseling, social work, nursing, family and consumer sciences, medicine, education) to foster professional growth and interests within the various fields.

STATEMENT 30   Human service professionals promote the continuing development of their profession. They encourage membership in professional associations, support research endeavors, foster educational advancement, advocate for appropriate legislative actions, and participate in other related professional activities.

STATEMENT 31   Human service professionals continually seek out new and effective approaches to enhance their professional abilities.

The Human Service Professional's
Responsibility to Employers

STATEMENT 32   Human service professionals adhere to commitments made to their employers.

STATEMENT 33   Human service professionals participate in efforts to establish and maintain employment conditions which are conducive to high quality client services. They assist in evaluating the effectiveness of the agency through reliable and valid assessment measures.

STATEMENT 34   When a conflict arises between fulfilling the responsibility to the employer and the responsibility to the client, human service professionals advise both of the conflict and work conjointly with all involved to manage the conflict.

The Human Service Professional's Responsibility to Self

STATEMENT 35   Human service professionals strive to personify those characteristics typically associated with the profession (e.g., accountability, respect for others, genuineness, empathy, pragmatism).

STATEMENT 36   Human service professionals foster self-awareness and personal growth in themselves. They recognize that when professionals are aware of their own values, attitudes, cultural background, and personal needs, the process of helping others is less likely to be negatively impacted by those factors.

STATEMENT 37   Human service professionals recognize a commitment to lifelong learning and continually upgrade knowledge and skills to serve the populations better.

Section II—Standards for Human Service Educators

Human Service educators are familiar with, informed by and accountable to the standards of professional conduct put forth by their institutions of higher learning; their professional disciplines, for example, American Association of University Professors (AAUP), American Counseling Association (ACA), Academy of Criminal Justice (ACJS), American Psychological Association (APA), American Sociological Association (ASA), National Association of Social Workers (NASW), National Board of Certified Counselors (NBCC), National Education Association (NEA); and the National Organization for Human Services (NOHS).

STATEMENT 38   Human service educators uphold the principle of liberal education and embrace the essence of academic freedom, abstaining from inflicting their own personal views/morals on students, and allowing students the freedom to express their views without penalty, censure or ridicule, and to engage in critical thinking.

STATEMENT 39   Human service educators provide students with readily available and explicit program policies and criteria regarding program goals and objectives, recruitment, admission, course requirements, evaluations, retention and dismissal in accordance with due process procedures.

STATEMENT 40   Human service educators demonstrate high standards of scholarship in content areas and of pedagogy by staying current with developments in the field of Human Services and in teaching effectiveness, for example learning styles and teaching styles.

STATEMENT 41   Human service educators monitor students' field experiences to ensure the quality of the placement site, supervisory experience, and learning experience towards the goals of professional identity and skill development.

STATEMENT 42   Human service educators participate actively in the selection of required readings and use them with care, based strictly on the merits of the material's content, and present relevant information accurately, objectively and fully.

STATEMENT 43   Human service educators, at the onset of courses: inform students if sensitive/controversial issues or experiential/affective content or process are part of the course design; ensure that students are offered opportunities to discuss in structured ways their reactions to sensitive or controversial class content; ensure that the presentation of such material is justified on pedagogical grounds directly related to the course; and, differentiate between information based on scientific data, anecdotal data, and personal opinion.

STATEMENT 44   Human service educators develop and demonstrate culturally sensitive knowledge, awareness, and teaching methodology.

STATEMENT 45   Human service educators demonstrate full commitment to their appointed responsibilities, and are enthusiastic about and encouraging of students' learning.

STATEMENT 46   Human service educators model the personal attributes, values and skills of the human service professional, including but not limited to, the willingness to seek and respond to feedback from students.

STATEMENT 47   Human service educators establish and uphold appropriate guidelines concerning self-disclosure or student-disclosure of sensitive/personal information.

STATEMENT 48   Human service educators establish an appropriate and timely process for providing clear and objective feedback to students about their performance on relevant and established course/program academic and personal competence requirements and their suitability for the field.

STATEMENT 49   Human service educators are aware that in their relationships with students, power and status are unequal; therefore, human service educators are responsible to clearly define and maintain ethical and professional relationships with students, and avoid conduct that is demeaning, embarrassing or exploitative of students, and to treat students fairly, equally and without discrimination.

STATEMENT 50   Human service educators recognize and acknowledge the contributions of students to their work, for example in case material, workshops, research, publications.

STATEMENT 51   Human service educators demonstrate professional standards of conduct in managing personal or professional differences with colleagues, for example, not disclosing such differences and/or affirming a student's negative opinion of a faculty/program.

STATEMENT 52   Human service educators ensure that students are familiar with, informed by, and accountable to the ethical standards and policies put forth by their program/department, the course syllabus/instructor, their advisor(s), and the Ethical Standards of Human Service Professionals.

STATEMENT 53   Human service educators are aware of all relevant curriculum standards, including those of the Council for Standards in Human Services Education (CSHSE); the Community Support Skills Standards; and state/local standards, and take them into consideration in designing the curriculum.

STATEMENT 54   Human service educators create a learning context in which students can achieve the knowledge, skills, values and attitudes of the academic program.

Glossary

Advice (p. 7)

- Advice should be based on comprehensive information (background, problem, goal, resources, beliefs, etc.).
- Phrase advice as recommendations, not demands.

Advising (p. 144)

Step 1. Identify the client's problem.

Step 2. Identify the client's goal.

Step 3. Solicit solutions.

Step 4. Present recommendation.

Anger (p. 88)

- The initial emotional reaction to hurt or loss

Anxiety (p. 90)

- Anticipating loss or hurt
- Feeling that one's physical or emotional safety or well-being is threatened

Ask one question at a time (p. 111)

- If a compound question comes to mind, break it into separate queries.
- Prioritize (separate) questions.
- Progressively adjust questions per responses.

Avoid asking accusatory questions (p. 118)

- Have courage. It's okay to tactfully explore tough issues.
- Probe issues in a sensitive, respectful fashion.
- Phrase questions nonjudgmentally.

Avoid asking biased questions (p. 121)

- Loading questions with an implicit right answer may solicit false confirmations.
- Assemble questions that do not carry a preferred response.

Avoid asking multiple-choice questions (p. 120)

- It can be challenging to assemble a comprehensive list of choices.
- Consider substituting with an open-ended question.

Avoid asking "Why?" questions (p. 119)

- Asking why is akin to demanding justification.
- May trigger defensiveness
- May derail emotional processes

Boundaries (p. 15)

- Focus remains on the client, not the therapist.
- Conversations should be goal-directed, addressing the client's needs.
- Contact should not extend beyond the therapeutic setting.

Brief verbals (p. 65)

Unobtrusively following or advancing the communication:

- *Uh-huh, mm-hmm, hmm, gotcha, okay, right, I get it, I see, go on*
- Selectively repeat key word(s) that the client said.

Buffering (p. 113)

- Avoid asking a rapid-fire succession of questions.
- Include meaningful commentary between questions.

Challenging (p. 137)

- Specifically identify contradictions or inconsistencies (facts, time lines, vagueness, etc.)
- Tactfully request clarification.
- *First you said X, and now you're telling me Y. I'm not understanding . . .*

Clarification (p. 77)

Requesting details on unfamiliar language, vagueness, discontinuous storytelling, or characters involved in the client's life:

- *What did you mean when you said . . . ?*
- *I'm not sure I understand . . .*

Close-ended question (p. 116)

Asking for a concise (objective) response (such as a *yes* or *no* question):

- *How old are you?*
- *Do you live with your parents?*
- *Are you a student?*

Confidentiality (p. 14)

- Disclose privileged communication only with client's or exclient's written consent.
- Office should be soundproofed.
- Paper files should be locked and data files encrypted.
- Protect client identity in peer consults.
- Consent is not required for legally mandated reporting.
- Know laws regarding subpoenas, depositions, and court orders.

Confronting (p. 139)

- Specifically identify and address discrepancies or implausibility.
- Encourage reconciliation of potentially misleading information.
- *This doesn't make sense to me . . .*
- *Here's what I'm understanding: . . . This doesn't sound right.*

Coping with prejudices (p. 100)

- Recognize the specific characteristics of your biases.
- Seek to dispel bias via establishing meaningful contact with such groups or individuals.

Coping with silence (p. 42)

Be patient; consider some prompts:

- *Take your time.*
- *What are you thinking or feeling?*
- *What do you want me to know?*
- *You seem . . . (distressed, thoughtful, etc.)*
- *You can start anywhere.*

Depression (p. 90)

- Hurt or loss that is held in and not vented or processed
- An interruption in the conveyance of (hurt) emotions

Emotional involvement (p. 9)

- Purposefully identify the client's feelings and your own feelings.
- Honor and process the client's feelings. The primary focus should be the client's feelings.

Empathy (p. 91)

- Conveying your perception of the client's emotional state:
- *You seem . . . (tense, sad, afraid, etc.)*
- *When you discuss your family, you seem prideful.*

Focusing (p. 128)

- Summarize the multiple issues raised in therapy, soliciting prioritized selection.
- Encourage concentrating on fewer substantial issues.
- *It sounds like there's a lot going on now: X, Y, Z. Which would you like us to concentrate on first?*

Fostering sensitive disclosure (p. 35)

- Create a supportive environment wherein it's safe to discuss difficult truths.
- Respectfully build and maintain genuine positive regard and nonjudgmental stance.
- Move at the client's pace.

Frustration (p. 88)

- Inability to gratify a desire
- Difficulty satisfying an urge or need
- Delays or encumbrances related to the accomplishment of a goal

Furthering (p. 106)

- Requesting additional details
- Spurs supplemental storytelling in an open-ended fashion
- *Tell me more about XYZ.*
- *You mentioned XYZ.*
- *I'm curious about XYZ.*

Generalizing (p. 133)

- Identify positive and negative trends and (re)actions.
- Cite specific events to support your generalization.
- *It seems like when X happens, it triggers Y.*
- *Considering X, Y, and Z, you seem to be the smart one in your family.*

Goal (p. 4)

- Collaborate with client to derive and pursue goals.
- Goals must concur with client's wishes, values, and belief system.
- Goals should be substantial, legal, and ethical.

Guilt (p. 90)

Feeling that one's emotions, lack of emotions, actions, inactions, or thoughts are unacceptable

Happiness (p. 88)

Feeling of personal satisfaction and contentment resulting from one's needs, wishes, or expectations being met

Hurt (see Anger)

Hurt = Loss (loss of person, love, admiration, esteem, respect, property, privilege, control, stability, power, etc.)

Informing (p. 142)

- Address relevant questions, incomplete information, or misconceptions.
- Consider citing sources or your level of expertise.

Initial contact (p. 3)

- Offer professional disclosure statement detailing your training.
- Client is given agency's policies (cancellations, fees, services).
- Client signs "consent for treatment" form.

Interpreting (p. 132)

Tentatively submitting your impression of the circumstances discussed:

- *Maybe X and Y are related.*

Introduction and ground rules (p. 40)

- Greet client warmly; exchange names.
- Welcome client's initial concerns or questions.
- Provide overview of agency rules.
- Discuss limits of confidentiality.

Involvement (p. 12)

- Actively engage in problem-solving process.
- Prudently limit your involvement. Encourage client action per principles of self-determination, empowerment, and self-efficacy.

Legal (p. 13)

- Know laws pertaining to your domain.
- Do not advocate illegal action.
- Submit mandated reports: child, elderly, or dependent abuse or neglect; Tarasoff warnings.

Managing countertransference (p. 99)

- Identify clients or issues that trigger strong feeling within you.
- Self-reflect; consider similar (unresolved) feelings within you.
- Confer with others (colleagues, supervisors, therapist, etc.).

Matching (p. 48)

- Tune your conveyance (vocabulary, voice tone, volume, emotional level, body language, formality or informality, etc.) to the client's communication style.

Monitoring your feelings (p. 99)

- Maintain awareness of your strong (positive and negative) feelings toward clients and subject matter. Such feelings may suggest issues within you needing resolution.

Nonjudgmental attitude (p. 18)

- Monitor and keep personal biases in check.
- Be open to the client's (unique) perspective or adaptation.
- Offer alternatives in a provisional manner.

Nonverbal attending (p. 63)

- Observe the client's nonverbal behavior.
- Use eye contact, facial expressions, nods, body language, posture, and gestures to demonstrate active listening.

Normalizing (p. 96)

Assuring the client that his or her condition or adaptation is not atypical or pathological per their circumstances:

- *That's actually a fairly common reaction.*
- *When XYZ happens, sometimes people do or feel . . .*

Objectivity (p. 9)

- Tend to the client's feelings.
- Your professional perspective can facilitate clarity, seeing potential solutions otherwise obscured by powerful emotions.

Observational cues (p. 60)

- Attend to verbal and nonverbal signals: voice tone, facial expression, eye contact, body language.

- Notice and discuss concordant (tears related to trauma) and discordant conveyances (smiling while discussing tragedy).

Open-ended question (p. 116)

Broadly prompting for expanded (subjective) storytelling:
- *What did you do this weekend?*
- *Tell me about your family.*

Open-ended requests (p. 109)

Questions phrased to suggest that there is more information available:
- *When else have you done XYZ?*
- *Who was with you?*

Paraphrasing (See **Reflection**)

Pausing (p. 66)

Patiently allow for some thinking or feeling space for the client and yourself:
- *I can see this is difficult for you. . . . Take your time with this.*
- *This is interesting. . . . Let me think about this for a moment.*

Personal contact (p. 11)

- Separate social from professional contacts.
- Avoid dual or multiple relationships.
- Limit contact with clients and ex-clients to session time and setting.

Perspective (p. 8)

- Strive for objectivity while recognizing your feelings and wishes for the client.
- Honor the client's right to self-determination in light of your standpoint.

Positive regard (p. 19)

- Actively recognize and articulate the value and inherent worth of the client.
- Convey your confidence in the client's capacity to grow, advance, or adapt.

Presenting problem (p. 41)

The initial problem that the client discloses:
- *How can I help you?*
- *Where would you like to begin?*
- *I understand from your file . . .*

Prompting (p. 108)

Brief verbal or nonverbal cues to request elaboration or to advance storytelling:

- *And ...*
- *Then what?*
- Nods, curious expression, gestures, etc.

Rapport (p. 33)

Anything you do or say to facilitate comfort, trust, and safety in an ethical and respectful manner

Re-asking a question (p. 114)

If the client is unresponsive or fails to clearly address the question, then tactfully rephrase and resubmit your question.

Recognizing your perspective (p. 98)

Be aware of your personal thoughts and feelings as you empathetically perceive the client.

Redirecting (p. 125)

Guiding the dialogue back to the focal topic:

- *Let's get back to XYZ.*
- *A few minutes ago, we were talking about XYZ.*

Reflection/Paraphrasing (p. 70)

Tentatively stating your perception of the client's story in your own words to demonstrate attentiveness and solicit corrections:

- *Let me see if I'm getting this straight. . . . Is that right?*
- *So after you got home ...*

Reframing (p. 130)

Proposing an alternate positive interpretation of neutral or negative circumstances:

- *It seems like you're being forced to grow in a way that you didn't bargain for.*

Rescind your ego (p. 10)

- The client is responsible for his or her own actions, inactions, and outcomes (or lack thereof).
- Avoid accepting too much credit or blame for the client's state.

Respect (p. 17)

- Regard the client's feelings, beliefs, and thoughts as highly as your own.
- Honor the client's right to self-determination.

Respect the client's boundaries (p. 46)

You may express your clinical opinions, but always honor the client's privilege to determine topics of discussion, therapeutic goals, choices, actions, and inactions.

Resuming (p. 123)

Picking up from where the last session ended:

- *Last week you mentioned that you were going to do XYZ.*

Returning (p. 122)

Going back to a point that the client mentioned before:

- *You mentioned XYZ.*
- *Tell me more about XYZ.*

Reverse reflection (p. 72)

Respectfully requesting the client to play back your (complex or detailed) message to verify and clarify comprehension:

- *I just want to make sure I'm clear. Could you please tell me, in your own words, what I just said?*

Sadness (p. 90)

The appropriate emotional expression associated with a (recent) hurt or loss

Scope of practice (p. 15)

- Provide only those services for which you have received appropriate training, certification, or licensure.
- Client cannot waive scope of practice principle.

Selection (p. 2)

- Client selection should be free of bias (age, ethnicity, culture, race, disability, gender, religion, sexual orientation, socioeconomic status, etc.).
- Clients may be assigned per therapist's expertise.

Self-disclosure guidelines (p. 25)

- Assess how comfortable you feel disclosing this particular piece of information.
- Reflect on how beneficial this self-disclosure would be to the client.
- Keep self-disclosures genuine.
- Consider using self-disclosure sparingly.

SOLER (p. 63)

Manage your physicality:

- Straight facing the client
- Open posture
- Lean forward occasionally
- Eye contact
- Relaxed demeanor

Specificity (p. 127)

Shifting from vague or overgeneralized statements to actual real examples:

- *You said, "Everything's insane at home." Can you give me a few specific examples of what's happening there?*

Start where the client is (p. 44)

- Meet the client on his or her (cognitive or emotional) ground.
- Respect the client's choice of entry point. Make what's important to him or her important to you.
- Be open to his or her storytelling.

Strength (p. 88)

A sense of personal surety and solidity

Summarizing (p. 75)

Tentatively presenting your perception of the client's story to demonstrate attentiveness, enable corrections, or advance storytelling; may span several stories or sessions:

- *It sounds like what's going on is . . .*

Termination (p. 161)

- Progressively address feelings and thoughts about the finite nature of the therapeutic relationship.
- Duration may be based on limited number of sessions or adequate resolution of clinical issue(s).

- Review progress achieved, issues requiring continued work, supportive resources.
- Client may terminate abruptly.

Time (p. 3)

- Appointments should begin and end on time.
- Sessions are typically 50 minutes.
- Sessions are typically not extended with the exception of genuine crisis situations.

Time commitment/responsibility (p. 17)

- Begin and end sessions on time.
- If total number of sessions is specified, collaboratively identify and prioritize client's issues.
- Work effectively within time constraints.

Topic of conversation (p. 6)

- Conversations should be therapeutically relevant and goal-oriented.
- May involve difficult issues. Be prepared to move slowly.

Underlying problem (p. 51)

- A problem that emerges after the (initial) presenting problem
- Be curious but not suspicious of potential underlying problems.
- Amend diagnoses, goals, and treatment plans accordingly.

Validation (p. 95)

Assuring the client that his or her feelings, actions, and thoughts are appropriate per their unique situation and perspective:

- *You have every right to feel that way.*
- *Given your circumstances, your reaction makes perfect sense to me.*

Vocal features (p. 49)

- Tend to the client's vocal characteristics (tempo, volume, emotionality).
- Convey in a complimentary fashion.
- If the client is unclear, model or respectfully request changes.

References

Anderson, S. C., Mandell, D. L. (1989). The use of self-disclosure by professional social workers. *Social Casework, 70*(6), 259–267.

Baker, F. M. (1988). Afro-Americans. In L. Comas-Diaz & E. E. H. Griffith (Eds.), *Clinical guidelines in cross-cultural mental health* (pp. 151–181). New York: John Wiley.

Baker, F. M., & Lightfoot, O. B. (1993). Psychiatric care of ethnic elders. In A. C. Gaw (Ed.), *Culture, ethnicity, and mental illness* (pp. 517–522). Washington, DC: American Psychiatric Press.

Bandura, A. (1986). *Social foundations of thought and action: A social cognitive theory.* Englewood Cliffs, NJ: Prentice Hall.

Barcus, C. (2003). Recommendations for the treatment of American Indian populations. In Council of National Psychological Association for the Advancement of Ethnic Minority Interests (Ed.), *Psychological treatment of minority populations* (pp. 24–28). Washington, DC: Association of Black Psychologists.

Barkham, M. (1989). Brief prescriptive therapy in two-plus-one sessions: Initial cases from the clinic. *Behavioral psychotherapy, 17*, 161–175.

Basch, F. M. (1980). *Doing psychotherapy.* New York: Basic Books.

Basch, F. M. (1988). *Understanding psychotherapy: The science behind the art.* New York: Basic Books.

Benjamin, A. (1987). *The helping interview with case illustrations* (4th ed.). Boston: Houghton Mifflin.

Berkman, C. S., & Zinberg, G. (1997). Homophobia and heterosexism in social workers. *Social Work, 42*(4), 319–332.

Bernal, G., & Gutierrez, M. (1988). Cubans. In L. Comas-Diaz & E. E. H. Griffith (Eds.), *Clinical guidelines in cross-cultural mental health* (pp. 233–261). New York: John Wiley.

Blinzinsky, M., & Reid, W. (1980). Problem focus and change in a brief treatment model. *Social Work, 25*, 89–93.

Bloom, B. L. (1997). *Planned short-term psychotherapy: A clinical handbook.* Needham Heights, MA: Allyn & Bacon.

Bohart, A., Elliott, R., Greenberg, L., & Waston, J. (2002). Empathy. In J. C. Norcorss (Ed.), *Psychotherapy relationships that work* (pp. 89–108). New York: Oxford University Press.

Bohart, A., & Greenberg, L. (1997). *Empathy reconsidered*. Washington, DC: American Psychological Association.

Bordin, E. S. (1979). The generalizability of the psychoanalytic concept of the working alliance. *Psychotherapy: Theory, Research and Practice, 16*(3), 252–260.

Brammer, L. M. (1993). *The helping relationship* (5th ed.). Needham Heights, MA: Allyn & Bacon.

Breuer, J., & Freud, S. (1955). Studies on hysteria. In *The standard edition of the complete psychological works of Sigmund Freud* (Vol. 2). London: Hogarth Press. (Original work published in 1895)

Brewer, M., & Brown, R. (1998). Intergroup relations. In D. T. Gilbert, S. T. Fiske, & G. Lindzey (Eds.), *The handbook of social psychology* (4th ed., pp. 554–594). New York: McGraw-Hill.

Cannell, C., Miller, P., & Oksenberg, L. (1981). Research on interviewing techniques. In S. Leinhardt (Ed.), *Social methodology* (pp. 389–437). San Francisco: Jossey-Bass.

Carkhuff, R., & Berenson, B. (1977). *Beyond counseling and therapy* (2nd ed.). New York: Holt, Rinehart & Winston.

Committee on Professional Practice and Standards. (1993). Record keeping guidelines. *American Psychologist, 48*(9), 984–986.

Cook, S. W. (1978). Interpersonal and attitudinal outcomes in cooperating interracial groups. *Journal of Research and Development in Education, 12*, 97–113.

Corey, G., Corey, M., & Callanan, P. (2006). *Issues and ethics in the helping professions* (7th ed.). Pacific Grove, CA: Brooks/Cole.

Council for Standards in Human Service Education, National Organization for Human Services. (1996). *Ethical standards for human service professionals*. Retrieved August 8, 2006, from www.nationalhumanservices.org/ethics.html

Couper, M. P., Singer, E., & Kulka, R. A. (1998). Participation in the 1990 decennial census: Politics, privacy, pressure. *American Politics Quarterly, 26*, 59–80.

Crenshaw, W., Bartell, P., & Lichtenberg, J. (1994). Proposed revisions to mandatory reporting laws: An exploratory survey of child protection service agencies. *Child Welfare, 73*(1), 15–27.

Dana, R. H. (1993). *Multicultural assessment perspectives for professional psychology*. Boston, MA: Allyn & Bacon.

Doster, J., & Nesbitt, J. (1979). Psychotherapy and self-disclosure. In G. Chelune & associate (Eds.), *Self-disclosure* (pp. 177–224). San Francisco: Jossey-Bass.

Eckert, P. A. (1993). Acceleration of change: Catalysts in brief therapy. *Clinical Psychology Review, 13*, 241–253.

Egan, G. (1994). *The skilled helper: A problem-management approach to helping* (5th ed.). Pacific Grove, CA: Brooks/Cole.

Egan, G. (2006a). *Essentials of skilled helping: Managing problems, developing opportunities*. Belmont, CA: Wadsworth.

Egan, G. (2006b). *Skilled helping around the world: Addressing diversity and multiculturalism*. Belmont, CA: Wadsworth.

Epstine, R. S. (1994). *Keeping boundaries: Maintaining safety and integrity in the psychotherapeutic process*. Washington, DC: American Psychiatric Press.

Evans, D., Hearn, M., Uhlemann, M., & Ivey, A. (1993). *Essential interviewing* (4th ed.). Pacific Grove, CA: Brooks/Cole.

Farber, B. A. (2003). Patient self-disclosure: A review of the research. *Journal of Clinical Psychology, 59*(5), 589–600.

Farber, B. A., & Hall, D. (2002). Disclosure to therapists: What is and is not discussed in psychotherapy. *Journal of Clinical Psychology, 58,* 359–370.

Garfield, S. L. (1989). *The practice of brief psychotherapy.* New York: Pergamon.

Gaw, A. C. (1993). Psychiatric care of Chinese Americans. In A. C. Gaw (Ed.), *Culture, ethnicity, and mental illness* (pp. 245–280). Washington, DC: American Psychiatric Press.

Goldfried, M., Burckell, L., & Eubanks-Carter, C. (2003). Therapist self-disclosure in cognitive-behavioral therapy. *Journal of Clinical Psychology, 59*(5), 555–568.

Goldfried, M. R., & Davison, G. C. (1994). *Clinical behavior therapy* (expanded ed.). New York: John Wiley.

Hackney, H., & Cormier, L. (2000). *The professional counselor: A process guide to helping* (4th ed.). Needham Heights, MA: Allyn & Bacon.

Harrigan, J. A., Osman, T. E., & Rosenthal, R. (1985). Rapport expressed through non-verbal behavior. *Journal of Non-Verbal Behavior, 9*(2), 95–109.

Harrigan, J. A., & Rosenthal, R. (1986). Non-verbal aspects of empathy and rapport with physician-patient interactions. In P. D. Blanck, R. Buck, & R. Rosenthal (Eds.), *Non-verbal communication in the clinical context* (pp. 36–73). University Park: Pennsylvania State University Press.

Hepworth, D. H., & Larsen, J. (1993). *Direct social work practice: Theory and skills* (4th ed.). Belmont, CA: Brooks/Cole.

Hermansson, G. L., Webster, A. C., & McFarland, K. (1988). Counselor deliberate postural lean and communication of facilitative conditions. *Journal of Counseling Psychology, 35*(2), 149–153.

Hill, C., Helms, J., Speigel, S., & Tichener, V. (1988). Development of a system for categorizing client reactions to therapist interventions. *Journal of Counseling Psychology, 35,* 27–36.

Ho, M. K. (1992). *Minority children and adolescents in therapy.* Newbury Park, CA: Sage.

Horvath, A. O., & Symonds, B. D. (1991). Relation between working alliance and outcome in psychotherapy: A meta-analysis. *Journal of Counseling Psychology, 38*(2), 139–149.

Howard, K. I., Kopta, S. M., Krause, M. S., & Orlinsky, D. E. (1986). The dose-effect relationship in psychotherapy. *American Psychologist, 41,* 159–164.

Ivey, A. (1983). *Intentional interviewing and counseling.* Monterey, CA: Brooks/Cole.

Jacobs, T. J. (1973). Posture, gesture, and movement in the analyst: Cues to interpretation and countertransference. *Journal of the American Psychoanalytic Association, 21,* 77–92.

Jewell, E. J., & Abate, F. R. (Eds.). (2001). *The new Oxford American dictionary* (1st ed.). New York: Oxford University Press.

Kadushin, A. (1990). *The social work interview: A guide for human service professionals* (3rd ed.). New York: Columbia University Press.

Kagle, J., & Kopels, S. (1994). Confidentiality after Tarasoff. *Health and Social Work in Education, 19*(3), 217–222.

Kleinke, C. (1994). *Common principles of psychotherapy.* Pacific Grove, CA: Brooks/Cole.

Knippen, J. T., & Green, T. B. (1994). How the manager can use active listening. *Public Personnel Journal, 23*(2), 357–359.

Lambert, M. J., & Ogles, B. M. (2004). The efficacy and effectiveness of psychotherapy. In M. J. Lambert (Ed.), *Bergin and Garfield's handbook of psychotherapy and behavior change* (5th ed., pp. 139–193). New York: John Wiley.

Leigh, A. (1998). *Referral and termination issues for counsellors.* London: Sage.

Lindsey, D. (1994). Mandated reporting and child abuse fatalities: Requirements for a system to protect children. *Social Work Research, 18*(1), 41–54.

Lukas, S. (1993). *Where to start and what to ask: An assessment handbook.* New York: W. W. Norton.

Maholick, L. T., & Turner, D. W. (1979). Termination: That difficult farewell. *American Journal of psychotherapy, 33,* 583–591.

Mahoney, M. (1991). *Human change processes: The scientific foundations of psychotherapy.* New York: Basic Books.

Mann, B., & Murphy, K. (1975). Timing of self-disclosure, reciprocity of self-disclosure, and reactions to an initial interview. *Journal of Counseling Psychology, 22*(4), 303–308.

Martinez, C. (1986). Hispanic psychiatric issues. In C. B. Wilkerson (Ed.), *Ethnic psychiatry* (pp. 61–87). New York: Plenum Medical.

Martinez, C. (1993). Psychiatric care of Mexican Americans. In A. C. Gaw (Ed.), *Culture, ethnicity, and mental illness* (pp. 431–466). Washington DC: American Psychiatric Press.

McClam, T., & Woodside, M. (1994). *Problem solving in the helping professions.* Pacific Grove, CA: Brooks/Cole.

Neukrug, E. (2002). *Skills and techniques for human service professionals: Counseling environment, helping skills, treatment issues.* Pacific Grove, CA: Brooks/Cole.

Nicholas, R. A., & Berman, J. S. (1983). Is follow-up necessary in evaluating psychotherapy? *Psychological Bulletin, 93,* 261–278.

Nugent, W. (1992). The affective impact of clinical social worker's interviewing styles: A series of single-case experiments. *Research on Social Work Practice, 2*(1), 6–27.

Paniagua, F. A. (2005). *Assessing and treating culturally diverse clients: A practical guide* (3rd ed.). Thousand Oaks, CA: Sage.

Peck, M. S. (1998). *People of the lie.* New York: Simon & Schuster.

Pendersen, P., Draguns, J., Lonner, W., & Trimble, J. (1996). *Counseling across cultures* (4th ed.). Thousand Oaks, CA: Sage.

Reik, T. (1948). *Listening with the third ear: The inner experiences of a psychoanalyst.* New York: Farrar, Strauss.

Richardson, E. H. (1981). Cultural and historical perspectives in counseling American Indians. In D. W. Sue (Ed.), *Counseling the culturally different: Theory and practice* (pp. 216–255). New York: John Wiley.

Rogers, C. (1957). The necessary and sufficient conditions of therapeutic personality change. *Journal of Consulting Psychology, 22,* 95–103.

Root, M., Ho, C., & Sue, S. (1986). Issues in the training of counselors for Asian Americans. In H. P. Lefley & P. B. Pedersen (Eds.), *Cross-cultural training for mental health professionals* (pp. 199–209). Springfield, IL: Charles C Thomas.

Rubin, A., & Babbie, E. (1993). *Research methods for social work* (2nd ed.). Pacific Grove, CA: Brooks/Cole.

Schlossberg, N. K. (1976). The case for counseling adults. *Counseling Psychologist,* 6(1), 33–36.

Seijo, R., Gomez, H., & Freidenberg, J. (1991). Language as a communication barrier in medical care for Hispanic patients. *Hispanic Journal of Behavioral Sciences, 13,* 363–376.

Sherer, M., & Rogers, R. W. (1980). Effects of therapist's nonverbal communication on rated skill and effectiveness. *Journal of Clinical Psychology, 30*(1), 696–700.

Shulman, L. (1977). *A study of the helping process.* Vancouver: University of British Columbia.

Simon, J. (1988). Criteria for therapist self-disclosure. *American Journal of Psychotherapy, 52*(3), 404–415.

Simonson, N. (1976). The impact of therapist disclosure on patient disclosure. *Journal of transpersonal psychology, 23,* 3–6.

Singer, E., Mathiowetz, N., & Couper, M. (1993). The impact of privacy and confidentiality concerns on survey participation: The case of the 1990 U.S. census. *Public Opinion Quarterly, 57,* 465–482.

Smith, E. J. (1981). Cultural and historical perspectives in counseling Blacks. In D. W. Sue (Ed.), *Counseling the culturally different: Theory and practice* (pp. 141–185). New York: John Wiley.

Sperry, L., Carlson, J., & Kjos, D. (2003). *Becoming an effective therapist.* Boston: Allyn & Bacon.

Stedman, T. L. (1987). *Webster's new world/Stedman's concise medical dictionary.* New York: Prentice Hall.

Sue, D. W. (1992). The challenge of multiculturalism: The road less traveled. *American Counselor, 1*(1), 6–14.

Sue, D. W., & Sue, D. (1990). *Counseling the culturally different: Theory and practice* (2nd ed.). New York: John Wiley.

Sue, D. W., & Sue, D. (Eds.). (2003). *Counseling the culturally different: Theory and practice* (4th ed.). New York: John Wiley.

Sue, S., & Zane, N. (1987). The role of culture and cultural techniques in psychotherapy. *American Psychologist, 42,* 37–45.

Sweeney, M., Cottle, W., & Kobayashi, M. (1980). Nonverbal communication: A cross-cultural companion of American and Japanese counseling students. *Journal of Counseling Psychology, 27,* 150–156.

Swenson, S. L., Buell, S., Zettler, P., White, M., Ruston, D., & Lo, B. (2004). Patient-centered communication: Do patients really prefer it? *Journal of General Medicine, 19*(11), 1069–1079.

Tharp, R. G. (1991). Cultural diversity and treatment of children. *Journal of Consulting and Clinical Psychology, 59,* 799–812.

Thompson, J., Walker, R. D., & Silk-Walker, P. (1993). Psychiatric care of American Indians and Alaska Natives. In A. C. Gaw (Ed.), *Culture, ethnicity, and mental illness* (pp. 189–243). Washington, DC: American Psychiatric Press.

Tourangeau, R., & Rasinski, K. (1988). Cognitive processes underlying context effects in attitude measurement. *Psychological Bulletin, 103,* 299–314.

Tourangeau, R., Rips, L. J., & Rasinski, K. (2000). *The psychology of survey response.* New York: Cambridge University Press.

Traux, C., & Mitchell, K. (1971). Research on certain therapist interpersonal skills in relation to process and outcome. In A. E. Bergin & S. L. Garfield (Eds.), *Handbook of psychotherapy and behavior change: An empirical analysis.* New York: John Wiley.

Ulman, K. H. (2001). Unwitting exposure of the therapist: Transferential and countertransferential dilemmas. *Journal of Psychotherapy Practice and Research, 10,* 14–22.

Viscott, D. (1976). *The language of feelings.* New York: Pocket Books.

Walker, R. D., & LaDue, R. (1986). An integrative approach to American Indian mental health. In C. B. Wilkerson (Ed.), *Ethnic psychiatry* (pp. 143–199). New York: Plenum Medical.

Watzlawick, P. (1967). *Pragmatics of human communication.* New York: W. W. Norton.

Wells, R. (1994). *Planned short-term treatment* (2nd ed.). New York: Free Press.

Wilkinson, C. B., & Spurlock, J. (1986). The mental health of Black Americans: Psychiatric diagnosis and treatment. In C. B. Wilmerson (Ed.), *Ethnic psychiatry* (pp. 13–59). New York: Plenum Medical.

Willis, G. (1997). The use of psychological laboratory to study sensitive topics. In L. Harrison & A. Hughes (Eds.), *The validity of self-reporting drug use: Improving the accuracy of survey estimates* (pp. 416–438). NIDA Monograph 167. Rockville, MD: National Institute on Drug Abuse.

Index

Note: In page references, *e* indicates exercise, *f* indicates figure, and *t* indicates table.

About the Author

Herschel Knapp, PhD, MSSW, is a psychotherapist and health science researcher in Los Angeles, California. His experience includes helpline work, acute care in hospitals (ER, ICU, CCU, oncology), and longer-term psychotherapy in both in- and out-patient settings with a diverse client population. He has served as a behavioral science representative advocating for quality of life on the Patient Care Committee, Palliative Care Committee, Ethics Committee, and Cancer Committee. He has taught at the university level, provided intern supervision, and presented numerous clinical trainings in hospitals, schools, and the community. He is currently involved in biobehavioral research directed at improving health care services to cancer patients and enhancing access to HIV testing. He is a member of the American Psychological Association and the National Association of Social Workers. His contributions to the field have earned him membership in Phi Kappa Phi Academic Honor Society; Phi Alpha National Honor Society for Social Work; and Who's Who Among Students in American Universities and Colleges.